Society and Literature
1945–1970

THE CONTEXT OF
ENGLISH LITERATURE

Society and Literature
1945–1970

EDITED BY
ALAN SINFIELD

HOLMES & MEIER
PUBLISHERS, INC
NEW YORK

First published in the United States of America 1983 by
HOLMES & MEIER PUBLISHERS, INC
30 Irving Place, New York, NY 10003

Library of Congress Cataloging in Publication Data

Main entry under title:
Society and literature, 1945–1970
(The context of English literature)
Bibliography: p.
Includes index.
1. English literature—20th century—History and criticism.
2. Social problems in literature.
3. Literature and society—Great Britain.
I. Sinfield, Alan.   II. Series.
PR479.S62S62   1983   820'.9'00914   83–12844

ISBN 0–8419–0903–2
ISBN 0–8419–0904–0 (pbk.)

Printed in Great Britain

Contents

Illustrations

Reproduced by courtesy of Keystone Press Agency.

Acknowledgements

The editor and publishers would like to thank the following for their permission to reproduce copyright material: Faber & Faber Ltd and Farrar, Straus and Giroux, Inc. for excerpts from 'The Barn' from (in the UK) *Death of a Naturalist* by Seamus Heaney, and (in the US) *Poems 1965–1975* by Seamus Heaney © 1966, 1980 Seamus Heaney; and for excerpts from 'Annus Mirabilis' from *High Windows* by Philip Larkin © 1974 Philip Larkin.

1 Introduction

ALAN SINFIELD

The study of recent history and literature is crucial to our understanding of current attitudes and events. Of course, present-day society has its roots in earlier history, but our expectations and the institutions through which we frame them were constituted in the recent past, and only through knowledge of that can we assess their influence and adequacy today. Literature, I shall argue, is involved in the process of self-understanding in the past and present. Sillitoe responds to the factory system, Lessing to the position of women, Murdoch to the existentialist movement, by developing, through the refractive lenses of literary conventions, constructions of conceivable lives. These are, inevitably, interpretations and evaluations of perceived possibilities in the real world. And these constructions are not just responses, they are interventions: their publication feeds back possible images of the self in relation to others, helping society (some sectors more than others) to interpret and constitute itself. The social identities so formed in recent history dominate our current perceptions.

Of course, we lack the guidance of a consensus upon what is the 'significant' recent literature (and, indeed, history). Yet the authoritative opinion that has congealed around earlier periods is, in reality, the promotion of a certain view of what is important and, therefore, the denial of other possibilities. Thus the centralizing of the modernism of the first half of the twentieth century serves to marginalize the (relatively) rationalist work of Wells and Shaw. Once the canon has become established (in the full range of that word) it seems 'natural' – so much so that the reader perhaps doubts my seriousness – and even people with different values will feel obliged to express them through the central 'tradition', though a radical reassessment might be more appropriate. It is therefore useful to examine literature while it is still warm – while we can still question, in even tones, whether Pinter presents the inevitable 'human condition', whether Orton is 'immature', whether 'pop poetry' merits attention. These issues were intensely important in the sixties, and we live in their aftermath. If they are still controversial, it is because they are still active constituents in our world-view today.

Yet the full implications of earlier literature for the present appear only when it is understood in its context. For a graduate to be running a sweet stall in a time of full employment (1956) indicates, depending on your point of view, either that he is a layabout or that without family and Oxbridge backing a graduate in that society had trouble discovering fulfilling work. Nowadays it might indicate either notable enterprise in creating some kind of work opportunity, or the waste of expertise in a recession (or both). The constant factor – a graduate running a sweet stall – we can envisage as well as the original audience of *Look Back in Anger*, but the significance is different: the play assumes, in every nuance, the context of 1956. We may read it without taking this into account, imposing our own context, but we thereby limit ourselves to reinforcing our own assumptions, rather than taking the opportunity to envisage a different kind of society. Although the world of 1956 is not ours, our society is derived from it; and the way to discern that derivation is not to assimilate but to distinguish. The full and specific character of *Look Back in Anger* in its original context challenges and informs our perceptions of ourselves.

If we insist on the context of literature, we must confront the prevalent idea of the artist as individual creator whose vision transcends society, and its corollary, that the proper study of important literature discovers its 'universal' dimension. In a period of such controversy – over standards, obscurity, élitism, political commitment, sexual explicitness, pop culture – we might wonder who is to decide which bits are detachable from their context as 'universal truth'. Like the established canon, the notion looks like a strategy for claiming special authority for one point of view. It appears more and more shaky as traditional wisdom is challenged by people (such as women and blacks) who have not hitherto been allowed to contribute to 'universal truth', and are now asserting their particular truth. Because we question the strategy whereby literature is evaluated separately from its context, this

book has no separate chapters on 'background'. It is not about literature *and* its context, but literature *in* its context.

To speak of literature and context is already to risk separating the
two. The writer is not distinct from society, any more than is the bus
driver or the bus driver's union or employer. Indeed, like those roles,
the very role of 'writer' is established socially, as is clear from the fact
that in different societies that role varies considerably and in some
societies does not exist at all. Integration in society does not deprive the
writer of insight or influence, any more than it does the shop steward,
the minister of religion or the student. Rather, it provides the conditions that make insight and influence possible.

The project of involving literature fully in its context seems unsatisfactory so long as we maintain a formulation like 'the individual versus
society' – in which the individual is imagined as essentially autonomous and society is envisaged as an undifferentiated external force.
But this formulation seems inadequate in each of its parts. First, the
individual exists and makes sense of himself or herself within society.
To imagine otherwise is like trying to imagine yourself dead: you think
you're doing it but actually you've reincluded yourself in the scene,
watching, impossibly, from one side. Surely, since we come to consciousness within a language and set of social arrangements, there can
be no self separable from social being.

Second, society is neither monolithic nor static; it is composed of
diverse groups whose interests, opportunities and attitudes interact in
complex ways in accordance with their relative power at different
points. To be sure, there are dominant ideologies which tend to legitimate some attitudes and disqualify or suppress others. In a society
which heaps indignities on certain of its members and often persuades
them that it is for the best, we could hardly suppose otherwise. But
there will also be scope for new kinds of relationships and understanding, for ideology is put together piecemeal during the process of living,
from the various components as they currently lie to hand. Otherwise
there would be no change; whereas in fact the contours of a dominant
ideology shift all the time, and its relationship with subordinate
tendencies is continually revised. Often these movements are ways of
heading off significant change, but sometimes they present genuine
new possibilities for living.

The relationship of the literary text to the particular pressures and
limits that condition it is identified through contextual study, which
demonstrates the relevance of the text to how people have actually

lived and thus helps us to appreciate its implications for ourselves. We might think of the literary work as a particularizing pattern laid across the (changing) grid of social possibilities. Through the mediation of literary conventions and cultural institutions, we may discern the work's emphases, as it heightens and affirms some customary structures, disconfirms others, and perhaps discovers new lines of force. We must not claim too much privilege for literature. The assertion of some theorists – that it always reveals the progressive potential in a culture, or that it always exposes crucial contradictions in the dominant ideology – cannot be sustained. What it does is vividly to represent certain possibilities; further, it draws us into those possibilities and makes us re-create their structures as we follow them through. It invites our assent that reality is *thus* or *thus* and so helps us to develop, by agreement, rejection or negotiation, our own understanding of the world and ourselves in it.

The *Evening News* saw in Jimmy Porter 'a character who could only be shaken into sense by being ducked in a horse pond or sentenced to a lifetime of cleaning latrines'; whereas Kenneth Tynan in the *Observer* welcomed 'the drift towards anarchy, the instinctive leftishness, the automatic rejection of "official" attitudes, the surrealist sense of humour'.[1] One critic identifies and sustains his own ideology by despising Jimmy, the other does so by celebrating him. The play is recognized as offering, through sympathetic involvement in an unaccustomed stance, a possible world-view; critics and then audiences reconstitute (in minute ways, perhaps) their senses of themselves in relation to a changed perception of possible personal and social identities. The range of negotiation is apparent in the reaction of Harold Hobson, who headed off disagreeable implications by concentrating upon Alison's predicament as 'the truly moving part of the play'.[2] (Interestingly, a feminist critique now might make the same point as Hobson's traditionalism. New contexts sometimes reassert old interpretations, though the implications will be different.)

Look Back in Anger provided a focus around which a new class fraction – educated and upwardly mobile but (as yet) without power – defined its frustrations (see Chapter 6). The origin of the process is discernible in Tynan's review, which refers to grant-aided students, *Lucky Jim*, the non-U intelligentsia, classlessness and youth, and sets them against Somerset Maugham, colonial injustice, racism, emotional inhibition and good taste. Similarly, Eliot's *Four Quartets* provided an acceptable self-image – conservative but questioning, liturgical but personal, mystifying but of intellectual repute – which helped an enfeebled Anglicanism to envisage its own continuance. The literary work is among the myriad pressures nudging people (in some instances decisively) into a particular way of thinking.

However, the cultural identification afforded by literature depends upon the mediation of literary forms and cultural institutions. The world-views that literature elaborates are not direct transcriptions of life, and the writer does not gain influence by reading out his or her work on the street corner. In these respects too the individual does not work independently of society, which is experienced, again, as both opportunity and confinement, with scope for negotiation in between. Of course, you probably won't be allowed to read your work out on the street corner, and whether you will be able to bring it to the notice of a significant audience depends upon institutions that are beyond the control of all but a few individuals. The point does not need labouring. Certain kinds of work will get published – not necessarily those that immediately match the dominant ideology, but those that find their way through an intricate network of predilections and decisions. Some of these involve explicit or implicit censorship, many are related to market forces, none is independent of social forces; their specific workings in the post-war period are discussed in Chapter 5.

Opportunities for expression vary with institutional changes. On a national scale, television, state subsidy and paperbacking develop while the cinema declines. In detail, a publisher decides that he or she can afford to encourage new work, while two firms merge and an outlet disappears; it is discovered that people will watch plays at lunchtime in pubs but not in the evening at repertory theatres; that people will listen to poetry if it is presented with jazz, folk or rock music, but that not many will buy slim volumes. And, almost without noticing, the writer tailors his or her work within the available options. Everyone knows that a long poem or novel is unlikely to be accepted, that television plays are rarely longer than 90 minutes, that a stage play's chances decrease hugely if it has more than a few characters and one or two simple sets, that sex helps to sell a book. It would be revealing to study specifically the conjunctures at which the prevailing 'rules' are broken, sometimes with lasting consequences.

The reception of literary works is also socially mediated. One has to know and respect the code of a particular form. The novel is not a 'natural' way of representing reality, as is clear from the fact that it has not always existed, even in Europe. To understand a novel – to appreciate and assess its version of reality – requires both practice and willingness. Novel reading is not equally distributed through society, though it is probably more widespread than theatre-going, which requires social skills not possessed or valued by everyone, and the reading of poetry, which requires linguistic skills that are actually an object of suspicion to many people. Literary practices are not ideologically neutral (very little is): they are part of the apparatus through which people demarcate their identities within society.

The concept of 'literature' is itself socially determined: its dominant modern meaning emerged in the eighteenth century, and even now widely different ideas of it are current. Does it include seventeenth-century sermons? *Fanny Hill*? Gibbon's *Decline and Fall*? Science fiction? Barbara Cartland? Television plays? Bob Dylan? These are not marginal questions; they imply divergent definitions of the whole enterprise, and different groups will prefer different answers. 'Literature' is not essentially *this* or *that* – a self-selecting line of poets (for instance) running from Chaucer to Eliot and awaiting the judgement of 'time' to decide the continuation – but a specialized sub-category of writing or (to include electronic media) communications, whose existence and content is socially defined and redefined by particular groups in relation to specific social forces (see Chapter 5).

For many people the placing of literature among other social practices involves the same kind of cultural break as happened in 1956 with the idea that Jimmy Porter might exist and have a point. Chapter 5 analyses the dominance of F. R. Leavis's view of culture: 'In any period it is upon a very small minority that the discerning appreciation of art and literature depends.'[3] But this élitist position has lost credibility. Literary culture is like going to church, football matches, popular or classical concerts; like having gnomes in your garden, health foods in your kitchen, punk records in your bedsit or gold-plated taps in your bathroom. It is developed by certain groups in ways that enable them to identify themselves through it; to others it is a matter of indifference and, to some, an object of detestation. While the prevailing literary culture offers great signifying power to its adherents, those who do not share its codes may actually define themselves in opposition to it. The privilege that is claimed for literature is actually the privilege, real or aspirant, of its enthusiasts.

If you were brought up to participate in literary culture or are in the process of acquiring it, it may be difficult to accept that it has only the same kind of validity as other cultural practices. But this analysis does not mean that the rich significance you might find in certain books is an illusion. On the contrary, they present probably the most highly and sensitively organized meanings experienced by the people who share their codes, and the present volume is partly concerned with investigating those meanings. Nor does it mean that value judgements are inappropriate. But we should recognize that the criteria we deem appropriate to the code of literature may not be transferable to the other cultural codes through which various groups of people interpret the world and their places in it.

The diversity of codes is probably healthy. What is not, I should say, is the tendency of each group to insist upon the exclusive validity of its particular mode. Looked at in this light, the privileging of literary over popular culture in schools is of a piece with Mrs Whitehouse's attempts to suppress work dealing with certain kinds of sexual experience, and with skinhead resentment of immigrant culture. Instead of availing ourselves of the unprecedented opportunities in modern society, we retreat into limited and exclusive identifications. These are often ratified institutionally (Radio 1/2/3/4; imagine bingo in the Covent Garden opera house in the afternoons), presumably following the tendency of commerce in seeking brand loyalty, increased market share and the destruction of competitors. So conflicts that are ultimately political are fought out at the level of culture.

The present volume is, of course, implicated in the confusion consequent upon such a radical contextualizing of literature: pointing out the social construction of certain categories and institutions does not release one from them. In this introduction I have used the term 'literature' in the way I imagine to be accepted by most readers. As long as we stay within our own circle, we all 'know what we mean' by it (that is what meaning is – an agreement within a community to use words in a certain way). It is when we move outside (perhaps into the Stock Exchange or a football crowd) that we find the concept of literature regarded quite differently (if it is regarded at all). 'The Context of English Literature' series is designed for students of literature following broadly traditional courses and for a portion of the general public which shares that orientation.

This book is therefore stretched across a cultural rift. It focuses, in great measure, upon high-cultural 'literature', charting its development as a partially autonomous practice and acknowledging its contribution to our understanding of ourselves in the post-war period. At the same time, it proposes a theory of context that undermines the currently privileged status of 'literature'. However, such a split focus is hard to avoid at a time when literary and cultural studies are changing rapidly, and new modes of understanding can be developed only through current categories and institutions. By treating the disjunction in attitudes to 'literature' explicitly and systematically, we intend to make it productive. The book represents in its structure the two main forms of contextualization. We may start with society and move towards literature, observing how events and attitudes in the real world are drawn (with all the indirection I have described) into writing. And we may start with literature and move towards the conditions by which it functions as a social practice.

Chapters 2–4 attempt the first of these approaches, taking society as their starting-point. They are organized round national experience in the period 1945–70, as this was perceived and lived – in domestic and world affairs, sexual and family relationships, and ideas of the nature of humanity and the universe. The literary text is not assumed to 'mirror' society or to be representative; it is regarded as the writer's interpretation of and intervention in the world as he or she perceived it. Chapter 2 discusses the attitudes of writers to particular events and more general movements in domestic and international affairs, finding in literature diverse projects within several broad concerns. Chapter 3 sets out the ideological parameters within which sexuality was conceived in the period, scrutinizes the major debates that took place and discusses how sexuality was constructed through a range of literary approaches. Chapter 4 considers how writers manifested and responded to a decline in religion and a crisis in secularism, describing how these issues were conceptualized through existentialism, and analysing the sixties 'counter-culture'. There is no complete uniformity of structure or emphasis in these chapters; they are breaking new ground in content and method, and an enforced orthodoxy would falsify the possibilities. But the organization throughout this part of the book is by themes and chronology of the period at large and not by specific literary institutions. Thus the same text may appear in more than one chapter, and in Part II as well; it is therefore possible to compare the different perspectives within which the same work may be regarded.

Part II starts from literature and moves towards the conditions of its production in society. Chapter 5 is about the processes by which literature comes about – both its material production and its production as a concept. The effects of market forces and public-sector interventions are analysed, and special attention is given to education and the mass media; finally, attempts to evolve alternative forms are considered. With this in view, chapters on theatre, poetry and novels call into question the autonomy and continuity of the genres and the constitution of the established canons. The dominant versions of how these things developed are regarded as themselves products of the period – as constructions placed upon experience in order to comprehend it and influence its future direction. In the case of the novel, these constructions are shown to have obscured what was in fact an uneven and diverse history, and to have fed back into further writing as disturbance and stimulus. With poetry, the establishment of a powerful orthodoxy is revealed, and the extent to which it becomes difficult to see or conceive of other kinds of work is discussed. With theatre, where audiences and institutions can be identified fairly specifically, the dominant movement is related to the development and growth of a particular class fraction, and its political significance is re-examined.

Is this radical contextualizing of literature not sawing off the branch we are sitting on? Quite probably, but that is better than sitting on the fence upon which the branch is going to fall anyway! To put it less facetiously, our project may contribute to the emergence of other, better places to stand.

Notes

1 Quoted in John Russell Taylor (ed.), *John Osborne, Look Back in Anger: A Casebook* (London: Macmillan, 1968), pp. 43, 50.
2 Ibid., p. 48.
3 F. R. Leavis, *Education and the University* (1943; London: Chatto & Windus, 1948), p. 143.

Further reading

Berger, Peter and Luckmann, Thomas. *The Social Construction of Reality*. New York: Doubleday, 1967. Harmondsworth: Penguin, 1967.
Eagleton, Terry. *Literary Theory: An Introduction*. Oxford: Blackwell, 1983.
Harris, Nigel. *Beliefs in Society*. London: Watts, 1968. Harmondsworth: Penguin, 1971.
Hebdige, Dick. *Subculture: The Meaning of Style*. London: Methuen, 1979.
Kernan, Alvin. *The Imaginary Library*. Princeton, NJ: Princeton University Press, 1982.
Morrison, Blake. *The Movement: English Poetry and Fiction of the 1950s*. London: Oxford University Press, 1980.

Sinfield, Alan. 'Against Appropriation'. *Essays in Criticism*, 31 (1981), pp. 181–95.

Widdowson, Peter (ed.). *Re-Reading English*. London: Methuen, 1982.

Williams, Raymond. *Culture*. London: Fontana, 1981.

Williams, Raymond. *Marxism and Literature*. London: Oxford University Press, 1977.

Wolff, Janet. *The Social Production of Art*. London: Macmillan, 1981.

Part I
Society in literature

2 Literature, politics and society

ALISTAIR DAVIES AND
PETER SAUNDERS

War and peace

The 1914–18 war is often referred to as the first 'people's war', in the
sense that it was fought between conscripted armies and caused
millions of deaths which struck at the heart of many ordinary families.
Yet in some ways the first genuine 'people's war' was that of 1939–45,
for not only were ordinary men and women conscripted into the armed
forces but those who stayed behind suffered directly from the sustained
bombing of cities.

After the First World War, Lloyd George had promised the returning troops that he would create homes fit for heroes, yet the inter-war
period turned out to be far from heroic. From the early 1920s, unemployment soared and was finally reduced only by conscription and
rearmament nearly twenty years later; social and welfare services
remained woefully inadequate and were subjected to degrading conditions of eligibility such as the infamous 'means test' and the rigorous
application of the 'genuinely seeking work' clause; and the gap
between rich and poor remained as wide and as visible as it had been in
the nineteenth century when Benjamin Disraeli had spoken of 'two
nations' in Britain.

The prolonged misery of the 1930s, coupled with the sacrifices which
those subject to this misery were called upon to make during the six
years of war, created a widespread feeling in Britain in the early 1940s
that a new start would need to be made when the war was over. A number of wartime committees were set up by the government to report

on how a variety of social problems could be tackled. The Beveridge Report proposed a new national insurance scheme which sought finally to overcome the main causes of poverty by insuring everyone against unemployment and sickness; the Butler Report recommended a new free system of compulsory secondary education which aimed to ensure that all children received as of right the education to which they were most suited; the Uthwatt Report suggested a new scheme for comprehensive land-use planning, designed to prevent speculative profit-making during the post-war reconstruction and to ensure public control over proposed building developments.

When the war finally ended, the popular mood for change proved irresistible, and the Labour Party was swept into office on a wave of euphoria and optimism. There was to be no going back to the 1930s, and for the first three hectic years the new Labour government set about implementing the wartime reports, laying the basis for free and universal national health, social security and education systems, as part of a new welfare state. During this period, the government also laid the foundations for what became known as the 'mixed economy' by nationalizing industries such as coal, iron and steel, gas and electricity, and the railways, many of which were rundown, under-invested and unprofitable, but all of which were crucial to any future economic revitalization. The euphoric mood did not last for long, however. Workers in the nationalized industries found that little other than the name on the factory gate had been changed. Other workers found that they could not get any employment at all as the post-war recession bit deeper, the pound was devalued, and memories of the 1930s began to return. A series of strikes, prompted by stagnant wages and rising prices, severely embarrassed the Labour government and strained its relationship with the trade unions. And, perhaps most visible and most resented of all, the rationing of basic foodstuffs reinforced the prevailing gloomy mood of austerity.

The determination to make a new start was evident too in international affairs. In 1944 the leaders of the major western allies met in America at Bretton Woods to agree on a new formula for ensuring stability in the international economy after the collapse of the gold standard during the inter-war years. As a result of this meeting, the World Bank and the International Monetary Fund were established to regulate international exchange rates and to aid countries whose economies were in recession. Both bodies were effectively dominated by America, and for twenty years after the war the dollar became the major unit of world currency, until it came under pressure from the late 1960s onwards, as a result of the growing strength of the German and Japanese economies and the weakening of the American economy which was due in part to vast military expenditure in Europe and South-East Asia.

The hegemony of the dollar in the international economy symbolized a much deeper change in international relations after the war, since Britain, for so long the 'world's policeman' and leading imperial and colonial power, could no longer sustain this role (although it took many years for the more chauvinist of its political and military leaders and intelligentsia to accept this). In 1947 India, the jewel of Victoria's crown, won independence from Britain, and over the next twenty years the empire disappeared, to be replaced, sometimes peaceably, sometimes less so, by a Commonwealth of independent nations.

Support for American foreign policy was generally unconditional, and this meant support for a drive against growing communist influence, particularly in the Third World. At the end of the war, Winston Churchill had spoken of an 'iron curtain' which now separated the 'free' countries of the west from the communist bloc in eastern Europe. By 1949 the imagery had been extended to that of a 'bamboo curtain' after the successful peasant revolution in China led by Mao Tse-Tung; and the western capitalist countries, organized through NATO under the direction of America, became increasingly uneasy about the threat to Europe posed by the Soviet Union and the threat to South-East Asia posed by the People's Republic of China, the new 'yellow peril'. The so-called Cold War (a state of hostility between east and west just short of war), had now become world-wide. In America, especially, fear of communist encroachment, both within and without, soon reached epidemic proportions. Preaching a crude but effective doctrine of 'Better dead than red', the government began a series of purges of communist sympathizers (real and imagined) within the country, with Senator Joe McCarthy playing the role of Witchfinder-General (Arthur Miller's powerful play, *The Crucible* (1952), drew a direct parallel between the paranoid purging of witches in sixteenth-century New England and the McCarthy senate hearings on 'unamerican activities'), while the application of the same doctrine abroad soon resulted in the deployment of American and British troops in Korea.

Most established writers found themselves out of sympathy with developments at home and anxious about trends in world affairs. When they considered the eagerness with which the British people had responded to Churchill's nationalistic rhetoric or had given up their freedoms during the wartime state of emergency, they were forced to speculate on the degree to which Britain had itself succumbed to that spirit which, elsewhere, had given rise to totalitarianism. Had the allied nations, in order to defeat Germany and Japan by mass mobilization and mass force, themselves become totalitarian? A victory won in Europe by the area-bombing of German cities and in the east by the atomic bombing of Japan neither merited celebration nor augured well for the future of the victorious states.

The most distinguished critic of the war effort was T. S. Eliot. In 'East Coker', 'The Dry Salvages' and 'Little Gidding', those of the *Four Quartets* composed during the war, Eliot set himself to define an England which, very different from that of wartime propaganda, might properly warrant allegiance in the struggle against Nazism. Eliot's vision of England – Anglican and Catholic, provincial and European – was an enabling Christian myth, designed to inspire assent and to guide action. For he wished to ensure that those who took up arms or participated in the struggle against Nazism did not themselves fall victim to the spiritual error that had given Nazism its birth. Nazism, Eliot had suggested in *The Rock* (1934), was quite simply a pagan lust for power, a new barbarism, growing in the void at the heart of western societies which had abandoned Christianity. Modern 'man', who feared that act of dispossession which followed from submission to God, preferred instead to magnify his ego by merging it with whatever promised him power and domination. Hence Eliot sought to show in his wartime *Quartets* another command which men at war might follow. Submission to a Christian sense of purpose, to a Catholic vision of England, would save men from falling prey to that totalitarian and chauvinist spirit which, Eliot felt, was inevitably present in a country mobilized for war:

> Thus, love of a country
> Begins as an attachment to our own field of action
> And comes to find that action of little importance
> Though never indifferent. History may be servitude,
> History may be freedom. See, now they vanish,
> The faces and places, with the self which, as it could, loved
>   them,
> To become renewed, transfigured, in another pattern.
>   ('Little Gidding', ll. 159–66)

Eliot was not alone in showing concern about the ready acceptance in Britain of wartime controls, arbitrary bureaucratic powers and militarism. The wartime poetry of Dylan Thomas and of the Apocalypse poets represented, in its excess and obscurity of language, a deliberate challenge to censorship and propaganda. Cyril Connolly argued in *Horizon* (1940–9), the most influential literary magazine of the period, that the arts would cease to flourish in a country whose writers voluntarily suppressed the imagination. In his famous 'Letter from a Civilian' (1944) Connolly complained that the war had brought in England the triumph of a vaunting and brutal military ethos: 'You may liberate Europe, but you cannot liberate me.'[1] In *Brideshead Revisited* (1945), written during 1944, Evelyn Waugh celebrated the country house of the Flyte family, making it a provocative symbol of an indulgent, aristocratic tradition which owed nothing to the vulgar calculation, the mean-spiritedness or the mediocrity which in his view had become rampant in wartime England.

Such criticism was at times well founded, but it is also clear that Eliot, Connolly (who declared his support for the post-war Labour government) and Waugh were more perplexed by the egalitarian than by the totalitarian spirit released by the war. Connolly argued in *The Unquiet Grave* (1944) and *The Condemned Playground* (1945) that in the generalized mediocrity of the post-war world the position of the artist would become even more tenuous than it had been before the war, while Waugh, with characteristic contempt, suggested that the sergeants were taking over. Eliot was perhaps the most outspoken in his anti-egalitarianism. In *Notes towards the Definition of Culture* (1948) he not only defended the notion of a cultured élite but also (in an obvious reference to the Butler Education Act of 1944) criticized the programme to establish a free system of compulsory secondary education. 'People can be persuaded to desire almost anything, for a time, if they are constantly told that it is something to which they are entitled and which is unjustly withheld from them,' Eliot argued in 'Notes on Education and Culture'. But familiarity would breed contempt if education became too readily available: 'A high average of general education is perhaps less necessary for a civil society than is a respect for learning.'[2]

However, not all those who were concerned about the totalitarian impulses released by the war effort within British political and cultural life were reactionaries. Some were, in the spirit of egalitarianism, concerned about the effect of the war effort on those on the Left. In *Animal Farm* (1945) George Orwell told of the rebellion of a group of farmyard animals against their neglectful owner. The outcome, however, was not as promised. The most intelligent of the animals, the pigs, quickly assumed control, and exploited their fellow animals even more ruthlessly than had their human masters. The allegory was thinly disguised, for Orwell feared that the war effort – which had, he believed, given the taste of power to the 'English russophile intelligentsia' of the Left – would lead, when the war was over, to a totalitarian, bureaucratic and profoundly inegalitarian socialism. It was, he argued in 'James Burnham and the Managerial Revolution' (1946), the secret wish of this intelligentsia 'to destroy the old equalitarian version of Socialism and usher in a hierarchical society where the intellectual can at last get his hands on the whip'.[3]

On its publication, *Animal Farm* was an immediate success. Many critics felt that writers of the pre-war Left were perhaps most able to take the measure of the immense changes that had come about in domestic and international life during the course of the war. In particular, they believed that such writers could supply the truest perspective on the division of Europe between the allies in the west and the Russians in the east, for, as socialists, they could better understand the nature and intentions of Soviet Russia than non-socialists. Arthur Koestler's *The Yogi and the Commissar* (1945), for instance, which stated that the west should have no illusions about Soviet Russia, was particularly influential because Koestler had been a leading pre-war communist. Soviet Russia, he insisted, was an empire, which had taken over eastern Europe and had designs upon western Europe as well. The west needed to stand firm against its erstwhile ally.

George Orwell was equally sanguine about the threat posed by Soviet Russia, but his view owed less to the belligerence of anti-Soviet rhetoric. He proposed in his essay 'Toward European Unity' (1947) 'a Socialist United States of Europe – the federation of Western European states'.[4] The purpose of such a federation would be to resist not only Soviet but also American domination of Europe. At the same time, he believed that a United States of Europe would allow socialists to transform the old relationships between the European states and their colonies. For, if the United States of Europe were to be 'self-sufficient and able to hold its own against Russia and America', it had to include Africa and the Middle East, not as dependencies but as partners. He looked forward to the end of a system which ensured that the high standard of living of the industrialized west was gained by the exploitation of the non-industrialized countries of the world.

Orwell's proposals – still as challenging now as in 1947 – followed from his conviction that the First and Second World Wars had been the result of an unbridled lust for domination set in train by the industrial revolution. He had found confirmation of these ideas in James Burnham's *The Managerial Revolution* (1942) and *The Machiavellians* (1943). Capitalism, Burnham argued, was disappearing, to be replaced not by socialism but by new managerial societies run by bureaucrats, technicians and soldiers. All societies in the future would be hierarchical, with an aristocracy of talent at the top and a mass of semi-slaves at the bottom. These societies would form great superstates, grouped round the main industrial centres in Europe, North America and Asia. They would fight among themselves for possession of the earth but would remain incapable of conquering one another completely. The prospect was of a state of continuous global war. If the future seen by Burnham was to be avoided, Orwell concluded, we needed not to amend advanced civilization but to recast its very material basis, by reducing the levels of consumption of industrial society. Socialists should seek to reduce, not to raise, the standard of living.

What intrigued Orwell particularly about Burnham's thesis was that it was put forward, with seeming resignation if not approval, by a man who had been a leading Trotskyite before he became a prominent conservative thinker. Did his vision not perhaps represent the wish-fulfilment of the bureaucratic Left, of the Left for whom world politics could be seen only in terms of power, of possession, of the struggle of forces? Accordingly, in his next and equally popular novel, *Nineteen Eighty-Four* (1949), Orwell presented his portrait of a future and ostensibly 'socialist' Britain which was not only a police state but also an island aircraft-carrier for Oceania (America) in its struggle with Eurasia (Soviet-controlled Europe) or with Eastasia (Chinese-dominated Asia) for control of Africa and the Middle East. The post-war Labour government, Orwell implied, had acquiesced in Britain's subordination to America; it had sacrificed Europe, particularly eastern Europe, to Russian domination; it had, above all, failed in its commitment to decolonization. He claimed, as a man of the libertarian Left, that the dominant tradition of British socialism, bureaucratic and officious, lacked both the imagination to create a socialist United States of Europe and the courage to re-establish social life upon a less exploitative material foundation than that of the imperialist-technological civilization that had been inherited from the nineteenth century. If Eliot, Waugh and Connolly charged that the Labour government had changed too much, Orwell (perhaps exaggerating, as we have seen, its freedom to act) charged that it had changed too little.

The fifties

At the 1950 general election, the Labour government was returned but
with a much-reduced majority, and by 1951 it had been replaced by a
Conservative one. For the next decade British politics were characterized by a remarkable consensus between both main parties. The new
Conservative government in 1951 was apparently just as committed to
the welfare state as the preceding administration had been (Harold
Macmillan's Ministry of Housing, for example, set itself ambitious
public-housing targets throughout the early to mid-1950s), and it
made little attempt to reprivatize the 'mixed economy' (iron and steel
and road haulage being the only industries that were returned to the
private sector). Furthermore, both major parties were committed to a
Keynesian 'demand-management' economic strategy, including the
use of public spending as a means of maintaining relatively full
employment, and the general elections of 1955 and 1959 (both of
which resulted in increasingly substantial Conservative victories) were
fought, not on the issue of capitalism against socialism, but on the
question of which party could better administer a society organized on
the principles of welfare-capitalism.

   This was the era of 'Butskellism' (a neologism derived from the
names of the Conservative Chancellor, R. A. Butler, and the Labour
Shadow Chancellor and later leader, Hugh Gaitskell). For what was, in
retrospect, a few fleeting years, Britain entered upon a new 'Elizabethan age' of stability and affluence. Indeed, some commentators
began to suggest with increasing confidence that the daunting problems of the inter-war years – mass unemployment, sharp class antagonisms, widespread poverty – had at last been overcome. Academics
such as Daniel Bell proclaimed 'the end of ideology', while politicians
like the Labour MP Richard Crossman spoke of the dawn of a 'post-
capitalist' society.

   The catchphrase for the 1950s was coined by Harold Macmillan, by
then Prime Minister, who told the British people in 1959 that they had
'never had it so good'. For some this was undoubtedly the case. The
economy was growing again (albeit at a much slower rate than that of
Britain's major industrial competitors such as the United States, West
Germany and later Japan), and this enabled the middle class and
sections of the skilled manual working class in the more affluent regions
of the country to improve their standard of living by buying consumer
goods which their parents could never have dreamed of owning. In the

space of a few years, ownership of television sets, refrigerators, washing machines and other consumer durables became the norm rather than the exception. Car ownership spread among both the middle class and the working class, and for the first time a 'home of one's own' became a realistic aspiration for a large section of the population (owner-occupation increased from around one-quarter of all households at the end of the war to half of all households by 1970). Underpinning this extended consumer boom was the fact of virtually full employment and a gradual but constant rise in real average incomes.

Three successive Conservative general election victories (in 1951, 1955 and 1959) began to fuel speculation that class divisions had been eroded, that the working class was undergoing a process of 'embourgeoisement', and that traditional 'cloth cap' loyalties to socialism had been washed away in a flood of consumerism. In the 1950s it seemed to many that the 'old' problems of poverty, malnutrition, ignorance, and hardship at times of illness and in old age had largely been overcome, and those who, like Richard Titmuss, suggested otherwise were generally ignored. It was only in the 1960s that poverty and deprivation were officially rediscovered, although in truth they had been present all the time.

The problems which seemed to preoccupy the country's political, intellectual and moral opinion-leaders were more those of affluence than of poverty. The young, especially, were now seen to enjoy more time and money than they had in previous generations but seemed to lack direction or 'moral purpose'. The teddy boys, with their drape jackets, duck's-arse hairstyles, winkle-picker shoes and loud juke-box rock 'n 'roll music, were simply the first in a long succession of youth-culture movements which developed from the mid-1950s onwards, to the evident distress of older generations and the delight of the Fleet Street headline writers. Church leaders, academics and politicians would regularly be questioned by the media about the causes of the 'decadence' of youth and the possibilities of overcoming it, and often their answers would refer to the new 'materialistic society' which was then being forged, and to the 'alienation' which became associated with it.

Many groups probably did feel a sense of alienation from the society which was being forged at that time. The teds hanging around the Espresso bars sought an identity in gang fights and found a hero in James Dean's 'rebel without a cause'. The assembly-line workers in the new light-engineering firms – notably the car industry – paid for their suburban homes stuffed full of consumer goods with long hours of mind-numbing tedium at work. Young mothers and elderly people alike rejoiced at being relocated from crumbling inner-city back-to-backs, only to find themselves isolated in new housing estates with no facilities, or in towering blocks of flats with nowhere for the children to play and with easily vandalized public spaces, miles away from family and friends and victimized by the 'tyranny of distance'. And newly arrived immigrants from the West Indies and the Indian sub-continent who had been lured to Britain by the promise of employment and the expectation of affluence were swiftly disabused of their illusions as they encountered racial antagonism from landlords, employers and fellow workers. Fondly referred to in an academic study of the time as 'dark strangers', immigrants began to encounter white racism and even official hostility, and in some cases (as in the Notting Hill riots of 1958) began to stir against it. But, elsewhere, there were few attempts to combat alienation. Those writers who explored such alienation most fully – Colin MacInnes and Alan Sillitoe – caught the frustration it evoked but hardly touched upon its deeper, social causes. In his *City of Spades* (1957) and *Absolute Beginners* (1959) MacInnes dealt with individuals – blacks or teenagers – who found themselves at odds with society, but he was too interested in the anarchic enjoyment of conflict successfully to explore the reasons for it. In *Saturday Night and Sunday Morning* (1958) Sillitoe presented an alienated lifestyle built around the pay packet, the pub and hedonistic sexuality with more than a little subversive sympathy, for the single male was at least provided with the means to enjoy himself, and to resist marriage and respectability for a while (see Chapters 3 and 8). Indeed, as we can see in 'The Loneliness of the Long-distance Runner' (1959), it was the drama of the hero's resistance to the system that oppressed him, rather than his understanding of it, which most concerned Sillitoe.

Yet in the 1950s most of these 'problems' were thought to be manageable, given the time, the will and the resources. The restiveness of the young could be channelled in a positive direction with the help of more youth clubs and organizations or (in the view of the more tough-minded) through compulsory national service. The tedium and monotony of the assembly line could be overcome by future technological developments which would render the most boring jobs fully automated. The *anomie* of the new housing estates would break down with the help of 'community' social work and more 'community' facilities. Growing racial tensions were merely teething problems and would disappear when the second and third generations of immigrant families became fully assimilated into British culture and society.

In short, British politicians, civil servants and political commentators were in the 1950s remarkably complacent. Such complacency, however, was not generally reflected in the literature of the period. Many English writers on the Right saw the immediate post-war period as a time of decline, if not of betrayal. The British, they suggested, had quite simply capitulated to the godless materialism of communism. In his trilogy, *Sword of Honour* (*Men at Arms*, 1952; *Officers and Gentlemen*, 1955; *Unconditional Surrender*, 1961), Evelyn Waugh described the growing disillusionment of a Catholic aristocrat, Guy Crouchback, with the conduct and outcome of the Second World War. In *Men at Arms* Guy had pledged himself on the sword of a knight-crusader to take up arms against the modern infidel, the materialism of both fascism and communism. For, at the outbreak of war in 1939, the Germans and the Russians were allies, until the German invasion of Russia in 1941 caused the Russians to seek Britain's help. In Waugh's view, the consequences of this wartime combination had been disastrous. In the significantly titled *Unconditional Surrender*, it is the Sword of Stalingrad, dedicated to the Russians for their wartime heroism by the King of England, which has pride of place in Westminster Abbey. During the course of the war, the godless sword of power, Waugh suggests, has replaced in British life the Christian sword of fidelity and of service. Similarly, Wyndham Lewis presented in *Monstre Gai* (1955) and *Malign Fiesta* (1955) a London that had fallen under the rule of satanic Bolshevism, its intellectuals willing adjuncts of satanic power, its population pacified and vacuously content with the benefits of the welfare state.

Such writing drew upon a hysterical and scaremongering rhetoric which Conservative politicians, most notably Winston Churchill, had employed in post-war attacks on the Labour Party. The terror felt by the political and the literary Right about the greater egalitarianism promised (and in small measure produced) by the welfare state found its expression in fantasies of collapse, conspiracy and takeover. We can measure the full degree of this terror in Waugh and Lewis if we compare their novels with Anthony Powell's gentle and anecdotal twelve-volume *A Dance to the Music of Time*, begun in 1951 with *A Question of Upbringing* and completed in 1975 with *Hearing Secret Harmonies*. Through the eyes of the melancholic Nicholas Jenkins, Powell deals with the decline of the English upper class, but it is a decline put into a much longer perspective than that provided by Waugh or Lewis. As Powell makes clear in *The Kindly Ones* (1962), the First World War had set in train the decline of the English upper class. Yet, even while taking a longer and more fatalistic perspective (for *A Dance to the Music of Time* suggests as a whole that change and decay are in the very nature of things), Powell too hints at conspiracy and betrayal. The ruthless Kenneth Widmerpool, the man of lower-middle-class origins whose irresistible rise to power is the main drama of the whole sequence, is not only elected after the war as a Labour MP in Attlee's government. He is also, it seems, a secret communist sympathizer, who may even have betrayed his country to the Russians.

However, those nominally on the Left were by no means uncritical enthusiasts of the welfare state. The qualification here is an important one. The disrepute of the Marxist tradition on account of Stalinism and the ineffectuality of the Labour Party after the defeat of the Labour government in 1951 meant that Britain had, in the early and mid-1950s, no coherent theoretical or political position for a young and radical intelligentsia (see Chapter 4). Such analysis of current developments as there was came from those who criticized the welfare state both for its failure to be sufficiently revolutionary and for its tendency towards an oppressive bureaucracy (though they were themselves, in all cases, its beneficiaries). They had absorbed enough élitism through their Oxbridge education to be wary of egalitarian aspirations, but not enough to feel comfortable with the traditionalism of Eliot and of Waugh. Accordingly, the radical young – the so-called Angry Young Men – appealed, in a highly selective and distorting fashion, to the work of George Orwell for their literary and political perspectives. (Indeed, Orwell was the only left-wing writer from the thirties to have an influence on the new post-war generation. W. H. Auden and Christopher Isherwood had lost credit by remaining in America during the course of the war, Louis MacNeice and Cecil Day Lewis seemed worthy but dull, while Stephen Spender was vilified for long-abandoned pro-Soviet views.) John Wain, Kingsley Amis, John Osborne and Thom Gunn all admired Orwell's scepticism and contempt for slogans, his praise of common sense and decency, and his forthright dismissal of literary modernism. Above all, they admired his analysis of the hidden lust for power in the russophile British Left of the thirties and forties. These men and women, the Angry Young Men believed, were now in control of British political and cultural life, oppressing, on the one hand, authentic feeling and experience, advancing, on the other, what was abstract, inauthentic and avant-garde.

In John Wain's *Hurry on Down* (1953) the hero, Charles Lumley, educated at a 'fake public school' and at Oxford – an education that leaves him 'unprepared for life' – finds himself down and out in a world of poverty, drudgery and, ultimately, crime. Yet his life in no way resembles that of 'the expensive young men of the thirties' who had turned 'their backs on the setting that had pampered them' so that they might 'enter and be at one with a vaguely conceived People, whose minds and lives they could not even begin to imagine, and who would, in any case, had they ever arrived, have made their lives hell.'[5] Lumley's journey is, by contrast, an inward Dostoevskyian one, compelled by his passion for a wealthy young woman whom he meets by chance in a pub: 'he would commit any crime . . . he would steal, kill, maim . . . for the sake . . . of giving himself even a remote chance of *possessing* her.'[6] He does, indeed, commit crime to gain money, but finds that the woman of his dreams is unworthy. By giving her up, by dispossessing himself of her image, he frees himself of illusion and of the inauthentic. At the end of the novel, Lumley finds himself 'in an uneasy truce' with society. But, in the course of the novel, he has himself experienced the oppressive power of class, money and bureaucracy. Significantly, it is as a patient and as an orderly in a hospital that he most particularly feels these oppressions. The hospital, pride of the welfare state, is rigidly stratified; its doctors, drawn from the public schools, behave 'like an *Herrenvolk*' among natives; its nurses bully the patients. When Lumley has an argument with a doctor, who accuses him of class betrayal because he works as an orderly, Lumley is 'frog marched' and thrown out of the door. Wain's language deliberately evokes an image of totalitarianism.

Kingsley Amis, likewise, continued the critique of the personnel and the institutions of the welfare state in *Lucky Jim* (1954), his satire upon life in a post-war provincial university. The university had been expanded to accommodate as staff and students those, like its hero, Jim Dixon, from working-class backgrounds. Yet power, as the fledgling lecturer Dixon discovers, remains firmly held by middle-class professors, such as his head of department, Welch. An exponent of the 'Merrie England' school of history and a devotee of the avant-garde, Welch is shown to idealize either a fictitious past or an indistinct future because he cannot in fact reconcile himself to the marginal social mobility brought about by the post-war Labour government he in theory supports. Egotistical and indifferent, tyrannical by temperament, Welch is a socialist in the abstract.

Lucky Jim (like *Hurry on Down*) is a picaresque novel. It conveys amusingly the rebellion of its youthful protagonist, Dixon, against the hypocrisies of comfortable, bourgeois middle age, and ends with an appropriately comic conclusion: Dixon decamps to a well-paid job in London with the girlfriend of Welch's son, Bertrand. Yet the novel employs a rhetoric of rebellion which is unlike that used by Orwell. The novel follows Orwell, it is true, by mocking the fellow-travelling world of the Welches for its snobbery, authoritarianism and innate hostility to social change, but it departs from him by mocking that world (often from a homophobic standpoint) for its physical, sexual and moral effeminacy. Dixon's rebellion, it seems, follows from his rediscovery of a natural, biological male vigour – a process similarly described in *Hurry on Down* and celebrated by Thom Gunn. 'I think of all the toughs through history', Gunn bragged' 'And thank heaven they lived continually' ('Lines for a Book', 1955).

At the beginning of the novel, we see Jim walking with Professor Welch in the college quadrangle:

> To look at, but not only to look at, they resembled some kind of variety act: Welch tall and weedy, with limp whitening hair, Dixon on the short side, fair and round-faced, with an unusual breadth of shoulder that had never been accompanied by any special physical strength or skill.[7]

Dixon's latent vigour, the one gift of his proletarian origins, has been curtailed by his participation in Welch's foolish academic routine. When he has broken free, to become private secretary to a successful businessman, Dixon openly derides Welch and his son for their effeminacy: 'standing rigid with popping eyes . . . they had a look of being Gide and Lytton Strachey.'[8]

What are we to make of the use of such language by the Angry Young Men (see also Chapter 3)? The celebration of masculine vigour and the contempt for physical and moral weakness had for them an ostensibly political purpose. The conservatives, they believed, had appeased Hitler; the socialists had appeased Stalin. Together they had lacked the courage to make fundamental social and political changes in Britain. Above all, they failed to face up to and challenge the indefinite totalitarian menace which, from within and without, confronted post-war Britain. The intention of the Angry Young Men, it is clear, was to follow Orwell's libertarian lead, but, as they did so, they failed to match his intellectual breadth or to show what was his most distinctive feature: his understanding of and compassion towards his fellow human beings. If Orwell had presented the vision of a socialist United States of Europe, they expressed a fierce and petty chauvinism. In *Lucky Jim*, Dixon takes a particular delight in hearing that Welch's younger son Michel (christened with a French name because of Mrs Welch's 'European' sentiments) had made himself ill while eating 'filthy foreign food'. If Orwell criticized the modernists for, among other things, their élitism and their right-wing politics, the Angry Young Men single-mindedly and somewhat absurdly attacked them for a 'cosmopolitan' vision which they associated with the homosexuality of some of the leading modernists. In *I Like it Here* (1958) Amis created a grand old man of modernism, John Wulfstan Strether, and mocked him not only for his domicile in Portugal but also for his homosexuality. If Orwell had stressed the importance of reason and compassion, the Angry Young Men emphasized the importance of instinct and will. What had in Orwell been coherently and positively formulated became with the Angry Young Men a curiously undirected and remarkably unstable fury.

Nowhere is this more evident than in John Osborne's *Look Back in Anger* (1956). The only prospect Jimmy Porter can see for himself in the 'Brave New-nothing-very-much-thank-you' world of the 'Butskellite' welfare state is one of stifling domesticity. 'No, there's nothing left', Jimmy laments to Cliff, 'but to let yourself be butchered by the women.' The men of the thirties had proved themselves in the Spanish Civil War; the men of the forties had defeated Hitler. In the fifties, in a world cynically divided between the superpowers and immobilized by fear of atomic war, there were no brave causes left in which young men might fight to prove themselves. It is significant that Jimmy feels himself powerfully drawn – even as he mocks them – to images of British imperial rule in India. What, however, makes Jimmy's plight singularly desperate is his recognition that this kind of action is now anachronistic. A young man who refuses to work in one of the bureaucracies of the welfare state can secure his independence only by running a sweet stall in a local market.

Suez and the bomb

Britain's final fling as an imperial world power came in 1956, when British, French and Israeli governments conspired in a hopeless plan to invade Egypt, in retaliation against that country's nationalization of the Suez Canal. This ill-advised act of aggression was condemned by the rest of the world, including (most significantly and hurtfully) America, and British troops were hastily withdrawn amid much confusion and embarrassment. The response of British writers was equally unfavourable. The Angry Young Men, in particular, opposed the Suez campaign, since it represented for them the mindless and bullying arrogance of the Conservative ruling class. Yet, at the same time, they were drawn to oppose what they saw as the increasing pacifism of the Labour Left. For Suez had been accompanied by the Hungarian invasion. When Russian tanks rumbled into Budapest to quash an anticommunist uprising, the British people and government listened helplessly to the radioed calls for assistance from Hungarian workers, and did and could do nothing. The inevitable retreat from empire, the Angry Young Men insisted, should neither give advantage to Russian aims nor weaken a western sense of resolve against totalitarianism.

Accordingly, John Osborne analysed in *The Entertainer* (1957) the decline of the ideals of British imperial culture with a curious and contradictory regret. The entertainer of the title, Archie Rice, is an old-fashioned music-hall artiste whose act draws heavily upon imperial sentiment. Contemptuous of the spinelessness of contemporary life (his elder son has, as a conscientious objector, refused to do his national service), Archie takes comfort from the example of his younger son Mick, who in his view is virile, uncomplicated and, above all, conscious of his duties to his country. Such a commitment runs counter to the 'I'm-all-right-Jack' selfishness rampant in Britain. The focus of the play is the fate of Mick (who is never seen on stage): Mick, his family learns, has been taken hostage in an imperial 'trouble-spot'; in the event, he is murdered. What affects Mick's family is not simply the cynicism of Britain's public representatives or Britain's evident power-lessness. It is that his death, on a soldier's duty, no longer has any meaning for a Britain of scrambling selfishness. 'Why should I care?' Archie asks at the close of the play.

The play expresses not so much a nostalgia for empire as frustration at the national impotence which followed from its loss; for the lesson of Suez was, quite simply, that Britain was no longer a world power, and control of events was now held by the Americans and Russians. Yet, for many Conservative and Labour politicians alike, all was not lost. Through the so-called 'special relationship' with America (which would survive the strains of Suez), they believed that Britain could still

play a major role in world affairs. This was a belief that most of the
Angry Young Men, who after the Hungarian uprising began to move
openly to the Right, fully accepted. However, their commitment to
America was a purely political one. Unlike English painters, who began
from the mid-fifties to emulate the pop art of American painters,
English writers in the period remained contemptuous of, and hostile
to, American literary innovation. It was paradoxically, as we shall see,
English writers of the sixties, often hostile to American power and to
the American way of life, who enthusiastically adopted American
forms. What the Angry Young Men found in the American alliance
was a ready and credible means of defence for a Britain in decline
against the threat of communism, either of the Russian or of the
Chinese variety.

In *One Fat Englishman* (1963), for instance – a novel set in America
– Amis satirized the anti-Americanism of the 'pinkish' intelligentsia,
epitomized by the figure of Roger Micheldene. Micheldene (whose
name is suspiciously Gallic) is not only effete, complacent and oppor-
tunistic but also blind to the effective decline of his own country as a
power in the world. Throughout the novel he patronizes his American
hosts for their brashness and lack of cultivation, unaware that it is the
expression of a natural vigour which he himself lacks. He cannot see
that the affected English he speaks is the expression of a culture in
decline. It is no longer the language of directness or of action but of
nostalgia and passivity: 'Americans pursue the dollar; the British had
an Empire. Fascinating to see the underlying assumptions and goals of
a culture laid bare in its idiom.'[9]

Meanwhile, the natural vigour and idealism of the Americans, which
Amis celebrated, and which Graham Greene in his novel set in Vietnam, *The Quiet American* (1955), brilliantly and incisively decried,
became increasingly manifest in a series of adventures in South-East
Asia and Latin America. The logic that had led to a succession of interventions in Korea (in the early 1950s), Cuba (with the abortive Bay of
Pigs invasion following Castro's communist revolution in 1958), Central and South America (where neo-fascist regimes in Argentina, El
Salvador and Haiti were given unquestioned support) and Cambodia
and Vietnam (where the Americans were to suffer a most costly and
humiliating defeat) was the 'domino theory'. According to this theory,
Russian and Chinese communism was intent on world domination.
The west could not afford (given its reliance on capitalist world markets
for buying its goods and producing cheap raw materials for its industries)

to allow even one more country to fall under communist influence, for the countries of South-East Asia were likened to a set of dominoes standing each on end which would successively collapse once the first in the line began to fall. After Korea, Vietnam. After Vietnam, Thailand. Then Singapore, perhaps. Then what? India? Even Australia was under threat!

Throughout the 1950s and 1960s the superpowers tangled with each other, directly or by proxy, throughout the Third World, while all the time holding back from open aggression towards each other's homelands. The constraint which held each of them in check was the ever-present threat of nuclear holocaust, for the awful image of the mushroom cloud, seen first in 1945 in the Japanese cities of Hiroshima and Nagasaki and subsequently in the proliferation of atmospheric H-bomb tests in the more deserted corners of the globe, lingered mockingly before hundreds of millions of people as a reminder of the inevitable conclusion of a third world war. The imagery and vocabulary of nuclear warfare entered the popular consciousness – the 'finger on the button', the 'four-minute warning' – while military and political leaders in America and Russia strained to keep the Cold War cold. Nationalism, chauvinism and jingoism ran high, and the spirit of national aggressiveness and indignation in the west was kept fuelled by a constant stream of stories of spy scandals, of the build-up of nuclear arms in the communist countries, and of refugees fleeing from the grey repression of eastern Europe at terrible personal risk.

Furthermore, the decline in Britain's influence in international affairs became even more marked. When in 1962 President Kennedy issued an ultimatum to First Secretary Khrushchev to withdraw Soviet missiles from Cuba, the British people and government could do no more than hold their breath and cross their fingers. Faced with the escalation of the Vietnam war later in the decade, the Prime Minister, Harold Wilson, fondly imagined himself in the role of mediator and peacemaker, but his offer to help provoked no more than an embarrassing and desultory silence on the part of the protagonists. When the Soviet Union again asserted its control over eastern Europe, this time in Czechoslovakia in 1968, the British response was no more effective than it had been twelve years earlier in Hungary. The locus of power in the west had shifted decisively and irreversibly to the other side of the Atlantic, and Britain's aspirations to a world role had to be limited to the maintenance of an 'independent' nuclear force which was neither independent (since it was purchased from America) nor affordable (given the declining state of the British economy), and to an unshake-able belief in the existence of a 'special relationship' with America.

Yet the most immediate outcome of Suez was the emergence in Britain of the Campaign for Nuclear Disarmament. Britain's pretensions to be a world power (given credibility by an 'independent' nuclear force) had been, it was argued, finally destroyed. We should recognize our changed status, J. B. Priestley suggested in an influential article in the *New Statesman* in November 1957, 'Britain and the Nuclear Bombs', and take the opportunity to act courageously and creatively by abandoning the arms race. We should abandon nuclear armaments unilaterally. This gesture would make Britain a great moral rather than military influence in the world. Although the Campaign for Nuclear Disarmament, with its annual march from Aldermaston (a nuclear research centre in Berkshire) to London, attracted supporters from all classes and age groups, its main political direction and effectiveness was given to it by left-wing members of the Labour Party. British political, economic and intellectual life, many on the Left felt, had been transformed by wartime participation in the development of the atomic bomb, and by the decision – taken in secret by the first post-war Labour government – to establish an independent nuclear force.

From 1957 onwards, C. P. Snow's eleven-volume chronicle of English political, social and moral life from the First World War to the present, *Strangers and Brothers* (1940–70), began to attract particular attention because its central figure, Lewis Eliot, was intimately involved (as had been C. P. Snow himself) in the development of a British atomic bomb. In *The New Men* (1954), for instance, Snow had presented a detailed account of the qualms of conscience and of the inevitable compromises of those engaged in the wartime development of the atomic bomb, while in *Corridors of Power* (1964) he dealt with the impact of the Suez fiasco on the defence policy of the Conservative Party. In the novel the newly appointed Conservative Minister of Defence, Roger Quaife, (somewhat improbably) puts forward the argument for the unilateral abandonment of the British atomic weapon. 'We can help', he says, echoing Priestley, 'swing the balance between a good future and a bad future, or between a good future or none at all.'[10] In the event, he fails to win support in his party, and is forced to resign.

Snow risked such improbabilities because he was, he insisted, a novelist of hope. He wished to make his readers aware, in his account of post-war British history, of what might have been as well as of what did happen. For the possibility of change had been and was still available. In 1957 Britain still had the opportunity to change the course of post-war world history by repudiating the arms race, and by turning its energies and resources to the problem of world poverty and under-development. Indeed, the bitterness of Snow's last two novels of the chronicle, *The Sleep of Reason* (1968) and *Last Things* (1970), came from his haunting sense of what might have been. The result of Britain's participation in the arms race, Snow suggested, had been to instil, in the generation of the sixties, a hopeless despair and a repudi-ation of reason itself. Convinced that those in authority had misused both power and knowledge, the young turned away from public affairs and from the faith, central to the pre-war generation, that science could cure the problems of mankind. Had Britain made the gesture of unilateralism, Snow implied, a whole generation might have been saved from an impotent and fruitless anger.

Snow's view that in the nightmare of the atomic age novelists of the Left had to be novelists of hope was echoed, even more forcefully, by Doris Lessing. Artists, she wrote in her personal statement in *Declaration* (1957), 'are the traditional interpreters of dreams and nightmares, and this is no time to turn our backs on our chosen responsibilities.' There were, she argued,

> only two choices: that we force ourselves into the effort of imagination necessary to become what we are capable of being; or that we submit to being ruled by the office-boys of big-business, or the socialist bureaucrats who have forgotten that socialism means a desire for goodness and compassion.

If we consent to such submission, 'we shall' – referring to the ever-present threat of atomic war – 'blow ourselves up.'[11]

Lessing's five-volume chronicle *Children of Violence* (1952–69) presented, as did Snow's *Strangers and Brothers*, an account of social, moral and political change from the First World War to the present. There are significant differences. Lessing's central figure, Martha Quest, is female, not male; an outsider, not (as Lewis Eliot is) an insider; a rebel, not a conformist. Above all, her childhood and early adulthood are spent not in inter-war England but in inter-war East Africa. The particular history which Lessing gives of this period of Martha's life is that of a white, colonial ruling class. But there are also important similarities. Like Snow, Lessing is a didactic novelist. By

giving an account of contemporary history from the point of view of
Martha Quest, an anti-colonial activist, a radical and a woman (living
first in East Africa, then in London), Lessing challenges established
preconceptions about the period. Situations, she reminds us throughout, were misread; opportunities in world politics were missed; hopes
were dashed. The unity of the fight against fascism gave way, under the
pressure of paranoia, to the divisions of the Cold War. It was during
that time, she notes in *The Four-Gated City* (1969), that

> Britain's bondage to America (begun in the Cold War while
> the nation's eyes were fixed, hypnotized on Russia) was con-
> firmed and built into an economic keystone; those years saw
> Britain's abject role in the Arms Race laid down; during those
> years occurred painfully ludicrous excursions into nineteenth-
> century colonial warfare – Kenya, Cyprus, Suez. Internally,
> the country ran down even further than it had during the war:
> the schools, hospitals, services, slumped into out-dated in-
> competence; old people died in impoverished neglect; science
> and technology were poor relations of the great money
> spender and breeder, war.[12]

What makes Lessing's *Children of Violence* distinctive, however, is
that it challenges not only the preconceptions of the Right but also (and
more intently) those of the Left. For, if the chronicle tells of Martha
Quest's growth and development as a radical, it also tells of her disillusionment with the political parties of the Left. In *A Ripple from the
Storm* (1958) we see Martha's involvement with the Communist Party
in 'Zambesia' (Southern Rhodesia), which she joined not only because
it opposed colonialism but also because it seemed inspired by that
dream of the unity of peoples which had haunted Martha from her
childhood. Communism in the Soviet Union, she firmly believes, has
abolished all forms of racial prejudice. However, as Stalin's atrocities
are revealed, Martha becomes convinced that communism, like fascism, expresses, in its spirit of hatred, particularity and opposition, the
sickness rather than the health of the collective psyche. 'The history of
the twentieth century', Martha declares in *The Four-Gated City*, 'as far
as we've got with it is of sudden eruptions of violent mass feeling, like
red hot lava, that destroy everything in its path – First World War, fascism, communism, Second World War.'[13] The collective psyche can, as
with the CND marches, still give expression to mankind's unconscious,
creative dream. But there were few 'in, or near or associated with these

columns of walking people', Martha feared, 'whose lives did not have a great gulf in them into which all civilization had vanished, temporarily at least.'[14] Even the young who had not known the First or Second World Wars had been conditioned by living under the shadow of a third and catastrophic atomic war.

However, Lessing's chronicle is not without hope. In *The Four-Gated City* Martha becomes sure, while nursing a woman labelled 'mentally ill', that the sickness of the individual and collective psyche arises from the hopelessly divisive and instrumental modes of perception and knowledge which modern humanity has inherited from the scientific revolution. The conscious mind has repressed the unconscious mind; the masculine has repressed the feminine. The novel ends, strangely, with a prophetic projection into the future. We learn from a series of documents dated from 1995 to 2000 that there has been an atomic war. Britain is devastated and abandoned. Martha, however, survived the war (although she is now dead). Stranded upon a remote island off the coast of Scotland, she had come upon children who had developed, as a result of radiation, hugely enlarged powers, both rational and telepathic. These children were 'grown up . . . mentally, emotionally',[15] beings who had absorbed and transcended the history of the century.

Paradoxically, these children, products and victims of the atomic era, were also its beneficiaries. For the atomic age is the age of relativity, of indeterminacy, of the dissolution of the dichotomies of pre-atomic science. These children are mutants, who have gone beyond the mental constrictions, the false dualities, inherited from the scientific revolution which had made the modern age. If atomic science has, through the arms race, provided mankind with the capacity to destroy all life upon the earth, it has also provided, through its revision of traditional scientific categories, the greatest spur to evolution since the Greeks.

The problems of liberalism

The Angry Young Men and the novelists of hope were not the only writers who began their careers in the fifties. During this period, Angus Wilson, Iris Murdoch, William Golding, Anthony Burgess and Muriel Spark published their first major works. Although these writers chose different styles, subject-matter and genres, they were soon taken by critics to form, if not a group, at least an identifiable association, for their work was marked by a philosophical explicitness and by an avowed commitment to liberal values. The era of *la littérature morale* has ended, Iris Murdoch wrote in 'Novelist as Metaphysician' (1950): 'there begins the era of *la littérature métaphysique.*'[16] They were influenced, in part, by Karl Popper's *The Open Society and its Enemies* (1945), which argued that fascism and communism, with their disastrous consequences for the present century, had their intellectual roots in a misplaced utopianism. If societies were to retain their freedom, they needed, Popper suggested, to preserve a sceptical temper.

The principal influences, however, came from the writings of the French existentialists: Jean-Paul Sartre's *Existentialism and Humanism* (1947), which insisted that all modern ideologies, fascist, communist and capitalist, were immoral because they regarded human beings as means rather than ends; Sartre's *What is Literature?* (1950), which emphasized that literature, arising in and working upon the imagination, was itself an ambiguous source of power; and Gabriel Marcel's *Being and Having* (1949) and Simone Weil's *The Need for Roots* (1952), which suggested that the ills of the century were in large measure due to the incalculable effects of the industrial revolution. Indeed, the existentialists shared the conviction that modern industrial society, based as it was upon technological power, had corrupted the moral sensibility of those who lived within it, for individuals, in their relationships with other individuals, adopted that spirit of domination and of exploitation which industrial organization inescapably engendered. All contemporary ideologies – whether communist, fascist or capitalist – needed to be rejected because they, the products of the industrial revolution, showed no concern for the moral being of individuals.

What encouraged interest among British writers in French existentialism was their belief that the British themselves (in spite of fighting against fascism in the war) were not immune from that very sickness, diagnosed by the existentialists, which had given rise to fascist violence and totalitarianism. William Golding, in particular, challenged the notion that the British were, in some peculiar way, different or special. In *Lord of the Flies* (1954) some English schoolboys find themselves abandoned, after a plane crash, on a tropical island. But they do not behave as we might suppose English schoolboys to behave, for soon a number of them take up hunting and become, by the end of the novel, a frenzied pack of killers. Yet, when Jack and Roger turn upon Piggy and Simon, they are, for Golding, simply making manifest the brutal and violent pattern of behaviour that underlies Britain's stratified and

bullying social order. In *Pincher Martin* (1956) he continued his un-
comfortable challenge to British assumptions. The mental processes of
a drowning Royal Navy lieutenant, whose ship has been sunk by the
Germans in the war, reveal *his* brutal and amoral personality.

Angus Wilson and Iris Murdoch, similarly, suggested that contemporary Britain, beneath its social and political surface, was a sinister and
unstable entity, in which the state, big business and even the press vied
for control. In Wilson's *Hemlock and After* (1952) Bernard Sands has
to win the blessing both of the state and of an ominously authoritarian
county and business set before he can establish his centre for writers; in
Murdoch's *The Flight from the Enchanter* (1956) the mysterious
tycoon, Mischa Fox, not only is an influential press baron but also
directly manipulates the political and administrative life of the
country. Those who seek power – James Sands in Wilson's *Hemlock
and After*, John Middleton in Wilson's *Anglo-Saxon Attitudes* (1956),
Lefty Todd in Murdoch's *Under the Net* (1954), Bill Mor in Murdoch's
The Sandcastle (1957) – seem marked by an egotism or by an authoritarian spirit singularly in tune with the brutal and morally impover-
ished modern industrial world in which they live.

What was, however, central to the work of Angus Wilson and of Iris
Murdoch was the questioning of the efficacy of the historic liberal
tradition in British politics and culture which placed the welfare and
wellbeing of the individual at the centre of its concern. Although they
were themselves liberals, Wilson and Murdoch wondered if the liberal
tradition, most recently epitomized by the members of the Bloomsbury
group, was able to cope, intellectually and morally, with the new forces
at play in contemporary society. Did this tradition amount to more
than the good intentions of the well-fed and the well-placed? Was it
not marked by the naïve meliorism of the nineteenth century? Even
after Hitler, Murdoch remarked, British liberals seemed constitution-
ally unable to imagine evil.

Certainly, in their early work, Wilson and Murdoch showed themselves to be remarkably pessimistic about the capacity of their fellow
liberals to deal with and to withstand the contemporary world. In
Hemlock and After (1952) Wilson presents the story of Bernard Sands,
a bisexual writer in the Bloomsbury fashion, who has throughout his
life concerned himself only with his own pleasures. He has ignored his
wife's mental collapse; he has failed, with smug self-satisfaction, to
question his own motives. Because he has failed to do this, he does not
understand, until it is too late, that his values, and the values of the

privileged cultural group of which he is a part, have been self-indulgent and irresponsible, creating a social and political void which has been filled by manipulative and authoritarian bureaucrats and capitalists. Before he can act, he dies. In *The Flight from the Enchanter* (1956) Iris Murdoch introduces into the cosy English world of liberal civil servants, scholars, wealthy socialists and elderly upper-class suffragettes a number of refugees from eastern Europe. This English world is effete, eccentric and innocent; the other world, of émigrés and survivors, is ruthless and amoral. Yet, in the course of the novel, the English liberals reveal themselves to be either unwilling or unable to resist the new and relentless spirit the outsiders represent. Some are strangely fascinated, wishing to submit to those who are amoral; others, displaced by ambitious bureaucrats and foreign tycoons, accept with resignation the loss of power and prestige. A whole social and political class seems, almost gladly, to participate in its own overthrow.

Yet the subsequent fiction of Wilson and Murdoch reversed this early pessimism. Liberals, they now asserted, once they had qualified their optimism about human nature and about inevitable human progress, could still play an active and important part in British social, political and cultural life. In *Anglo-Saxon Attitudes* (1956) Wilson analysed – on an ambitious scale – the failures of the English liberal political and cultural tradition since the First World War. The novel examines the consequences, upon Gerald Middleton and his family, of his refusal, as an individual and as a professional man, to face up to the unpleasant truth of human wickedness. The gifted but unbalanced son of a distinguished archaeologist had once told Middleton, while they were both drunk, that he had mischievously planted a pagan symbol in the tomb of an early Christian which his archaeologist father was then excavating. Middleton, who has himself since then become a leading historian, has remained silent about the deception, convincing himself that he does so out of loyalty to his friend, who had soon afterwards been killed in the First World War. But we see clearly that he has remained silent because he cannot accept the fact of deliberate human wickedness and deceit. In old age, Middleton, recognizing that he has shirked his responsibility to confront painful reality, sets out to put the record straight. Middleton, unlike Bernard Sands, finally does act and acts decisively: the liberal tradition, albeit in a chastened and more realistic form, is shown still to be valid. The issues might seem minor, but Wilson, in the course of the novel, makes it clear that the kind of self-willed blindness that Middleton practised had led liberals like him to deceive themselves about the threat posed in the thirties by European fascism.

What distinguished *Anglo-Saxon Attitudes*, however, was not simply the assertion of the validity of the liberal tradition in the second half of the present century. It was that, by his explicit parody in the novel of the art and attitudes of the Bloomsbury group, Wilson put forward his comic-realistic mode of fiction as the most suitable vehicle for the chastened and more worldly liberalism he proposed. For in his characterization of Gerald's Scandinavian wife, Inge, he made deliberate (and very successful) mockery of Virginia Woolf's Clarissa Dalloway and Mrs Ramsay. Even when it is manifestly impossible, Inge wishes all those in her orbit to love one another. If liberal fiction was to survive, it too had to avoid the illusions and the sentimentalities of its early practitioners.

Similarly, Iris Murdoch challenged in *The Sandcastle* (1957) the ethics and aesthetics of Bloomsbury. In the novel, an unhappily married middle-aged schoolmaster, William Mor, falls in love with a young portrait painter, Rain Carter, who has come to his school to paint a portrait of the former headmaster. Not only did Rain Carter's occupation allow Murdoch to present in detail views on the purpose and nature of art which are opposed to Bloomsbury's doctrine of art for art's sake, but Mor's infatuation with Rain Carter also raised questions about the ethics of action and of choice. For, from the point of view of Bloomsbury, Mor is presented with a straightforward opportunity for self-realization and self-fulfilment: Rain is an object of beauty and of desire. Yet this point of view is challenged explicitly within the novel by Mor's colleague, Bledyard:

> There is such a thing as respect for reality. You are living on dreams now, dreams of happiness, dreams of freedom. But in all this you consider only yourself. You do not truly apprehend the distinct being of either your wife or Miss Carter.[17]

Ethical action – unselfish action – can only follow from a 'respect for reality'. We need to recognize the 'distinct being' of others, and we ignore at our peril the needs of others as well as of ourselves.

In these two novels, Wilson and Murdoch established themselves as the exponents of a revised liberal tradition – a tradition which, while it continued to emphasize the centrality of the individual, was aware not only of the psychological complexity of the individual but also of the individual's social and political obligations. The wellbeing of a 'civilized' society – one in which the rights and the welfare of the individual were paramount – could be sustained only by the active and critical participation of individuals. Accordingly, in 'A House of Theory' (1959) and 'Against Dryness' (1961), Murdoch described the dangers of mass technological society and proposed in *The Bell* (1958) and 'The Idea of Perfection' (1964) a socialism of the small-scale. It is by working with our hands, in small communities, she suggested, that we shall find peace and satisfaction. In *Late Call* (1964) Wilson similarly explored the spiritual emptiness not only of the new town in which the novel is set but also of the technological civilization that had inspired its ideal of 'social engineering', while in *No Laughing Matter* (1967) he examined the gains and the losses which the technological revolution had brought during the present century. In *No Laughing Matter*, however, Wilson stressed that the technological revolution now affected all parts of the world: the English liberal novelist should no longer restrict his or her analysis to English experience or to English circumstances.

The sixties: Europe

Although we should be wary of periodizing history too tightly and precisely, there is a sense in which 1964 represented a watershed, if only because it was in October of that year that the Labour Party returned to power. As in 1945, so in 1964 there was a popular mood for change coupled with a revolt against complacency. Gradually academic, journalistic and dramatic work began to reflect the view that the old problems of the inter-war years had not been overcome after all. Television programmes such as *Cathy Come Home* alerted the national consciousness to the continuing housing problem, just as academic research by Fabian socialists such as Peter Townsend established that millions of people were still suffering poverty and that gross inequalities of life chances were as real twenty years after the war as they had been twenty years before it. Increasingly it was argued that the reforms introduced by the post-war Labour government needed now to be vastly extended if material security and equality of opportunity were to be achieved.

The election campaign of 1964 vividly expressed the contrast between the 1950s and 1960s. Campaigning on the slogan of 'thirteen wasted years under the Conservatives', Harold Wilson epitomized youth, energy and optimism, while the incumbent Conservative Prime Minister, Alec Douglas-Home, seemed almost decrepit by comparison.

The Conservative government, tarnished by the Profumo scandal (ostensibly concerning a security risk involving a Conservative minister but actually significant more for its sexually titillating qualities), seemed tired and listless. In its place, Wilson offered the prospect of a new era (decried in advance, as we have seen, by the liberal intelligentsia) in which rational centralized planning, linked to the 'white heat' of the new technological revolution, was to provide the instrument for forging a new Britain. Cloth-cap socialism had been replaced by white-collar corporatism, and the choice in 1964 seemed as simple as it was stark; progress versus reaction, change versus tradition, the confident eloquence of Wilson, with his pipe and Gannex raincoat, versus the bungling incompetence of the fourteenth Earl of Home. The result was tight, but Labour scraped in with a majority of four. Eighteen months later Wilson won a landslide victory and remained in office until 1970.

It was the government's dual concern with the country's economic decline and its lack of international political significance which resulted in a series of attempts throughout the 1960s to join the six-member European Economic Community. The EEC countries at that time comprised the richest nations of western Europe, a market of some 200 million affluent consumers whose demand for British goods would (it was hoped) regenerate British industry. But 'Europe' was always more than just a market to those in Britain who wished to join. It represented an 'ideal' of international co-operation in which national self-interest would gradually be eclipsed, and it represented a power bloc which potentially could come to rival that of the USA and the USSR. If Britain was to regain a voice in the modern world, it could only be as a member (albeit a dominant member, or so it was assumed) of a united European supernation. Some who still shared Orwell's hope for a socialist Europe were particularly enthusiastic.

The case for British membership was always contentious, and the reality turned out to be somewhat more messy and less idealistic than its more committed supporters had hoped. National pride took a severe knock when the first two applications to join the EEC were rebuffed by the French President de Gaulle's veto, and throughout the 1960s there remained considerable opposition to membership from within Britain as well. On the one hand there were the nationalists, dismissed by pro-Europeans as 'little Englanders', who held that political sovereignty should not be ceded to Brussels and that Britain's historical links lay not with its traditional enemies and rivals in Europe but with its traditional friends and allies in North America and the white Commonwealth.

This argument was somewhat undermined by the fact that the United States government was keen to see Britain join the EEC in order to strengthen western Europe in opposition to the communist bloc to the east; but it did strike a chord in the popular consciousness, which had been nurtured for generations on jingoistic sentiments celebrating the superiority of the British 'island race' *vis-à-vis* the Krauts, Frogs and Wops on the other side of the 'English' Channel. Notwithstanding the spread of foreign language teaching in schools and the growing popularity of continental package holidays, there was in Britain in the 1960s still a strong sense of separation from Europe, and newspapers like the *Daily Express* did their best to keep this alive with disparaging comments about Brussels bureaucrats, decimal money, metrication and driving on the right.

At the other end of the political spectrum from the nationalist Right were the internationalist Left who also opposed British membership of the EEC, though for very different reasons. For them, the Common Market represented a rich countries' club concerned only with mutual self-interest economically and militarily, uninterested in the Third World, and resolutely hostile to socialist policies and genuine internationalism. Such sentiments were not widely shared in the population as a whole, although they were manifest among some leading trades unionists, the Labour-Left and in the pages of the *New Left Review*.

In a symposium on the EEC in *Encounter* (December 1962–January 1963), Kingsley Amis argued that 'the English-speaking countries (which we helped to found) belong to the future, whereas Europe is a place we have spent much of our history trying to extricate ourselves from.' John Osborne too found nothing attractive in the Common Market's 'chromium pretence' or its 'grasping businessmen and technocrats'. He was prepared to settle for 'a modest, shabby, poor-but-proud Little England any day'. In the same symposium, Angus Wilson expressed his deep reservations about British entry to the Common Market, while Iris Murdoch expressed her outright opposition, maintaining the historic attachment of the liberal tradition to international institutions by her support for the Commonwealth. Indeed, in *The Old Men at the Zoo* (1961) Wilson presented an Orwellian fantasy of the takeover of Britain by a 'uni-Europe' movement, eager to enjoy the benefits of French and German economic success. 'In throwing off the puritan legacy', one uni-European insisted, 'we get closer to the rich vein of Mediterranean brutality on which our European legacy so much depends.'[18] If Britain's puritanical, illogical and sentimental legacy made it uncompetitive, it also, in Wilson's view, made it compassionate, and manifestly superior to 'brutal' Europe.

Of those in favour, the most positive (and perhaps least surprising) advocate was T. S. Eliot. But he was not alone. In the 1960s other writers (not consulted by *Encounter*) expressed their support. In *A Clockwork Orange* (1962) Anthony Burgess presented another Orwellian fantasy, but of an Americanized Britain in which the technological spirit was in total and nightmarish control. All resources of language and feeling had been obliterated. Burgess made it clear in *Inside Mr Enderby* (1963) and *Enderby Outside* (1968) that these resources – European resources – had to be revived in Britain if the world of *A Clockwork Orange* were to be avoided. In *The Mandelbaum Gate* (1965) – a novel set in Jerusalem – Muriel Spark examined the transcendence of the divisions of class, nation and race by the powers of love. She stressed that we must seek unity if we are, in Europe as well as in the Middle East, to overcome the madness of particularity. It is hardly surprising, therefore, that her hero, a middle-aged British diplomat, Freddy Hamilton, insists that Britain (to avoid such particularity) must join the Common Market.

The 'Swinging Sixties': hope, experiment, illusion

Every decade is associated with certain evocative images and symbols – the Charleston in the twenties, the dole queue in the thirties, the austerity of the ration book and the wailing of the air-raid siren in the forties. Such images are to some extent clichés, but they do help to capture and represent the spirit of a particular period, whether it be the flippancy of the affluent strata in pre-depression America or the stoicism of Londoners during the Blitz.

The image of the 1960s is above all that of youthful rebellion and rapid social change. It was a time when the stifling smugness of the fifties came to be challenged and when the future seemed to offer immense promise. The freshness and radicalism of energetic youthfulness seemed for a time to carry all before it. In popular music the Beatles led the way with inventive and deceptively simple lyrics and melodies which were bouncily optimistic and zestful. In fashion Mary Quant opened a series of boutiques aimed specifically at teenagers, and Twiggy – six and a half stone and virtually shapeless – emerged as the antithesis to the buxom stereotype of female sexuality which had dominated during the 1950s. On television David Frost, Lance Percival,

Millicent Martin and others scandalized the old establishment with satirical programmes such as *That Was The Week That Was*, and in the process rapidly themselves became part of the new establishment. A succession of 'swinging London' films portrayed this new, young establishment disporting itself in nightclubs and in garishly painted Rolls-Royces, while back in the real world teenage girls celebrated a new era of pill-liberated sexuality and teenage boys with Beatle haircuts did their awkward best to take advantage of it. The Mods with their sharp mohair suits, parkas, pep-pills and dazzling Lambrettas took over the bank holiday beaches and The Who expressed their triumph in the song, 'My Generation': 'Hope I die before I get old!'

As working-class youth became caught up in the Mod phenomenon, so their middle-class contemporaries came to take their cue from San Francisco and the 'mystical' east. Male students in universities and art colleges grew their hair long – a symbol of defiance to authority no less potent than the chains and leather jackets of the Rockers or the exaggerated smoothness of the Mods. The hippies of 1966 and 1967 proclaimed peace and love with V-signs, adorned themselves with beads and body paint, indulged in free love at free rock concerts, discovered themselves through 'acid', expressed themselves in mantras and eastern-influenced music, communicated among themselves in the pages of *Oz* and *International Times* with a language all their own, and (in America if not in Britain) took on the armed might of the state with flowers: 'All across the nation, there's a new expectation, people in motion, people in motion.'

The mood of the sixties was one of rebellion – in the quest for self-expression, for liberation, for 'doing your own thing'. Writers, film directors, painters and musicians experimented with new forms and subject-matters, seeking what was for them most truthful, most authentic, most alive to contemporary experience. Not surprisingly, this led to headlong assaults upon established forms and values. In poetry, for instance, Al Alvarez argued in his preface to *The New Poetry* (1962), 'The New Poetry or Beyond the Gentility Principle', that English poets, too much bound by the decency and politeness of the English tradition, had failed to come to terms with the 'forces of disintegration' at work in man, forces whose 'public faces are those of two world wars, of the concentration camps, of genocide, and the threat of nuclear war.'[19] Alvarez claimed that some of the English and American poets included in his anthology – Ted Hughes, Sylvia Plath and Robert Lowell – were aware of these forces in a way that, in

Alvarez's phrase, the 'genteel' poetry of Philip Larkin (who was also anthologized) was not. Others, such as the Liverpool poets, Roger McGough, Adrian Henri and Brian Patten, wished to bring poetry back to its folk roots by emphasizing that poetry (like pop music) should be performed in public before a live audience (see also Chapter 5). Adrian Mitchell and Michael Horovitz, meanwhile, modelled themselves upon the American beat poets who were exploring the links between poetry and jazz.

In fiction, likewise, novelists tried to break out of the constricting forms of the English novel by assimilating the modes and techniques of foreign writers – particularly French and American writers. In *The Foot of Clive* (1962) and *Corker's Freedom* (1964) John Berger examined the relationship between the private and the social self in the manner of Jean-Paul Sartre; in *The Death of William Posters* (1965) Alan Sillitoe presented the revolt of Frank Dawley against a dreary marriage and debilitating job, not in the style of his earlier, realist fiction, but in the violent (and nihilistic) style of Norman Mailer; in *The Decline of the West* (1966) David Caute analysed the psychology of European imperialism in Africa in the terms which Sartre had developed from his reading of black writers; in *Gog* (1967) Andrew Sinclair drew upon the model of Thomas Pynchon's *The Crying of Lot 49* to describe the quest of an amnesic, 7-foot giant for his roots amidst the multiple signs and symbols which made up the culture of 'Great Britain'; and in *Between* (1968) Christine Brooke-Rose enlisted French structuralism to explore the relationships between language, mind and consciousness. Indeed, the creative interplay between the English novel and other literary and intellectual traditions was not only one of the major features but is also one of the major legacies of the writing of the sixties.

However, it was in drama, written for television as well as for the stage, that the most striking innovations were made (see also Chapter 6). The plays of Arnold Wesker, John Arden, Harold Pinter, David Mercer and Edward Bond brought a new seriousness of content and of purpose to drama, making the theatre the principal vehicle in the decade for debate and discussion about social and political issues. Perspectives were often contradictory. The pessimism of Pinter with his imagery of collapse, of decline, of menace, was countered by the bleak optimism of Bond, the resignation of Wesker by the activism of Mercer and Arden. Indeed, Mercer's trilogy for televison, *The Generations* (1961–3), can be seen as a deliberate rejoinder to Wesker's *The Wesker Trilogy* (*Chicken Soup with Barley*, 1959; *Roots*, 1959; *I'm Talking about Jerusalem*, 1960). For, while Wesker concluded that we can now find Jerusalem only through intense, private living, Mercer asserted that there was no escape, except by suicide or madness, from the pressure of public responsibility. Yet such explicit argument between playwrights themselves showed how confident dramatists had become that contemporary drama could and should deal with social and political questions.

There was in 1960s Britain a new liberalism. Falteringly, and sometimes half-heartedly, progressive legislation was introduced on a range of moral issues, shifting the responsibility for moral judgements from the state to the individual. Suicide was decriminalized in 1961 (although it remained an offence to help somebody to commit suicide). Homosexual relations between consenting adults were legalized (although the age of consent was set at 21 – five years older than that governing heterosexual relations – and discrimination against gays by police and employers continued unchecked). Abortion law reform vastly extended the grounds on which women could legally seek termination of pregnancy (although abortion on demand – a 'woman's right to choose' – was denied). Racial discrimination in housing and employment was outlawed (although the legislation proved largely ineffective and was in any case undermined by a further tightening of implicitly racist immigration laws). The government even set up a committee to investigate the decriminalization of so-called 'soft' drugs such as cannabis (although all such drugs remained illegal, and custodial sentences continued to be imposed on those deemed to be 'pushers').

The sixties, therefore, brought new freedoms and new responsibilities. Some, such as Margaret Drabble in *The Millstone* (1965), examined with compassion (although, for more recent readers, too tamely) the dilemmas these new freedoms posed, particularly for women; others, such as Kingsley Amis and Donald Davie, fulminated against the new and freer morality. For the younger generation, Amis declared in *I Want it Now* (1968), the concept of freedom amounted to no more than easy enjoyment of promiscuous sex, money, travel and drugs, while Davie, in his poem 'England' (1969), seemed almost hysterical in his conviction that the 'permissiveness' of the young was undermining social and cultural order. The love of knowledge, the disinterested inquiry of the past, he feared, had gone:

Gone, gone as the combo
starts in digging the beat

and the girls from the nearest College
of Further Education
spread their excited thighs.

Behind all this, however, there remained the persistent and worsening problems of the British economy. Economic policy in the early Wilson government was dominated by a concern with the foreign exchange rate of the pound sterling and the associated question of the balance of payments. In retrospect, it is clear that the pound (fixed at that time at a rate of US $2.8) was overvalued, given the declining relative productive capacity of the British economy. Recurring bouts of speculation in the world's money markets necessitated repeated interventions by the Bank of England in an attempt to prop up its value, and Wilson referred bitterly in Parliament to the faceless 'gnomes of Zürich' whom he saw as responsible for the sorry state of British fiscal policy.

For two and a half years the Labour government struggled to maintain the value of sterling, thus aiding those financial institutions which held the currency, but at the same time crippling British industry (whose products became overpriced in foreign markets) and jettisoning the much-heralded National Plan along the way. Eventually, in 1967, the pound was devalued, but this was too little too late, for deep and enduring problems of under-investment and archaic labour relations had by then fundamentally weakened large sections of British industry in comparison with its competitors in countries such as West Germany and Japan.

Unable to control the 'gnomes of Zürich', the government turned to confront a different enemy – organized labour. An attempt at regulating wage rises had already been made through the establishment of a Prices and Incomes Board, and this was now followed by a strategy for regulating trade-union practices in the form of a White Paper, *In Place of Strife* (1968). The aim of the proposed legislation was to outlaw unofficial strikes and to shift the balance of power in the unions from the increasingly influential shop stewards back to the national leadership. Such a strategy was entirely consistent with the government's centralized corporatist philosophy: the economy was to be managed through tripartite collusion between big capital, organized labour and the state, and shopfloor militancy represented an obstacle to the implementation of agreements arrived at by the heads of the big union bureaucracies.[20]

The proposals set out in *In Place of Strife* never reached the statute book because of the widespread and hostile reaction from the unions themselves to what was seen as an unwarranted and illegitimate intrusion into their own mode of operation. The proposals were, however, significant, not only because they demonstrated clearly how far the Labour government had strayed from its own industrial working-class base (it is interesting that many of the proposals in *In Place of Strife* were later resurrected by the Conservative administration of Edward Heath in the equally ill-fated Industrial Relations Act of 1971), but also because they represented the 'final straw' for many on the Left in Britain, whose disenchantment with the Labour Party in particular, and with the parliamentary system in general, had been mounting with each successive failure since 1964.

By 1968 – the year when students and workers rioted in Paris and nearly toppled the French government, and when the anti-Vietnam-war movement came to a head in America with street battles between police and demonstrators outside the Democratic Party convention in Chicago – radicals in Britain had generally lost faith in parliamentary socialism. A bewildering variety of left 'fringe' parties – IMG, SWP, RWP, RSL and many more – was spawned at around this time, and revolutionary student leaders such as Tariq Ali argued forcefully for an insurrectionary road to socialism with students in the vanguard of the struggle. A spate of occupations and demonstrations over issues as diverse as the confidentiality of student files and the use of the army in Northern Ireland brought the era of flower power on the campuses to an abrupt end.

The youthful optimism of the early mid-sixties had disappeared. The language of racial politics, first voiced in 1964 by Peter Griffiths in his successful election campaign at Smethwick ('If you want a nigger neighbour, vote Labour'), took on an added vicious thrust with a speech in which a senior Conservative politician, Enoch Powell, declared, 'like the Romans, I seem to see "the River Tiber flowing with much blood"'. In London the dockers marched in support of 'Good Old Enoch', and neo-fascists were not slow to take their cue in organizing openly and arrogantly through white-supremacist parties such as the National Front.

Across the Irish Sea, the Civil Rights Campaign among Catholics in Derry and Belfast escalated into riots and civil unrest unparalleled for nearly fifty years. In 1968 James Callaghan, then Home Secretary, sent British troops to Ulster as a 'temporary measure' to help the overwhelmingly Protestant Royal Ulster Constabulary (in a profoundly ambiguous phrase) to 'keep the peace'. This, in turn, fuelled a resurgence of terrorist activity among both republican and loyalist groups, and the troops have remained there ever since.

By the end of the decade, the Labour government's programme had been almost totally discredited. When Harold Wilson left office in June 1970, his administration could boast that it had at last got the balance of payments into surplus, but balance sheets are not the stuff that socialist dreams are made of. Centralized corporate planning had failed. The technological revolution had not materialized (despite vast investment in new plate-glass universities and polytechnics). The towering blocks of flats which had been built to replace the inner-city slums had proved immensely unpopular with all connected with them, except for the building firms and architects who made millions during this period. The big new comprehensive schools had done little to increase the educational opportunities of working-class children, and fiscal and social policy had done even less to reduce the inequalities of income and wealth which still divided the classes.

The dawn of the 1970s heralded the so-called 'me' decade. Collectivism, centralism, corporatism, statism – all were now discredited. Small was beautiful. People began to contemplate their navels, and Woody Allen became the new cult figure. Politically, this move from hope to 'hard-nosed realism', from collectivism to individualism, from altruism to egoism, was reflected in the emergence of 'Selsdon Man' – a new breed of political animal heralded by a Conservative working party at the Selsdon Park Hotel, Croydon, in 1970. The new Conservative Prime Minister, Edward Heath, who surprisingly won the general election later in the year, personified the type (although his successor as leader of the Conservatives and, later, as Prime Minister, Margaret Thatcher, was to prove an even more ruthless example). For he appealed not to the electorate's principles but to its pockets, committing his government to rolling back the state, controlling the unions, reprivatizing the mixed economy, cutting welfare and abandoning Keynesian policies aimed at maintaining low levels of unemployment. By June 1970 the principles established immediately after the war had lost their aura of sanctity and the consensus established by 'Butskellism' had been forgotten. What had been gained, in the post-war period, was not enough; but what was now in jeopardy was manifestly too much.

Notes

1 Cyril Connolly, 'Letter from a Civilian', *Horizon* (September 1944).

2 T. S. Eliot, 'Notes on Education and Culture', *Notes towards the Definition of Culture* (London: Faber, 1948), p. 100.

3 George Orwell, 'James Burnham and the Managerial Revolution', in *The Collected Essays, Journalism and Letters of George Orwell*, vol. 4: *1945–50* (Harmondsworth: Penguin, 1971), p. 212.

4 George Orwell, 'Toward European Unity', in ibid., pp. 423–9.

5 John Wain, *Hurry on Down* (Harmondsworth: Penguin, 1979), p. 42.

6 Ibid., p. 113.

7 Kingsley Amis, *Lucky Jim* (Harmondsworth: Penguin, 1977), p. 8.

8 Ibid., p. 251.

9 Kingsley Amis, *One Fat Englishman* (Harmondsworth: Penguin, 1975), p. 147.

10 C. P. Snow, *Corridors of Power* (Harmondsworth: Penguin, 1972), p. 334.

11 Doris Lessing, 'The Small Personal Voice', in Tom Maschler (ed.), *Declaration* (London: MacGibbon & Kee, 1957), p. 16.

12 Doris Lessing, *The Four-Gated City* (St Albans: Panther, 1972), p. 494.

13 Ibid., p. 495.

14 Ibid., p. 428.

15 Ibid., p. 662.

16 Iris Murdoch, 'Novelist as Metaphysician', *The Listener*, 16 March 1950.

17 Iris Murdoch, *The Sandcastle* (St Albans: Panther, 1979), p. 195.

18 Angus Wilson, *The Old Men at the Zoo* (St Albans: Panther, 1979), p. 310.

19 A. Alvarez, *The New Poetry* (Harmondsworth: Penguin, 1962), p. 26.

20 See J. Winkler, 'Corporatism', *European Journal of Sociology*, 17 (1976), pp. 100–36.

Further reading

Bogdanor, Vernon, and Skidelsky, Robert. *The Age of Affluence 1951–1964*. London: Macmillan, 1970.

Calvocoressi, Peter. *The British Experience 1945–75*. London: Bodley Head, 1978. Harmondsworth: Penguin, 1979.

Cox, C. B., and Dyson, A. E. (eds). *The Twentieth Century Mind*, vol. 3: *1945–1965*. London: Oxford University Press, 1972.

Havighurst, Alfred F. *Britain in Transition*. Chicago, Ill.: Chicago University Press, 1979.

Hewison, Robert. *In Anger: Culture in the Cold War 1945–60*. London: Weidenfield & Nicolson, 1981.

Holloway, John. 'English Culture and the Feat of Transformation'. *The Listener*, 77 (1967), pp. 47–9, 85–9, 126–32.

Marwick, Arthur. *British Society Since 1945*. Harmondsworth: Pelican, 1982.

Morrison, Blake. *The Movement: English Poetry and Fiction of the 1950s*. London: Oxford University Press, 1980.

Ryder, Judith, and Silver, Harold. *Modern English Society*. Rev. edn. London: Methuen, 1977.

Sissons, Michael, and French, Philip (eds). *The Age of Austerity 1945–1951*. London: Hodder & Stoughton, 1963. Harmondsworth: Penguin, 1964.

Sked, Alan, and Cook, Chris. *Post-War Britain: A Political History*. Harmondsworth: Penguin, 1979.

Wilson, Elizabeth. *Only Halfway to Paradise: Women in Postwar Britain 1945–68*. London: Tavistock, 1980.

Ziegler, Heide, and Bigsby, Christopher (eds). *The Radical Imagination and the Liberal Tradition: Interviews with Contemporary English and American Novelists*. London: Junction Books, 1982.

3 The challenge of sexuality

JONATHAN DOLLIMORE

Ideological parameters

Sexuality, transgression, subversion In his diary for March 1967 Joe Orton records an exchange with his lover, Kenneth Halliwell, on the subversive potential of 'complete sexual licence':

> 'It's the only way to smash the wretched civilization,' I said, making a mental note to hot-up *What the Butler Saw* when I came to rewrite. . . . Yes. Sex is the only way to infuriate them. Much more fucking and they'll be screaming hysterics in next to no time.[1]

The entry is to be explained not solely in terms of Orton's personal desire to scandalize; he is subscribing to a view widely held in the post-war period, namely that sexual transgression and deviance could radically challenge an existing, repressive social order. Even in Orwell's *Nineteen Eighty-Four* (1949), as Winston is making love with Julia, the revolutionary potential of sexuality is affirmed: 'simple undifferentiated desire: that was the force that would tear the party to pieces'.[2] But the most inspired advocates of the idea were the Freudian Left, particularly Herbert Marcuse. Elevated almost to the status of prophet by the sixties counter-culture, Marcuse held that the sublimation of sexuality was a precondition for capitalism's successful transformation of the body into an instrument of labour (see *Eros and Civilization*, 1955; *One Dimensional Man*, 1964). In *Life against Death* (1959) Norman O. Brown argued that civilization, on the brink of self-annihilation through nuclear warfare, must save itself through the abolition of repression, the resurrection of the body (see also Wilhelm Reich, *The Sexual Revolution*, trans. 1951). This philosophy was embraced eagerly by the youth movements in America and Europe: if the sublimation of eros is the means whereby a repressive civilization is maintained, then what revolutionary change might not be inaugurated by its liberation?

Law Lord Patrick Devlin also acknowledged the subversive power of sexuality – not, however, in order to liberate it, but in order more effectively to suppress it. In *The Enforcement of Morals* (1959) – a prominent contribution to the contemporary debate between emergent liberalism and conservative reaction – Devlin actually associated 'immorality' with treason: just as the latter constituted sedition from within, so the former generated social disintegration from within. Therefore, Devlin asserted, 'the suppression of vice is as much the law's business as the suppression of subversive activities'[3] (the liberal position was represented by H. L. A. Hart in *Law, Liberty and Morality*, 1963). Strikingly, then, Devlin, though diametrically opposed to the political position of Marcuse, nevertheless shares with him one assumption: sexuality is possessed of an inherently subversive power. Whether that power was to be liberated or controlled depended on whether it was seen as representative of repressed human potential or, conversely, of the evil human condition; as potentially revolutionary or fatally disintegrative. But that it existed was beyond the doubt of the most disparate sections of society, from Orton to Devlin, from Marcuse to Mary Whitehouse.

This was not, however, the assumption of a third political position, more important perhaps than either the authoritarian or the libertarian – namely, liberal reformism. Apologetic, piecemeal and often inconsistent, it was hardly a movement as such; nevertheless, it was responsible for promoting – though not necessarily initiating – legislative and ideological changes that were significantly to improve many people's lives. In the process, albeit unwittingly, it also facilitated the emergence of more radical forces for social change. Indeed, the very contradictions within liberal reformism – in particular, the extent of its complicity with the ideological assumptions it was ostensibly challenging – are themselves crucial for understanding the history of this period.

The *Chatterley* trial is an important point of departure for at least three reasons: it illustrates the contradictions in liberalism; as a major censorship issue it is a glaringly 'material' instance of the intersection of literature, sexuality, politics, ideology and law; and it constitutes a fascinating record of contemporary attitudes – especially authoritarian attitudes – to sexual transgression (the trial was in 1960, one year after Devlin's book). Lawrence's novel, alleged the prosecution, exalted adultery and promiscuity – activities transgressive enough in themselves, but here the more so (it was constantly implied) because they involved two further factors: the initiative of a woman, and a relationship with a servant. So, in his opening address for the prosecution, Mr Griffith-Jones described *Lady Chatterley's Lover* as about 'a sex-starved girl' who satisfies herself with a man 'who also happens to be her husband's gamekeeper'.[4] Griffith-Jones intended the jury to infer that this woman's behaviour violates not just her personal duty to her husband but, worse, the whole order of society – an order in which, from the patriarchal perspective, servants, especially *gamekeepers*, are as sacrosanct as wives. Thus Griffith-Jones asked the jury, 'Is it a book that you would even wish your wife or your servants to read?'[5]

At the same time, homosexuality was becoming a contentious issue, considered by many to be more subversive of right order even than female infidelity. In 1965 Field Marshal Lord Montgomery asserted in the House of Lords:

> If these unnatural practices are made legal a blow is struck at the discipline of the British armed forces at a time when we need the very highest standards of morale and discipline with these forces serving throughout the world. . . . Take a large aircraft carrier with 2000 men cooped up in a small area. Imagine, what would happen in a ship of that sort if these practices crept in.

Homosexuality in the ranks is chaos come again; literally overnight, inversion will breed subversion.

The views expressed by Griffith-Jones and Montgomery are no longer dominant, but they cannot be discounted. First because Montgomery won his case: homosexuality in the armed forces is still illegal and offenders are court-martialed, dismissed and even imprisoned. Second, reform, when it came in 1967, constituted not so much acceptance of homosexuality as tolerance of it, the gift of the superior to the inferior; it was to be quarantined as far as possible from the majority of the population and permitted only between 'adults' (those over 21), and then only in private with no more than two at any one time. Third, many of Griffith-Jones's assumptions about women and sexuality were shared by the defence. As C. H. Rolph remarked, it was not Lawrence's book so much as the woman, Lady Chatterley, that was on trial. The defence evidence exemplified, says Elizabeth Wilson, 'how a Puritan, humanist view of marriage dominated radical intellectuals and Christians alike'; even within a genuinely progressive discourse – which, in historical terms, the defence undoubtedly was – there was no space for women to speak *as such*.[6] In fact, the view of Lawrence which the defence advanced seems as archaic as that of the prosecution when set against the devastating critique of Lawrence in Kate Millett's *Sexual Politics*. This classic of the women's movement, published in Britain in 1971, perceived in Lawrence not the quasi-mystical wholeness of self for which he was celebrated in the fifties and sixties but a phallocentrism at once sadistic and misogynistic.

Lastly, any suggestion that Lawrence's book constituted a celebration of sexuality *per se* was (had to be?) denied by the defence witnesses, some of whom even argued that the novel meted out a kind of poetic justice to those who indulged in promiscuity for its own sake. 'Promiscuous intercourse', said one, is shown as 'unsatisfactory, giving no fulfilment, no joy, and as really rather disgusting';[7] by another as 'barren of satisfaction'.[8] The defence case made acceptable sexuality always *signify something else* – for example: 'a beauty which cancels lust'.[9] This beauty was often described in religiose terms; 'sacred' was a word often used. Richard Hoggart defended the novel as being 'virtuous and puritanical',[10] while Norman St John-Stevas put Lawrence among 'the great literary moralists . . . essentially trying to purge and to cleanse and to reform'.[11]

Sexuality and nature   Conservative arguments for the control of sexuality typically anchor notions of a correct *social* order in notions of a correct *natural* order. Historically this has been one of the most important mechanisms of ideological control: by being designated as 'natural', a particular social order or practice is legitimized, since anything natural must surely be unalterable and therefore beyond question. Conversely, whatever is thought to contravene that order or practice is stigmatized as 'unnatural', and outlawed. Even when the appeal to nature appears secularist, its roots are likely to be in the Christian tradition.

The unnatural then becomes a most insidious and paradoxical manifestation of evil: it is at once alien to, and yet mysteriously inherent within, 'the human condition'. This contradiction surfaces in two especially revealing (and related) anxieties of the post-war period. The first concerns the family, which was presented on the one hand as incontrovertibly natural and on the other as terribly vulnerable to deviant sexual desire, especially from within. The second concerns the homosexual, who was seen on the one hand as a monstrous invert utterly alien to normal beings and on the other as capable of corrupting such beings (especially children and soldiers) almost on sight. Hence, of course, Montgomery's fear of the consequences of what he called 'these unnatural practices' being permitted in the forces. But a yet more revealing instance of this contradiction can be observed in the ideological appropriation of nature which occurs in the *Chatterley* trial. Cecil Day Lewis, for the defence, had suggested that Lady Chatterley's sexual behaviour was 'perfectly natural'; Griffith-Jones retorts, incredulously, ' "Perfectly natural" that Lady Chatterley should run off to the hut in the forest on every occasion to copulate with her husband's gamekeeper? Not "perfectly natural", sir!' Day Lewis: 'Yes; it is in her nature.' Griffith-Jones: 'It is in her nature because she is an oversexed and adulterous woman; that is why it is in her nature, is it not?' Day Lewis: 'No.'[12] Griffith-Jones's incredulous response implies that Lady Chatterley's behaviour, far from being in accord with the 'perfectly natural', outrageously contravenes it. That which is outrageously contravened must, by implication, be not only transparently obvious to all, but obviously right. Yet in the next breath he uses 'nature' to mean the opposite – 'sinful nature': 'it is in her nature because she is an over-sexed and adulterous woman'.

Perhaps Griffith-Jones would have concurred with Richard Burton's declaration of 360 years ago: 'Of women's unnatural, unsatiable lust, what country, what village doth not complain?'[13] From Burton's day to ours, 'nature' has worked mysteriously to privilege in men what is outlawed in women. 'It's only natural for a man like him to be laying a different woman each night,' says Judith of Maurice in David Storey's *This Sporting Life* (contemporary with the *Chatterley* trial). That Judith is speaking of her own husband indicates one of the most significant things about sexual ideology: those whom it oppresses often subscribe to it as willingly as those who use it to oppress. Such 'self-oppression' (a less authoritarian term than the older 'false consciousness') was to become within a few years a central concern of sexual politics, especially in the women's and gay movements.

If those radical movements showed the possibility of escaping in political terms (that is, collectively) from such oppression, Margaret Drabble's

2 View of newly opened motorway – the Western Avenue extension, London (1970)

novels written in the sixties register the virtual impossibility of escaping from it in individualistic terms. Sarah is the heroine of Drabble's first novel, *A Summer Bird-Cage* (1963). Privileged in class and education, she finds unjust what Storey's Judith accepts. Even so, because she in turn still fatally conflates the natural and the social, biology and gender, she finds it impossible to escape her destiny as 'woman':

> I looked at myself in fascination, thinking how unfair it was, to be born with so little defence, like a soft snail without a shell. Men are all right, they are defined and enclosed, but we in order to live must be open and raw to all comers. What happens otherwise is worse than what happens normally, the embroidery and the children and the sagging mind. I felt doomed to defeat. I felt all women were doomed. Louise thought she wasn't but she was . . . because she was born to defend and depend instead of to attack.[14]

Sexuality and authenticity   For Michel Foucault the idea that there exist 'complex, obscure and essential relationships between sex and truth' is found in psychiatry, psychoanalysis, psychology and current opinion generally. It is manifested in two crucial beliefs: first, that a deviation from the norm is a deviation from truth, so that even if sexual deviants are to be tolerated 'there is still something like an "error" involved in what they do . . . a manner of acting that is not adequate to reality'; second, that 'it is in the area of sex that we must search for the most secret and profound truths about the individual'.[15] As we shall see, both beliefs are strikingly foregrounded, but also rendered intensely problematic, in Lessing's *The Golden Notebook*. There and in other novels of the period, the second belief becomes the subject for sustained attention, reflecting, in Britain at least and in the widest sense of the term, a Protestant heritage.

Once again it is at the *Chatterley* trial that we find the idea put unequivocally (by Richard Hoggart): 'For Lawrence the [sexual] act is meaningless unless it relates to one's whole being; in other words, back to God.'[16] Many who would balk at letting God in on the act would nevertheless agree with the first part of Hoggart's statement – that sexuality does lead to a manifestation of the discovery of one's essential, authentic self, the unity of one's being. But what is found, all too frequently, is not authenticity but a whole new dimension of conflict and contradiction – though never perhaps as much as critics subsequent to Hoggart have found in Lawrence himself.[17]

So far I have outlined three important ideological constructions of sexuality: those concerned with its transgressive potential, its represen-
tation in terms of the natural/unnatural dichotomy, and its status as the source and haven of the authentic, unitary self. They constitute, I believe, three of the main parameters within which sexuality was constructed during this period, and hence they are crucial for understanding the continuities, and equally the discontinuities, between its literature and the concurrent public discourses on sexuality.

Public debates

> Sexual intercourse began
> In nineteen sixty-three
> (Which was rather late for me) –
> Between the end of the *Chatterley* ban
> And the Beatles' first LP.
>
> Up till then there'd only been
> A Sort of Bargaining,
> A wrangle for a ring,
> A shame that started at sixteen
> And spread to everything.
>
> (Philip Larkin, 'Annus Mirabilis', 1974)

The changes Larkin evokes were not limited to sexual intercourse, or to the Marvellous Year 1963. But his sense of liberating transition – especially of what is displaced – seems right: in the post-war period sexuality became, to an unprecedented extent, a topic for public debate. Once released from the closet, its power to signify seemed in-
exhaustible – and worrying: that which once seemed relatively clear-
cut became problematic. (Powerful literary evocations of pre-1963 sexual poverty include Orwell's *Keep the Aspidistra Flying* (1936) and Stan Barstow's *A Kind of Loving* (1960).)

From the debates of the sixties there emerged real achievements in the causes of personal freedom generally and sexual liberation in par-
ticular, including a sequence of important legal reforms, mostly during the Wilson administration of 1966–70: the facilitating of birth control and divorce, the permitting of abortion and homosexuality, the abolition of hanging and theatre censorship, and the Obscene Publications Act (1959) which led to the *Chatterley* trial. Nevertheless all this should not be seen as a straightforward displacement of dominant conservative

attitudes by emergent progressive ones. As in the *Chatterley* defence case, the emergent ideology often retains assumptions of the dominant, with the subordinate – not necessarily in a minority – perhaps being allowed no representation at all. Nowhere is this more apparent than in relation to the family.

The family   As an institution the family has been jealously guarded; to suggest that something was inimical to family life was to condemn it. The family was seen as the indispensable unit for emotional stability, mature psychosexual development and responsible citizenship; it helped to ensure the survival of all that was best in a culture, and was a powerful mainstay against the corruptions of the modern world. Whether the family actually fulfilled all these functions is questionable; but it had usually been assumed to possess them. The far-reaching social, economic and ideological changes in which it participated after the war therefore aroused considerable alarm.

There were several main factors. A more open attitude to sexuality gradually developed; its enjoyment became more permissible, albeit within an insistently defined conjugal context; sex manuals became franker and more widely acceptable; and there was some acknowledgement of female sexuality. Pornography and sex education in schools were both growth areas. There was an increase in the availability of contraception and contraceptive advice. Female chastity became less important, and fashion eroticized the body more explicitly. Divorce increased and in the process lost some of its stigma. Correspondingly, the Christian ideal of the permanence of the marriage bond was displaced, as was, to some extent, the authoritarian and patriarchal conception of family structure. More and more women were entering paid work. Teenage children acquired greater economic independence.

Such changes fed a growing controversy in the fifties and sixties over the state of the family. It focused, for example, upon 'latch-key' children – those whose mothers had been drawn into waged work and who were supposedly starved of the stability and affection only a mother could provide; it focused too on the apparent breakdown of kinship networks and the emergence of the supposedly less stable, more isolated nuclear family; and on the 'generation gap' and the increased affluence and hence independence of children, leading to fears (ungrounded) that they were becoming more promiscuous – in effect, adolescent independence (a loosening of parental control) was interpreted as adolescent irresponsibility (a lack of parental control).

Once again, however, this was a controversy within the parameters of conservatism and liberalism. Sociologists, teachers, social workers, politicians, journalists and churchmen conducted a debate marked by unquestioned assumptions like those in the *Chatterley* trial. The sexual division of labour, for example was taken for granted.[18] Again, although female sexuality was being recognized in a way it had not been before, it was still being constructed from the point of view of the male.[19] Furthermore, there was a persistent consensus about the necessity of the family: the point at issue was whether or not it was in dissolution. This can be clearly seen in the way familial ideology was built into the theory of the welfare state, where benefits were (are) conditional upon conventional moral behaviour and were denied to women living with men who were not their legal spouses.[20]

There developed in the sixties a radical critique of the family. The anti-psychiatry movement, associated especially with R. D. Laing, saw the family as the source of mental illness – in particular, schizophrenia. Even more fundamental, at the end of the period, was the sexual politics of the women's and gay movements. The family's narrow channelling of sexuality, its socializing of children into rigid gender roles and its oppression of women in the domestic roles of wife and mother – these were just some of the criticisms. The common ground was an analysis of the family as incorporating in its very structure – and thus perpetuating – the negative elements of society at large. It gained many adherents, and not only among fringe radicals; Edmund Leach's contention in the 1967 Reith Lectures that the family, 'with its narrow privacy and tawdry secrets, is the source of all our discontent' aroused frantic controversy because the radical analysis had become publicly thinkable.[21]

Wolfenden Between 1939 and 1953 prosecutions for prostitution and male homosexual offences rose quite dramatically (the former sixfold, the latter fivefold), even though there was little evidence to show any increase in the actual number of offences.[22] What this suggests is that, if one condition for a freer discourse on sexuality was that it be seen to be contained within the family, another condition was that behaviour thought to threaten the family (such as prostitution and homosexuality) be even more effectively controlled. The Wolfenden Committee, appointed to review the law on homosexuality and prostitution, was in part a response to this second condition. Not surprisingly, then, it designated homosexuality 'reprehensible from the point of view of the family'. Its punitive recommendations on prostitution became law very quickly – the 1959 Street Offences Act increased penalties for public soliciting – while its progressive recommendations on homosexuality were not taken up in legislation until a decade later.

The crucial contribution of the Wolfenden Report was to propose the demarcating of a private sphere of sexual morality (this is the case Devlin rejected) – or, rather, that homosexual behaviour in certain circumstances be decriminalized. Progressive as this undoubtedly was, it had authoritarian implications as well: 'by ceasing to be the guardian of *private* morality, the law would more effectively become the protector of *public* decency and order. . . . The key point is that privatization did not necessarily involve a diminution of control.'[23] In fact, the Wolfenden Report was part of a general movement away from the legal control of deviance of all kinds and towards a more diffuse form of social surveillance via the medical profession and the social services. Thus it recommends further research into the 'aetiology of homosexuality'.

This in turn was involved with a wider shift – away from seeing sexual deviance as a sin and towards seeing it as a regrettable condition of sickness, mental disturbance or maladjustment of some vaguer kind. Among the professional discourses involved in this, Freudian psychiatry was powerful; here the natural, now in quasi-scientific guise, was restated in terms of 'normal' psychosexual development and maturity. Such shifts (it may be repeated) represented a stage in liberalization while at the same time sanctioning powerful new forms of surveillance and control. Thus in 1965 a poll showed that more people than ever before were in favour of homosexual law reform (63 per cent), but 93 per cent thought homosexuality a form of illness requiring medical treatment.[24] This kind of consensus, though it did not cause, was undoubtedly a precondition for, the application of one of the most objectionable ways of inducing conformity to the norm: aversion therapy. Developed initially for alcoholism, in the fifties and sixties it was attempted with various kinds of sexual deviant.

The Kinsey Reports and sexual diversity   Typically it is in a conceptual slide between 'norm' in its descriptive or statistical sense and 'norm' in its prescriptive sense that a dominant practice is legitimated: via 'normality' it is rendered natural. Instrumental in debunking this particular appeal to nature in sexual matters were the Kinsey Reports – *Sexual Behaviour in the Human Male* (1948) and *Sexual Behaviour in the Human Female* (1953). These reports didn't attack the dominant/ natural equation as such; rather, by showing that deviant behaviour was far more widespread than hitherto believed, they showed the dominant itself to be something of a myth and thereby also problematized the concept of the natural. Conducted in America but widely publicized in this country, they were the focus, both here and there, of much controversy. Perhaps the most significant of Kinsey's discoveries was the sheer diversity of sexual practice; but most controversial was his finding that 37 per cent of his male respondents and 13 per cent of his female respondents had experienced homosexual relations to the level of orgasm. Kinsey also revealed that other deviant behaviour, hitherto thought very rare, was in fact relatively widely practised. Additionally, he provided evidence which could be used to defend pre- and extra-marital intercourse; which revealed the differing effects of class on sexual behaviour; which suggested that marriage was at odds with the facts of sexual ageing (the high point of sexual activity in males was put at 16–17 years); which helped discredit the idea of vaginal orgasm; which found that for women masturbation and homosexuality were more 'reliable' than heterosexual intercourse. In short, Kinsey's findings 'were of a nature to shatter the self-esteem of the American male and undermine the authority of the husband'.[25] (Others interpret Kinsey differently: Andrea Dworkin, for example, finds that he construed the social as the biological and so reproduced women's social oppression in terms of 'facts' about their biological nature.[26])

Masters and Johnson drew conclusions similar to Kinsey's. In *Human Sexual Response* (1966) they sought to refute the idea that women's sexuality simply replicates men's; on the contrary, female sexual capacity appeared both greater than male and more diverse. They also vindicated masturbation, especially for the female, and emphasized the importance of the clitoris as the primary focus of female sexual response. Thus they prepared the ground for a challenge to 'the myth of the vaginal orgasm' (the title of Anna Koedt's book on the subject) – a challenge which has had far-reaching implications for female sexuality, particularly by undermining the traditional assumption that it must centre upon the phallus.

The work of these researchers, naïvely empirical as it may seem now, called into question prevailing ideas about sexuality, not least the naturalness of monogamous heterosexual genital intercourse. One consequence was a freer emphasis on sexuality as pleasure. Yet so deep-seated in our culture has been the appeal to nature that many – perhaps the majority – felt unable to surrender the belief that there must be *some* universal norm in matters sexual. A growth in the influence of Freudian theory may have helped to contain the challenge of Kinsey by reconstituting the norm in psychoanalytic terms. Thus the manifestations of sexual desire which Kinsey represented as relatively disorganized were reorganized by Freudian theory: 'it located sexuality within the family while Kinsey showed it to be free-roaming.'[27]

But the questioning of the ideological use of nature was to continue. Like Roland Barthes in France, many rejected the belief that if we scratch history we find the bedrock of nature beneath. Barthes said we must reverse the terms and constantly interrogate nature, its laws and its limits 'in order to discover history there' and, finally, to establish nature itself as an ideological construct.[28] The effect of this undermining of nature has been far-reaching, not least in changing the identifications of the sexuality and status of the two groupings we have considered here, women and homosexuals. 'Anatomy is destiny,' Freud declared. But are the determinants of this 'destiny' natural or historical? – necessary or contingent? In *The Second Sex* (trans. 1953) Simone de Beauvoir voiced the proposition which was to shift questions of sexuality and gender on to a radically new terrain: you are not born a woman, you become one. In the mid-seventies the implications of that proposition, substantiated by sociological and anthropological research, were to be even more boldly stated; Kenneth Plummer echoes a maxim of Marx: 'Rather than sexuality determining our social being – as many writers suggest, especially Freudian ones – it is the other way round: social meanings determine and affect our sexuality. Sexuality has no meaning other than that given to it in social situations.'[29]

Literary constructions

Sexuality, cool and angry   Fifties 'Movement' poetry (Larkin, Amis, Wain, Davie, Gunn) aimed to debunk Victorian prudery, romantic solemnity and Lawrentian humourlessness. It affected a more casual attitude to sexuality: 'Why pretend / Love must accompany erection?' (Thom Gunn, 'Modes of Pleasure'). Yet, as Blake Morrison has shown,[30] it foregrounded other attitudes as well, including misogyny and anxiety about sexual prowess. Thom Gunn was exceptional in his attentiveness to the complexity of erotic signification. His early verse, in particular, represents desire playing across and eroticizing images of youth, freedom and escape, and also (and often inseparably) images of power and violence:

> The lips that meet the wound can finally
> Justify nothing – neither pain nor care;
> Tender upon shoulders ripe with blood.

('The Beaters')

In the 'angry' literature sexuality is explicitly linked with class antagonism. In Eliot's *Waste Land* (1922) occurs that famous act of sexual intercourse whose alienated sordidness is inseparable from the class and social identity of those who perform it: a 'typist' and 'a small house agent's clerk. . . . One of the low'. In the mid-fifties the low speak back; in John Osborne's *Look Back in Anger* (1956) a cross-class marriage becomes a site of 'challenges and revenge' in the class war.[31] This literature likewise foregrounds themes of misogyny and sexual anxiety. In *Look Back* Jimmy says of his wife, Alison: 'she has the passion of a python. She just devours me whole every time, as if I were some over-large rabbit. . . . She'll go on sleeping and devouring until there's nothing left of me.'[32] Jimmy's anger is traced to the death of his father: no one else cared, not even his mother: 'all she could think about was the fact that she had allied herself to a man who seemed on the wrong side in all things.'[33] Now he holds women responsible not just for his own angry helplessness but for the emasculation of the whole post-war world: 'there aren't any good, brave causes left' – nothing, in fact, 'but to let yourself be butchered by the women'.[34] Male bonding, between Jimmy and Cliff and Jimmy and Alison's father, is valued because it may help to retard the process.

Contempt for women finds its counter-image in their idealization. *Look Back* and *Room at the Top* both echo the ancient dichotomy of woman as madonna/whore. These are opposite sides of the same coin; the madonna mode involves an idealization which, like the contempt, distances and thereby 'objectifies' women. The prominent placing of this contradictory estimate of 'woman' in these books is evidently related to the social and sexual insecurity of the male, and it perhaps marks a crucial point of strain in patriarchal ideology.

Jimmy's fondness for Hugh's mother is real enough, but it is of the kind which thrives on limited personal involvement and a corresponding idealization of what she represents: a tragic victim in *his* war: 'She was alone, and I was the only one with her. And when I have to walk behind that coffin on Thursday, I'll be on my own again.' The idealization

3 Queue in Camberwell, South London, during potato shortage (1947)

4 Fans besiege
Buckingham
Palace when the
Beatles receive
their MBEs
(1965)

67

feeds Jimmy's self-pity and his self-righteousness; it facilitates a dichotomization in which Alison is made to represent both the other side of woman and the unfeeling middle class: 'that bitch won't even send her a bunch of flowers'.[35]

In John Braine's *Room at the Top* (1957) sexual domination and submission are the explicit counterpart and consequence of class antagonism. This is working-class Joe at last gaining possession of middle-class Susan:

> 'I love you, you silly bitch, and I'm the one who says what's to be done. Now and in the future.'
>
> 'Let me go,' she said. 'I'll scream for help. You can't make me stay against my will.' She started to struggle. . . . I shook her as hard as I could. I'd done it in play before, when she'd asked me to hurt her, please hurt her; but this time I was in brutal earnest. . . . Then I kissed her, biting her lip till I tasted blood. . . .
>
> 'You hurt me,' she said when I came to my senses afterwards. . . .
>
> 'Oh Joe, I love you with all of me now, every little bit of me is yours. You won't need *her* any more, will you?'[36]

Her is Alice, the woman Joe really loves but whom he is sacrificing for what he came to Warley to get: 'an Aston-Martin . . . a three-guinea linen shirt . . . a girl with a Riviera suntan'.[37] But Joe's attitude to Susan is not merely predatory, for she is also his ideal madonna: 'Even apart from her money, she was worth marrying. She was the princess in the fairy stories, the girl in old songs, the heroine of musical comedies';[38] 'I wanted simply to admire what is, after all, a very rare human type: a beautiful and unspoiled virgin'.[39] To complete the pattern we need woman-as-whore, and Joe in fact feeds his self-righteousness by contemplating 'the disgust which any man one stage above the apes is bound to feel when he unites with a woman whom he despises'.[40]

Joe finally opts for Susan, while Alice, suicidal and drunk, crashes her car; she suffers appalling injuries and crawls around for hours before dying. Horrified and guilt-ridden, Joe wanders drunkenly into a working-class neighbourhood, where his remorse is intensified by sordid encounters with a woman (whore?) whom he successfully seduces and a homosexual who tries (of course, unsuccessfully) to seduce him. Joe is thus made to experience a 'dark night of the soul', a supposedly cleansing plunge into the deep reality of evil. At this point we can see how *Room at the Top* foregrounds, and so in certain respects demystifies, sexuality as the site of class struggle and exploitation, yet at the same time sanctions more complex forms of mystification and exploitation which facilitate rather than challenge patriarchal power. Thus the death of Alice is seen by Joe as a consequence of the 'fallen human condition' – his own, that of the working class he is abandoning, in fact everyone's:

> I licked my dry lips, looking round the bus at the other passengers, sleek rosy, whole, stinking of food and tobacco and sleep . . . it was an attack of the truth: I saw quite clearly that there were no dreams and no mercy left in the world, nothing but a storm of violence.[41]

With Alice as a dead (and thus impossible) ideal; with a grim fatalism born of guilt and remorse; with the recognition of the sordid human condition which reassuringly implicates all: far from preventing Joe from arriving at the top, these convenient mystifications will enable him to get there.

Arthur, the hero of Alan Sillitoe's *Saturday Night and Sunday Morning* (1958), is having affairs with two married women but vows that if any wife of his behaved as they are doing he'd 'kill her'. And, what's more,

> My wife'll have to look after any kids I fill her with, keep the house spotless. And if she's good at that I might let her go to the pictures now and again and take her out for a drink on Saturday. But if I thought she was carrying on behind my back she'd be sent back to her mother with two black eyes.[42]

The novel manifests the debunking realism of the Angry Young Man – a realism that insists on what is actually and obviously the case over against the lies of politicians, trade unions, bosses and the rest; a realism in the service of anarchic individualism. At the same time, more is disclosed, especially in the realm of the sexual. In Arthur's universe almost everything to do with sexuality is simply assumed. That women are positioned somehow off-centre in relation to men is just a fact of life (natural); thus men are strongly individuated, whereas women exist primarily to ratify men – as sex partners, mothers or quite literally as onlookers. Even so, the attitude towards women is ambivalent. On the one hand they are appreciated as givers of pleasure: 'Arthur, in his more tolerant moments, said that women were more than ornaments and skivvies: they were warm and wonderful creatures that needed and deserved to be looked after.'[43] On the other hand they threaten to trap and tame the male, to curtail his freedom and, worse, become parasitic upon his virility. In this novel too, anxiety on the last score quickly flares into misogyny:

> Dave got a woman into trouble who had turned out to be the worst kind of tart, a thin, vicious, rat-faced whore who tried to skin him for every penny he'd got – until he threatened to chuck her over Trent Bridge one dark night, and she settled for a quid a week out of court.[44]

Arthur insists on identifying women as complicit with the system he is fighting – 'fighting every day until I die. . . . Fighting with mothers and wives, landlords and gaffers, coppers, army, government';[45] but, in so far as his anarchic aspirations are actually realized, it is only with and at the expense of the women in his life. This contradiction is only an aspect of a more general one: Arthur's aggressive, anarchic individualism is actually enabled by the very system he believes it to be opposing, or at least resisting. His kind of individualism, stubbornly anti-political, becomes dependent upon – actually exploits and reinforces – many of the conditions of his and his class's oppression, even as that individualism is acted out as a challenge to that oppression. So, when Arthur's workmate Jack is 'promoted' to the night shift, Arthur sleeps with Jack's wife, believing that it serves him right for being a 'slow husband'.[46]

This suggests what is, in retrospect, so important about the 'angry' literature: the destructive and unjust operations of power that its male protagonists identify and attack in society at large are reproduced and sanctioned (more or less unconsciously) by those protagonists in their personal lives and relationships. There is here something more important than hypocrisy. Patriarchy is arguably as fundamental as class, and inseparable from class. In these books, power in its class manifestations is being overtly criticized and foregrounded, and in the very process power in its patriarchal manifestations is being implicitly endorsed and yet drawn into unintended visibility. Moreover, to see the full extent of patriarchal power in the personal sphere is to see how pervasive it is in the public sphere too and so, finally, to collapse the distinction between private and public. Thus both the family unit and sexual relations are disclosed to be, not havens of retreat from the world of power relations, but two primary sites of their operation.

Lessing and the authentic self Debate about sexuality and the family occurred also through a number of novels about the nature and roles of women, in part anticipating issues taken up by the women's movement. The most ambitious and controversial was *The Golden Notebook* by Doris Lessing (1962). Published just two years after the *Chatterley* trial, it contradicts almost all its normative statements about sexuality. One of the novel's many levels concerns the way women suffer in their relationships with men, not only because of men's callousness, aggressive insecurity and self-deception, but also because of women's vulnerability: 'it remains', says Elizabeth Wilson, 'perhaps the most complete exploration possible of what it "meant" and "means" to be a woman today'.[47]

The character of Richard, a powerful businessman, and his exploitative relationships with the women in the book are brilliantly done, especially the scene in his office with Anna. Richard is complaining of his wife's new-found independence – of him and, relatedly, of alcohol:

> Richard said hotly: 'She doesn't care for me . . . I might just as well not be there at all.' Wounded vanity rang in his voice. And Anna was amazed. For he was genuinely wounded. Marion's escape from her position as prisoner, or fellow-victim had left him alone and hurt . . . that's his way of loving someone, and he doesn't understand anything else. And it's probably what Marion understands too.[48]

Here and throughout the novel we see how gender identity is in-formed by wider social relations and roles, and how masculinity especially is constituted through relations of power. By identifying gender roles as authentic selfhood, both women and men perpetuate the contradictions, conflict, oppression and self-oppression that characterize their lives.

When *The Golden Notebook* was first published, it was mistaken, said Lessing ten years later, for a tract about the sex war; in her view its central theme was personal breakdown (p. 8). The book is indeed an indefatigable anatomy of the self in search of its essential truth; breakdown is the consequence of the quest for authenticity. At this level the book strikingly substantiates the argument that in our time sexuality, subjectivity and truth are inextricably related. Lessing defends her relentless subjectivity on the grounds that 'one's unique and incredible experience is what everyone shares' (p. 14); in effect, preoccupation with the self becomes a preoccupation with the human condition. But in the novel the self becomes problematic: it seems increasingly to be predicated upon a central absence, a lack, a pervasive sense of failure (e.g. p. 253). Therefore, as with so much existentialist literature, what validates the self is not its positive discovery but the heroism of the search for it: 'I keep trying to write the truth and realizing it's not true,' says Anna (p. 272). To be vulnerable, to suffer, involves an integrity of its own: 'neurotic means the condition of being highly conscious and developed. The essence of neurosis is conflict. But the essence of living now, fully, not blocking off to what goes on, is conflict' (p. 456; cf. p. 79). Behind this is the fear that truth equals *nothing but* conflict, that there is no essential, unitary soul to be discovered (e.g. p. 272). The climax of this tension is breakdown: the failure to authenticate the self is compensated for by investing failure itself with authenticity.

Full selfhood is conceived of mainly as self-integration through love, the relationship that will render Anna's identity secure by allowing her to be her 'real' self. And for that she needs what she repeatedly refers to as a 'real man' (pp. 383, 470, 543). Along with this goes a prescriptive and normative insistence on vaginal orgasm as 'the only . . . *real* female orgasm', experienced when 'a man, from the whole of his need and desire takes a woman and wants all her response' (p. 220; cf. pp. 444, 446). Anna's quest for authenticity leads her to reaffirm the very gender stereotypes that underly the misery from which she is courageously trying to escape. *The Golden Notebook* shows, then, the extent to which we carry in our sexual identities the contradictions of our social existence; the irony of its section headings – 'Free Women', 1–4 – grows increasingly resonant. Like most kinds of normative prescription, Anna's is made through exclusion: against *real* vaginal orgasms and *real* men are set homosexuals. They are a source of anxiety in Anna (pp. 92, 567, 590) and are stereotyped by her as unattractive, unnatural and parasitic. She asks:

> What's the use of protecting [her daughter]? She will grow up in England, a country full of men who are little boys and homosexuals and half-homosexuals . . . but this tired thought vanished in a wave of *genuine* emotion – By God, there are a few *real* men left and I'm going to see she gets one of them. (p. 395; my italics)

Anna identifies the feeling of self-disgust as a specifically homosexual one (p. 590), perhaps explaining why, in a diary sequence almost epic in its inclusiveness, lesbianism is not addressed. Anna's prejudice is subjected to self-criticism, but mostly of the kind that aims to substantiate the prejudice in terms of her integrity, 'normal love' and 'the healthy female influence'.

At another level *The Golden Notebook* powerfully documents a transition from political commitment to despairing political disillusionment in the context of the traumatic impact upon the Left of Stalinism. In the novel the failure of political commitment is fatalistically conceived and tends to justify the abandonment of political engagement for existential integrity. Thus the Marxist charge against a preoccupation with subjective authenticity – namely, that it is a bourgeois neurosis of interiority – is pre-empted: politics has been tried and has failed. Political failure takes on the attributes of the classic tragic backdrop, but for the purpose of a modern tragic point: fatal, unalterable, it becomes the absolute guarantee of foregrounded subjectivity. It sanctions also the impossible absolutes which characteristically promote existentialist despair: further failure is almost guaranteed in advance by making only the impossible acceptable. Just before he tries to kill himself Tommy asks Anna what they are living for. She replies, 'We're a sort of latter day stoic . . . our kind of people' (p. 269). Tommy lacks an absolute and envies the milkman's son just because 'He hasn't got a hundred opportunities. He's got just one. But he really knows what he wants. He isn't suffering from paralysis of the will.' Anna: 'You're envying Reggie Gates for his handicaps?' Tommy: 'Yes. And do you know, he's a Tory.' Tommy shoots himself and though he survives is blinded. This 'handicap' gives him his purpose.

The Golden Notebook is about different and traumatic experiences of social, political and personal failure and about how, in the wake of that failure, the source of value and meaning is made impossibly subjective. Contrary to expectation, sexuality, perceived through this grid of subjectivity, offers not an escape from failure but only an intensely subjective experience of it. Sexuality here reveals not the spontaneous self but a gender identity informed by the dictates of power; not straightforward 'love', but need complicated by insecurity and commitment complicated by betrayal.

Finally, then, according to Foucault, 'sexuality is not fundamentally what power is afraid of, but . . . that through which power is exercised.'[49] Much literature of the fifties and sixties, even when it is premised upon the first proposition, must be seen to disclose the truth of the second. Likewise with the actual debates around sexuality: the authoritarian (Devlin) *was* afraid of sexuality; the libertarian, the anarchist, the Freudian Left *did* believe sexuality could challenge power; others, including liberals, believed they could escape politics and power altogether, finding authenticity in the domain of the sexual.

Homosexual as outsider   Homosexuals are among the sexual deviants who, according to Marcuse, would help effect the 'Great Refusal':[50] they are potentially revolutionary because marginalized and excluded. On this view the dis-location of deviants, their unsuccessful socialization, gives them an enforced independence of the dominant ideology – of 'normality' and 'nature' – which keeps the majority within the system. The homosexual as revolutionary outlaw does not appear in mainstream English literature of the period – at least, not with the vividness found in Jean Genet (*Our Lady of the Flowers*, *The Thief's Journal*), William Burroughs (*The Naked Lunch*, *The Wild Boys*) and John Rechy (*City of Night*, *The Sexual Outlaw*).

English novels of the immediate post-war period treat homosexuality with extreme caution and indirection. In Mary Renault's *The Charioteer* (1953) it is an affliction to be endured and ultimately triumphed over by the human spirit. At one point Alec, a doctor, is having trouble with his boyfriend and he tells his friend Laurie: 'I don't know how I can go on like this.' Laurie replies: 'You'll be all right, because you're more of a doctor than you're a queer.' Alec: 'you know that's the first sensible remark anyone's made to me all day.'[51] If this suggests the public/private dichotomy of liberal reformism, it also carries the further implication that privatization of one's sexuality involves a triumph of the will and even (to the extent that Alec will be a better doctor for harnessing his homosexual desire) a service to mankind. In Angus Wilson's *Hemlock and After* (1952) homosexuality does become the vehicle of a social criticism made possible to an extent by the alienation of the homosexual 'hero'. But this takes second place to the use of homosexuality to identify an evil prior to and deeper than the problems of society: the evil of the human condition.[52] As the appalling implications of Bernard's sado-masochistic desire well up from the depths of his corrupt human nature – 'the reflection of his own guilt, of his newly discovered hypocrisy, his long suppressed lusts'[53] – tragedy becomes inevitable.

Wilson continued to place homosexuals at or near the centre of his novels but, as public attitudes changed in the sixties, so these characters took on more positive identities. In *No Laughing Matter* (1967), for example, Marcus emerges with a resilience and wisdom lacked by others in his family. This becomes a familiar theme of English fiction and the closest it gets to the Marcusean idea of deviance as positive refusal. Another example is Iris Murdoch's *A Fairly Honourable Defeat* (1970). Hilda and Rupert are blissfully content as they celebrate their twentieth wedding anniversary. This relationship is set against that of the homosexual lovers Simon and Axel, Rupert's brother and friend respectively. Hilda is critical of homosexuals: 'all queers are a bit sly . . . all queers do like trouble.'[54] For Hilda the shortcomings of such people derive from their homosexual nature; consequently 'queer relationships are so unstable', especially when contrasted with 'normal relationships'[55] (with relatives like this, who needs enemies?). If Hilda is thoughtlessly expressing the kind of prejudice that makes for the very instability she scorns, instability nevertheless becomes a source of strength for Axel and Simon while, conversely, the 'normality' and stability of the Rupert–Hilda relationship is revealed to be a kind of bourgeois hubris leading to tragedy. The added irony, in a novel resonant with irony, is that the son of this model marriage ends up undergoing 'prolonged psychoanalysis'.[56] But Murdoch does not suggest that the homosexual lovers survive because the nature of their love is intrinsically better. On the contrary, their sex and gender is shown finally to be irrelevant to their love; it is their social insecurity which is mainly responsible both for their vulnerability and, eventually and consequently, for their strength. As Rupert tells Hilda, reprovingly yet complacently, homosexuals 'run more hazards of an external social kind'.[57]

The inadequacy of the family and marriage as *prescribed* conventional forms of relationship and behaviour is a recurring theme in Murdoch's fiction (see *The Bell*, 1959; *An Unofficial Rose*, 1962; *The Black Prince*, 1973). She believes 'the general consciousness today to be ridden either by convention or by neurosis'; it is difficult to escape from the one without invoking the other, and together they constitute 'the two enemies of understanding, one might say the enemies of love'.[58] *A Fairly Honourable Defeat*, teasingly inconclusive in many respects, seems unambiguous here: the unorthodox relationship has a head start in resisting convention and neurosis and most chance of love. This suggests something important: if the revealing absence in the working-class 'angry' literature was a consciousness of the relation between power and gender identity, then the corresponding absence in the preponderantly élitist literature dealing with sexual transgression tends to be the relation between sexuality and class (or, at the very least, the way that differences in power and self-determination are determined in part by social location). Murdoch's privileging of the homosexual outsider is much more cautious than Marcuse's, but those who have experienced imprisonment, aversion therapy and other less violent but nevertheless powerful forms of oppression might find both the liberal and the libertarian complacent. As George, the homosexual protagonist of Christopher Isherwood's novel, *A Single Man* (1964), puts it:

> Do you think it makes people nasty to be loved? You know it doesn't! Then why should it make them nice to be loathed? While you're being persecuted you hate what's happening to you, you hate the people who are making it happen; you're in a world of hate. Why, you wouldn't recognize love if you met it![59]

This notwithstanding, *A Single Man* is equally insistent on the possibility of love, both in spite of *and because of* the unconventional, stigmatized relationship. Arguably then, this constitutes the liberal-humanist alternative to the more provocative construction of the sexual deviant as subversive outlaw.

If the Wolfenden Report represented the legal pole of the liberal-humanist attitude to deviance, perhaps these novels are oriented towards its ethical pole: the first tolerates deviance through a process of quarantining it, the second tolerates it through a process of appropriating it, by allowing it to signify only to the extent that it confirms, or can be aligned with, the values of the dominant. In the case of Murdoch's novel it may even be seen to revitalize those values. In liberalism, what often passes for integration is in effect colonization (of the subordinate by the dominant).

The validity of George's claim about the effects of discrimination is memorably attested to in the American James Baldwin's *Giovanni's Room* (1956), which is roughly contemporaneous with, yet incomparably better than, English fiction like *The Charioteer*. Baldwin's novel explores the effects on a relationship of a guilt nurtured socially in the name of the natural and right order of things. In that order, the hatred of which Isherwood's George speaks has become internalized as self-hatred, self-oppression. David is a white American living out a crippling contradiction between his homosexual desire and an equally powerful need to conform to the American ideal of heterosexual masculinity. In Paris he meets and falls guiltily in love with Giovanni. Giovanni is uninhibited and unashamed by his sexuality, although his love for David is fatally complicated by his own vulnerability (he is socially displaced and penniless).

David's guilt makes him increasingly ambivalent; because Giovanni has reawakened his homosexual desire David experiences 'a hatred for Giovanni . . . as powerful as my love . . . nourished by the same roots'.[60] Eventually he leaves Giovanni to marry his fiancée Hella, 'to give myself something to be moored to'.[61] She and Giovanni are not the only casualties of David's guilt. There is Joey, his boyhood friend who for one weekend was his lover, something for which David cannot forgive himself or Joey; and there is Sue, the lonely, ageing one-night stand ('do you suppose we could do this again sometime?').[62]

At one level *Giovanni's Room* puts homosexuality at the centre of a tragic-romantic lament for the distressed human condition; at another it aims at an almost Brechtian conception of the tragic: that is, it sees the failure of love not in terms of the distressed human condition (or its corollary, the *intrinsic* inadequacy of homosexual love) but in terms of the social and historical conditions of its possibility or, as in this case, its impossibility. The two levels correspond to the novel's contradictory attitude to guilt. According to one attitude, guilt and remorse are profoundly redemptive, the consequence of original sin but also, eventually, the source of David's salvation and atonement for the human wreckage left behind him; thus David sees his body even in its 'vileness' as 'the incarnation of a mystery', and he resolves to believe in 'the heavy grace of God, which has brought me to this place' and which is all that can carry him from it.[63] According to the other attitude, guilt is a poisoned self-consciousness, the heritage of a puritan culture which withers everything it touches, and especially innocence. All the casualties of David's guilt epitomize innocence, albeit in complex and different ways. David's is, moreover, a narcissistic and self-sustaining guilt: he is a survivor, not in spite of but because of his self-hatred (Hella tells him, 'How you love to be guilty!').[64] As so often (also for instance, in *Room at the Top*), the guilty are shown to be parasitic upon the innocent and to survive at their expense. Both conceptions of guilt inform the novel but the second – simply by being articulated – constitutes a demystification of the first and therefore to a large extent displaces it.

Some critics have read the failure of love in *Giovanni's Room* as a consequence of the *nature* of the love itself. Thus Colin MacInnes saw the poverty of the room as 'a symbol: that of the sterility and self-destruction of homosexual love'.[65] It should be seen more literally: Baldwin attempts to show how the failure stems from actual poverty and specific power relations. Both David and Giovanni are in a kind of exile but neither vindicates the romantic ideal of the outsider. David, as white American male, has power, and it is used not to transform society but to destroy his lover.

Orton's black camp Joe Orton's intention was to outrage. Had he been alive he would doubtless have been delighted at the response of the leading conservative theatre critic to *What the Butler Saw* (1969): 'Orton's terrible obsession with perversion, which is regarded as having brought his life to an end and choked his very high talent, poisons the atmosphere of the play. And what should have been a piece of gaily irresponsible nonsense becomes impregnated with evil.'[66] In fact, this play isn't nonsense but it is, quite precisely, gayly irresponsible:

> [DR] RANCE. When Dr Prentice asked you to pose as a woman did he give a reason?
> NICK. No.
> RANCE. Didn't you consider his request strange?
> NICK. No.
> RANCE. Have you aided other men in their perverted follies?
> NICK. During my last term at school I was the slave of a corporal in the Welsh Fusiliers.
> RANCE. Were you never warned of the dangers inherent in such relationships?
> NICK. When he was posted abroad he gave me a copy of 'The Way to Healthy Manhood'.

By insisting on the arbitrariness and narrowness of gender roles, and that they are socially ascribed rather than naturally given, Orton expresses a central motif in the sexual politics of the period. *What the Butler Saw* becomes an orgy of confused and *refused* gender identities:

> GERALDINE [dressed as a boy]. I must be a boy. I like girls.
> RANCE. I can't quite follow the reasoning there.
> PRENTICE. Many men imagine their preference for women is, *ipso facto*, a proof of virility.

Cross-dressing leads to wholesale gender confusion:

> RANCE. Were you present when Dr Prentice used this youth unnaturally?
> NICK. What is unnatural?
> RANCE. How disturbing the questions of the mad can be. (*To* NICK [disguised as a girl]) Suppose I made an indecent suggestion to you? If you agreed something might occur which, by and large, would be regarded as natural. If, on the other hand, I approached this child – (*He smiles at* GERALDINE [disguised as a boy]) – my action could result only in a gross violation of the order of things.

Dr Rance's precisely inappropriate assumptions about madness, the natural and the order of things discredit the claims of psychiatry. In the sixties the psychiatry that had developed after the war was, like the family, attacked: it was perceived as a form of social policing which, with the aid of pseudo-scientific categories, mystified socially desirable behaviour as natural, and undesirable behaviour as the result of abnormal psychosexual development (a deviation from 'The Way to Healthy Manhood'). As R. D. Laing put it in *The Divided Self*:

> Psychiatry can so easily be a technique of brainwashing, of inducing behaviour that is adjusted, by (preferably) non-injurious torture. . . . I would wish to emphasize that our 'normal' 'adjusted' state is too often the abdication of ecstasy, the betrayal of *our true potentialities*, that many of us are only too successful in acquiring a false self to adapt the false realities.[67]

Orton goes much further than Laing, for his plays transgress accepted norms at every point but refuse to replace them with 'our true potentialities'; Laing is still preoccupied with the authentic self, the repressed human essence. In the *Chatterley* trial, similarly, Lawrence was defended as puritanical on the grounds that he had to transgress moral respectability in order to be moral at a deeper, more authentic level dictated by personal conscience. Orton refuses this long-established model of *legitimate* transgression – nonconformist yet revalidating the dominant order's lapsed moral conscience. Even the indignation of satire usually assumes the same moral perspective as that of the order being challenged, or at least an alternative to it. But, as his diaries show, Orton's indignation was too anarchic to be recuperated in such terms.

In *What the Butler Saw* sexuality, like language, becomes decentred and therefore radically contingent: it escapes continually from medical and legal attempts to define and regulate it.

Not surprisingly, Orton's anarchic irresponsibility becomes the ultimate confirmation for those who agree with Devlin about the dangers of vice. Even for liberals and some radicals, he took the Great Refusal too far, not just in what he actually *did*, but in the refusal in his work to confront established morality with an earnest moral alternative. What we find instead is a kind of delinquent or black camp. Susan Sontag in her brilliant 'Notes on Camp' remarks that its essence is 'love of the unnatural: of artifice and exaggeration'; it is characterized by travesty, impersonation and theatricality.[68] But the point at which Orton's camp eludes Sontag's account is precisely where it becomes black and potentially subversive. Camp, says Sontag, 'is a solvent of morality. It neutralizes moral indignation, sponsors playfulness.'[69] Orton's camp is indeed constituted by playfulness and it acts as a solvent of morality – but it does this to provoke rather than disarm moral indignation. 'No first night of the sixties was more volcanic than that of *What the Butler Saw*,' says Orton's biographer, John Lahr; while Stanley Baxter, who played Dr Prentice, has recalled the 'militant hate' of the audience, some of whom 'wanted to jump on the stage and kill us'.[70]

Conclusion

For many Orton now seems *passé*. For others the evil he personified has continued unabated. Mary Whitehouse, writing in 1977, warns that the liberationists of the sixties, by undermining chastity, marriage and the family, by championing promiscuity and 'gay liberation . . . that most insidious of all pressure groups', effectively 'destroy the community and emotional stability which is essential to childhood security *and social cohesion*'.[71] Belief in the socially disintegrative power of unrestrained and/or transgressive sexuality survives to an extent unforeseeable in 1970, and does so as the spearhead of an attempt to reassert authoritarian control of sexuality. In fact, conservative sexual ideology was held throughout by many people, and they responded at once to liberal developments through new organizations like Whitehouse's Clean Up TV Campaign (1963) and the Society for the Protection of the Unborn Child. This mid-sixties reaction was part of 'the exhaustion of consent' which Stuart Hall and others have elucidated, and it therefore needs to be seen in relation to other fears: a general anxiety and sometimes hysteria over 'permissiveness' and the alleged breakdown of law and order, as well as more specific fears of, for example, racial contamination and the corruption of youth by drugs.[72] Yet again, sexuality becomes the site for new efforts of social policing which extend far beyond the sexual. The defence of the family was, as usual, top priority, and abortion and pornography drew special attention. The anti-abortionist lobby came close in 1980 to getting the 1967 Act drastically amended, and there have been successful prosecutions for obscenity and even for blasphemy (e.g. the *Oz* and *Gay News* trials). In March 1982 Prime Minister Margaret Thatcher blamed 'the fashionable theories and permissive claptrap' of the sixties for some of the present social ills, adding: 'For years there was no riposte, no reply. The time for counter-attack is long overdue.'[73]

Few on the other side of the fence now believe in the revolutionary potential of sexuality. It has, however, experienced new impetus from continental theories. Deleuze and Guattari in *Anti Oedipus: Capitalism and Schizophrenia* (1972; trans. 1977) declare: 'desire is revolutionary in its essence . . . no society can tolerate a position of real desire without its structures of exploitation, servitude and hierarchy being compromised.'[74] Under the different influences of, in particular, Jacques Lacan (*Écrits*, 1966; trans. 1977) and Michel Foucault (*The History of Sexuality*, 1976; trans. 1978) ideas of sexuality have undergone a radical revision. No longer are we to believe that as individuals we possess a given, unitary sexual nature which may liberate us from a repressive social order: 'there is no single locus of great Refusal, no soul of revolt, source of all rebellions, or pure law of the revolutionary.'[75] On the contrary, our sexuality, like other aspects of human behaviour and consciousness once thought to be rooted in our human nature, is rooted in society. Far from finding our liberation, our authentic selves, in the long-repressed realm of the sexual, we find instead only deeper evidence of our social construction. And because our sexuality is in-formed by the social and ideological structures into which we are born, rebellious desire can be expressed only in and through the existing forms of its subjection. Such desire will therefore encounter – become involved with – new contradictions, even as old ones are escaped. On this view, sexuality ceases to be a utopian alternative, and its simple 'release' no longer promises to transform the social order. It appears instead as one site of our social construction and, therefore, of our potential subjection. In other words, on this view, sexuality becomes truly understood only when it is finally and radically demystified.

The demystification of sexuality has proved as distressing to the defenders of high culture as to the representatives of 'the moral majority'. Peter Conrad insists that sexuality is 'a fate and a compulsion' and that 'freedom from repression means a further imprisonment in desire'. He revels in the agony of sexuality and 'the riveting experience of self-obliteration and estrangement from society which the great lovers in literature know it to be'.[76] So there we have it: the demystification of sexuality robs literature of one of its eternal and most highly charged themes. The idea that literature thrives on such romantic–tragic mystification may have encouraged many who have grown up in the post-war world to leave it to those of Conrad's persuasion and to the educational institutions they inhabit. But others have felt that they cannot afford to do this, any more than they can afford to leave morality to Whitehouse.

There is an alternative; it has gained ground in the post-war period, and Thatcher, Conrad and Whitehouse are reacting against its successes. It involves a determined and democratic questioning of conservative constructions, not just of literature and sexuality, but of the political and social realities of which they are inextricably a part. It is a questioning to which I for one am grateful and to which this chapter has tried to do justice. The tradition of all the dead generations still weighs upon the living, but because of such questioning it does so less heavily.

Notes

1 Quoted in John Lahr, *Prick Up Your Ears* (Harmondsworth: Penguin, 1980), pp. 135–6.
2 George Orwell, *Nineteen Eighty-Four* (Harmondsworth: Penguin, 1954), p. 103.
3 Patrick Devlin, *The Enforcement of Morals* (London: Oxford University Press, 1968), pp. 13–14.
4 In C. H. Rolph (ed.), *The Trial of Lady Chatterley* (Harmondsworth: Penguin, 1961), p. 18.
5 Ibid., p. 17.
6 Elizabeth Wilson, *Only Halfway to Paradise: Women in Postwar Britain 1945–1968* (London: Tavistock, 1980), p. 136.
7 Rolph (ed.), op. cit., p. 62.
8 Ibid, p. 190; cf. p. 159.
9 Ibid., p. 184.
10 Ibid., p. 92.

11 Ibid., p. 137.
12 Ibid., p. 153.
13 Richard Burton, *The Anatomy of Melancholy*, Everyman's Library (London: Dent, 1972), vol. 3, p. 55.
14 Margaret Drabble, *A Summer Bird-Cage* (Harmondsworth: Penguin, 1967), pp. 28–9.
15 Michel Foucault, *Herculine Barbin* (Brighton: Harvester, 1980), pp. x–xi.
16 Rolph (ed.), op. cit., p. 102.
17 See Paul Delaney, *D. H. Lawrence's Nightmare* (Brighton: Harvester, 1979); Kate Millett, *Sexual Politics* (London: Virago, 1977).
18 See Wilson, op. cit., ch. 4.
19 See Rosalind Coward, 'Sexual Liberation and the Family', *M/F*, 1 (1978).
20 See Jeffrey Weeks, *Sex, Politics and Society* (London: Longman, 1981), p. 235.
21 Edmund Leach, *A Runaway World?* (London: BBC Publications, 1968), pp. 44 and 97.
22 Weeks, op. cit., pp. 239–40.
23 Ibid., pp. 243–4.
24 Ibid., p. 265.
25 Wilson, op. cit., p. 87.
26 Andrea Dworkin, *Pornography: Men Possessing Women* (London: The Women's Press, 1981), pp. 179–98.
27 Wilson, op. cit., p. 108.
28 Roland Barthes, *Mythologies* (St Albans: Paladin, 1973), p. 101.
29 Kenneth Plummer, *Sexual Stigma: An Interactionist Account* (London: Routledge & Kegan Paul, 1975), p. 32.
30 Blake Morrison, *The Movement: English Poetry and Fiction in the 1950s* (London: Oxford University Press, 1980), pp. 179–85.
31 John Osborne, *Look Back in Anger* (London: Faber, 1960), p. 67.
32 Ibid., pp. 37–8.
33 Ibid., p. 57.
34 Ibid., pp. 84–5.
35 Ibid., p. 73.
36 John Braine, *Room at the Top* (Harmondsworth: Penguin, 1959), pp. 198–9.
37 Ibid., p. 29.
38 Ibid., p. 57.
39 Ibid., p. 72.
40 Ibid., p. 166.
41 Ibid., pp. 220–1.
42 Alan Sillitoe, *Saturday Night and Sunday Morning* (London: Pan, 1960), p. 126.
43 Ibid., p. 36.
44 Ibid., p. 65.
45 Ibid., p. 191.
46 Ibid., p. 36.

47 Wilson, op. cit., p. 158.
48 Doris Lessing, *The Golden Notebook* (St Albans: Panther, 1972), p. 376; page references to this edition are subsequently given in the text.
49 Michel Foucault, 'The History of Sexuality: Interview', *Oxford Literary Review*, 4, 2 (1980), p. 9; first published in *Le Nouvel Observateur*, 12 March 1977.
50 Herbert Marcuse, *Eros and Civilization* (London: Sphere, 1969), p. 171.
51 Mary Renault, *The Charioteer* (London: New English Library, 1968), p. 346.
52 Angus Wilson, *Hemlock and After* (Harmondsworth: Penguin, 1956), p. 25.
53 Ibid., p. 148.
54 Iris Murdoch, *A Fairly Honourable Defeat* (Harmondsworth: Penguin, 1972), pp. 15, 18.
55 Ibid., pp. 18, 17.
56 Ibid., p. 443.
57 Ibid., p. 18.
58 Iris Murdoch, 'The Sublime and the Beautiful Revisited', *Yale Review*, 49 (1959), pp. 254, 256.
59 Christopher Isherwood, *A Single Man* (London: Magnum, 1978), pp. 59–60.
60 James Baldwin, *Giovanni's Room* (London: Corgi, 1963), p. 64.
61 Ibid., p. 8.
62 Ibid., p. 77.
63 Ibid., pp. 126–7.
64 Ibid., p. 123.
65 *Encounter*, 21 (August 1963).
66 Harold Hobson, in *Christian Science Monitor*, 19 March 1969, alluding to the fact that Orton was beaten to death with a hammer by his homosexual lover.
67 R. D. Laing, *The Divided Self* (Harmondsworth: Penguin, 1965), p. 12; my italics.
68 Susan Sontag, 'Notes on Camp', *Against Interpretation* (New York: Farrar, 1966), pp. 275, 280.
69 Ibid., p. 290.
70 Lahr, op. cit., pp. 333–4.
71 Mary Whitehouse, *Whatever Happened to Sex?* (Hove: Wayland, 1977), pp. 9, 66 (my italics); see also *Pornography: The Longford Report* (London: Coronet, 1972).
72 Stuart Hall *et al.*, *Policing the Crisis: Mugging, the State and Law and Order* (London: Hutchinson, 1978), esp. pp. 218–72.
73 *Sunday Times*, 28 March 1982, p. 1.
74 G. Deleuze and F. Guattari, *Anti Oedipus: Capitalism and Schizophrenia* (New York: Viking Press, 1977), p. 116.
75 Michel Foucault, *The History of Sexuality*, vol. 1: *An Introduction* (New York: Vintage Books, 1980), pp. 95–6.
76 *The Times Literary Supplement*, 20 February 1976, p. 190.

Further reading

Barrett, Michèle. *Women's Oppression Today: Problems in Marxist Feminist Analysis*. London: New Left Books, 1980.

Carter, Angela. *The Sadeian Woman: An Exercise in Cultural History*. London: Virago, 1979.

Foucault, Michel. *The History of Sexuality*, vol. 1: *An Introduction*. New York: Vintage Books, 1980.

Gay Left Collective (ed.). *Homosexuality, Power and Politics*. London: Allison & Busby, 1980.

Gorer, Geoffrey. *Sex and Marriage in England Today*. London: Nelson, 1971.

Hall, Stuart, *et al. Policing the Crisis: Mugging, the State and Law and Order*. London: Hutchinson, 1978.

Heath, Stephen. *The Sexual Fix*. London: Macmillan, 1982.

Hocquenghem, Guy. *Homosexual Desire*. London: Allison & Busby, 1978.

Marcuse, Herbert. *Eros and Civilization*. Boston, Mass.: Beacon Press, 1966. London: Sphere, 1969.

Millett, Kate. *Sexual Politics*. London: Virago, 1977.

Mitchell, Juliet. *Psychoanalysis and Feminism*. London: Allen Lane, 1974. Harmondsworth: Penguin, 1975.

Pearson, Geoffrey. *The Deviant Imagination*. London: Macmillan, 1975.

Poster, Mark. *Critical Theory of the Family*. London: Pluto, 1978.

Robinson, Paul. *The Modernization of Sexuality*. London: Elek, 1976.

Rolph, C. H. (ed.). *The Trial of Lady Chatterley*. Harmondsworth: Penguin, 1961.

Rowbotham, Sheila, *et al. Beyond the Fragments: Feminism and the Making of Socialism*. London: Merlin, 1979.

Turkle, Sherry. *Psychoanalytic Politics: Freud's French Revolution*. London: Burnett Books/Deutsch, 1979.

Weeks, Jeffrey. *Coming Out: Homosexual Politics in Britain from the Nineteenth Century to the Present*. London: Quartet, 1977.

Weeks, Jeffrey. *Sex, Politics and Society*. London: Longman, 1981.

Weeks, Jeffrey. Preface to Hocquenghem, *Homosexual Desire*, pp. 9–33.

Wilson, Elizabeth. *Mirror Writing: An Autobiography*. London: Virago, 1982.

Wilson, Elizabeth. *Only Halfway to Paradise: Women in Postwar Britain 1945–1968*. London: Tavistock, 1980.

Important journals include:

Feminist Review (14 Sumner Buildings, Sumner Street, London, SE1).
I and C (1 Woburn Mansions, Torrington Place, London, WC1).
M/F (69 Randolph Avenue, London, W9 1DW).

4 Varieties of religion

ALAN SINFIELD

Between two worlds

We have to start from the Church of England, because in 1945 most people still did, though the social structure which had needed it was changing rapidly. It was not at once apparent that Christianity was under increased threat. Until the mid-fifties, surveys showed, nine out of ten people said they belonged to a church or sect, seven to eight out of ten said they believed in God, and Sunday attendances increased slightly. In 1957 a quarter of the population were at a service once a month and an eighth went weekly. More than half of all parents sent their children to Sunday school.

The established literary culture, as Chapter 2 shows more fully, was eager to distance itself from pre-war political commitment but could see little that was congenial in post-war society. One answer, which seemed especially powerful at Oxford, was a conservative high Anglicanism. John Wain describes how it 'suddenly became the adventurous spearhead of English intellectual and artistic life' and C. S. Lewis and his friends undertook 'the interpretation of English poetry along Anglican lines'.[1] In the face of the egalitarian spirit fostered by the war, it was an attempt to assert a past world where Christianity, literature and society made sense of each other within a relatively stable, hierarchical social system, grouped in parishes round a church and manor house. Lewis believed that, 'if we had not fallen, patriarchal monarchy would be the sole lawful government' and that, 'unless we return to the crude and nursery-like belief in objective values, we perish'[2] (overlooking the fact that most people had never been in a nursery). In *The Craft of Letters in England*, a survey edited by John Lehmann in 1956, we read that 'Among intellectuals Christian belief is widespread and may be growing' and that Arnold's 'Sea of Faith' has begun to turn (L. D. Lerner, Maurice Cranston).[3]

Four Quartets (1942) and verse drama were the main imaginative focus of this religious, social and literary conservatism. In her book *The Art of T. S. Eliot* (1949) Helen Gardner offered a formalist reading of *Four Quartets*, celebrating the *stability* she found in it: 'the word's life is preserved almost miraculously by art, in a kind of true life beyond its life in speech; it is there stable, not in itself, but in its relations to all the other words in the poem.'[4] Eliot's poem explicitly invites such an interpretation, but looking at it in context we can see also the alarm of a conservative at the approach of and experience of the war; this is what must be transcended by art. 'Burnt Norton' begins: 'Time present and time past / Are both perhaps present in time future': 'perhaps' hints a reservation about a future which will not respect its past, which may be unrecognizable. The poem rings with this anxiety: 'the hills and the trees, the distant panorama / And the bold imposing façade are all being rolled away' ('East Coker'); 'the past is all deception, / The future futureless'; 'We cannot think . . . of a future that is not liable / Like the past, to have no destination' ('The Dry Salvages'). The movement of the poem is epitomized in the evocation of

> Years of living among the breakage
> Of what was believed in as the most reliable –
> And therefore the fittest for renunciation.
>
> ('The Dry Salvages')

Distress at the fracturing of an older, stable social order which is felt to be necessary to civilization stimulates the move towards renunciation, transcending a world that seems now to offer so little.

The imagery of the poem is often concrete and its locations specific, but its powerful lyrical impetus is always directed away from the present. We may 'lean against a bank while a van passes' but if we don't come too close we can time-slip into Sir Thomas Elyot's world ('East Coker'); our visit to Little Gidding merges into that of 'a broken king'; 'distress of nations and perplexity / Whether on the shores of Asia, or in the Edgware Road' ('The Dry Salvages') at first jars us with the juxtaposition of the remote and the familiar, but the outcome is a

transcending of the circumstantial. Eliot asks 'Why should we celebrate / These dead men more than the dying?' ('Little Gidding'), and
the dead men indeed get far more attention. The sole consolation for
living in the present is that only thus can we be conscious of the past:
'only in time can the moment in the rose-garden . . . / Be remembered' ('Burnt Norton').

In the immediate post-war period it was easy to read *Four Quartets* with
reference to a current disturbance of order, hierarchy and 'values', for
Eliot tends to couple spiritual desolation with the modern world generally and the bulk of ordinary people. The London Underground is the
image for 'disaffection' – the people coming up are 'Eructation of un-
healthy souls / Into the faded air' ('Burnt Norton'); it is in these unfortu-
nate users of public transport that 'you see behind every face the mental
emptiness deepen' ('East Coker'). Eliot specified the sense in which 'conditions . . . seem unpropitious' ('Burnt Norton') in *Notes towards the
Definition of Culture* (1948). There he asserted that civilization depends
upon uniformity of religious doctrine and 'upper middle class society',
and that both must be defended against egalitarianism – for instance,
the extension of secondary education in the Butler Act of 1944. He
evoked the threat of 'barbarian nomads of the future' in their 'mechan-
ized caravans'.[5] The religious transcendence proposed in *Four Quartets*
encouraged a consolatory spiritual élitism. It was one way of dealing with
a rapidly changing world: 'the intersection of the timeless moment / Is
England and nowhere. Never and always' ('Little Gidding'); for Eliot
and his followers the moment out of time was preferable to England now.

The nature and context of this conservative movement are described
in Chapter 2. Evelyn Waugh (who had embraced Catholicism as the
most traditional religion) gave his version of the start of the period in
Unconditional Surrender (1961). The novel suggests that during the
war a cynical communist (and homosexual) conspiracy undermined
society and hence religion. Everyone in the novel who is not an upper-
class conservative is assimilated to this supposed conspiracy, which
Waugh calls 'the dismemberment of Christendom'. A concluding
image for this disaster is a party during the Festival of Britain where
'Some of the men wore hired evening-dress; others impudently presented themselves in dinner-jackets and soft shirts.'[6]

The decline of religion

Christianity's grip weakens not when its improbabilities are exposed
(for that has been done throughout its history) but when, because of

changes in the world, it no longer seems relevant. Since about 1600 a secular – rationalist, pragmatic, instrumental – approach to the world has been gaining ground. Secularism assumes that human and natural affairs can be explained (if at all) without the hypothesis of God. Its principal discourses are natural science, the human sciences and politics. It was involved (as both cause and effect) with industrialization, which revolutionized the class structure, moved people from their localities, occupations and loyalties, and showed that secularism *works*. Colonialism fed back information about other cultures which tended, eventually, to relativize the imperial culture. The church gradually relinquished its role in education, welfare provision and social control; it became marginal. In the late fifties this process seemed to be accelerating.

The economic growth and all-party commitment to welfare-capitalism in the fifties have been described in Chapter 2. They involved people more and more in value systems that ran counter to religion and encouraged an openness to new attitudes. By 1956 commercial television had begun and television licences had increased more than tenfold to 4½ million; they doubled again by the end of the decade. Advertising grew at 13 per cent a year; in 1957 the aggregate hire-purchase debt reached £442 million, and by 1962 it was double that. John Osborne indicted the church's failure to compete with consumption, advertising and the media when he compared it to a vacuum cleaner: 'When the Jesus jingles came on, most people simply switched off their responses automatically, and waited for the next programme. They knew that the people selling the product were themselves utterly incapable of making the damned thing *work*.'[7] Surveys showed that, the more people were implicated in the modern economy, the less likely they were to be religious. Secularism was stronger among men than women, in cities than in the country, among the middle-aged than the old or very young, in industrial than traditional occupations. Employers and politicians no longer appealed to 'Christian values'; they had personnel managers, industrial-relations specialists, advertising agencies, opinion polls, arguments from 'economic reality'. Peter Berger concluded that 'church-related religiosity' was strongest 'on the margins of modern industrial society'.[8]

What these changes signify is disputed. One point of view, represented by David Martin (*Religion in Secular Society*, 1966) and Harvey Cox (*The Seduction of the Spirit*, 1974), holds that the religious impulse is a constant in human life and that while the churches have declined the impulse comes out in other ways. The other view, which seems to me correct, is that we have experienced a decline in religious attitudes – basically, that is, in the idea of ultimate reference to super-natural authority. Bryan Wilson demonstrates in *Religion in Secular Society* that 'religion – seen as a way of thinking, as the performance of particular practices, and as the institutionalization and organization of these patterns of thought and action – has lost influence'. Even in the United States, where religious institutions seem not to have declined, they have transformed themselves 'to organizations which embody all the rational bureaucratic authority assumptions of other, non-religious organizations in advanced society'.[9]

'Religion implies the farthest reach of man's self-externalization, of his infusion of reality with his own meanings. Religion implies that human order is projected into the totality of being.'[10] Religion claims absolute validity for a theory of our origins, a history, an ethic, a psychology and a sociology, all supported by institutions and rituals, and ratified, supernaturally, by the supposed cosmic structure. The conservative-minded and sociologists following Durkheim (sometimes the same people) hold that society must have such a stable, comprehensive structure of common belief, reinforced by supernatural sanctions, to give it authority and cohesion. Religion *legitimates* society's arrangements, makes them seem part of 'the way things are'. It is not always remarked that such legitimation works, by definition, in the interest of those who benefit most from current arrangements.

It seems, then, that we have largely lost this sacred legitimation. The religious symbols and practices that used to supply it no longer speak adequately, for most people, to a society that has changed beneath them. This caused much anxiety in the period. But we must be careful. First, it may be that most people long since stopped relying upon official religion to 'explain' their world (if they ever did). A Mass Observation survey in 1947 showed that nearly half the churchgoers disbelieved in or were undecided about life after death, and that only half believed in the divinity of Jesus and his birth from a virgin. Even more strangely, a sixth of the people who said they didn't believe in God and a fifth who said they thought Jesus was no more than a man held nevertheless that he was born of a virgin.[11] According to Richard Hoggart, the attitude of working-class people towards the parson was 'likely to be faintly cynical; he is in with the bosses'; and religion 'Just would not work in "real" life'.[12]

Second, it may be that modern societies manage quite well without religious legitimation – that they thrive upon flexibility, and the comprehensive stability of religion is unnecessary. Technology and bureaucracy require us to operate in diverse specialized roles, to commute between discrepant and provisional sets of expectations. We develop a fluency and sophistication incompatible with a single worldview. This does not mean that anything is allowed. Alternatives are ceaselessly classified and evaluated, especially by the media, so as to limit possibilities for change. But this is all negotiation of detail by implication, and it does not involve reference to a generally legitimating structure of belief.

Third, as religion becomes manifestly irrelevant in the public world of business and government, transcendent value is located, by contrast, in personal experience. In fact, readers may assume that this is the natural province of religion. In the period this book deals with, the development of the self, especially in and through personal relationships, became the focus of many people's most intense commitments, and it often attracted religious language (see also the discussion of sexuality and authenticity in Chapter 3). But such *privatization* represents an important change: 'The world-building potency of religion is thus restricted to the construction of sub-worlds, of fragmented universes of meaning, the plausibility structure of which may in some cases be no larger than the nuclear family.'[13] Privatized religion engages only in limited ways with society at large. Business and government proceed in the secularist manner they prefer, while we invest our 'real' selves in personal experience.

Broadly, then, organized religion declined, and people seemed not to need sacred legitimation. The churches still attracted enthusiasts (perhaps those disposed towards traditional values), and occasional bursts of fervour remained possible. With unprecedented publicity, Billy Graham filled Harringay Stadium for twelve weeks in 1954. American evangelism is organized on business lines and appeals to modern society on its own terms: 'Earn your money, as much as you can, according to God's laws, and spend it to carry out his commands.'[14] English churchmen were embarrassed, first by the vulgarity of the campaign, then by its success. But generally people just neglected to think about religion.

This was less true in intellectual and high-cultural circles. Hence the attention to Colin Wilson's 'Outsider' who, Wilson says in his *Declaration* article, 'can fight his way back from the sense of meaninglessness and futility to a religion'.[15] Much of the writing discussed in this chapter is involved in anxiety at the loss of, or an attempt to reassert the authority of, a religious sensibility. This may be because it is in literary circles that a coherent account of human purpose in the world was valued in the first place, but we may also perceive a persistent backward-looking tendency in literary institutions of the period, based perhaps on a belief that the conditions for intellectual and creative work were better before, when the church was central in English life. Consequently in literature of the period we repeatedly find religion *recuperated* – recovered, often in privatized form, when it appears irretrievable.

These attitudes are addressed in Larkin's poetry, whose characteristic tone is a bemused alienation from the modern world. In 'Church Going' (discussed also in Chapter 7) he admits, it appears, to no involvement with the building he enters:

> Another church: matting, seats, and stone,
> And little books; sprawlings of flowers, cut
> For Sunday, brownish now; some brass and stuff
> Up at the holy end.

We might suspect in the last phrase that Larkin is exaggerating his ignorance so as to provoke us into asserting that spiritual meaning still resides in the church. He is preparing us to envisage that there should be a positive outcome to his 'Wondering what to look for'; and so to credit the thought of the concluding stanza:

> A serious house on serious earth it is,
> In whose blent air all our compulsions meet,
> Are recognized, and robed as destinies.
> And that much never can be obsolete . . .

Personal religiousness is rescued, and the church, stripped of its doctrinal and institutional significance, is reasserted as its proper venue.

Privatized religion is discovered also in 'An Arundel Tomb'. The earl and countess hold hands in effigy; they did not envisage that this would become the only meaningful part of their monument:

> The stone fidelity
> They hardly meant has come to be
> Their final blazon, and to prove
> Our almost-instinct almost true:
> What will survive of us is love.

Personal feeling was peripheral to the original purposes of the tomb, but now the authority of religious awe and physical endurance combine with the poet's personal perception to discover in it transcendental value. (It has recently been pointed out that the earl and countess were made to hold hands only in a nineteenth-century restoration. A religion of personal feeling has even less basis in tradition than Larkin supposed.)

In Iris Murdoch's *The Bell* (1958) the complacent religiosity of an Anglican community is destroyed by interpersonal tensions which expose the inadequacy of traditional formulas ('We know in very simple ways, ways so simple that they seem dull to our subtle moral psychologists, what we ought to do and what avoid';[16] these are Lewis's nursery values). Above all, Catherine, who is exalted as perfect innocence (comparable in candour to the bell which, like her, is to enter the abbey), experiences sexual obsession, tries to kill herself and is diagnosed as schizophrenic. The bell is sounded, inadvertently, by the worldly, unassuming and constructive Dora, who has been patronized by the community. Secularism seems better and more successful.

Yet Murdoch wants to retrieve religious experience and the church. The abbey is not criticized; indeed, the abbess is wise and a young nun rescues the drowning. Dora has a 'mystical experience' in the National Gallery and interprets it as evidence of the existence of objective goodness: 'When the world had seemed to be subjective it had seemed to be without interest or value. But now there was something else in it after all.'[17] So she returns to the community, which is said eventually to have helped its members towards personal autonomy. The personal experience in the gallery is projected on to a universal plane as 'a revelation', and then given further realization, witnessed in Dora's personal development, through the abbey. So religion is recuperated in privatized terms. In fact, Murdoch is unable to make her story enact this encouraging outcome, for it is stated only in an extended, tidying-up coda ('Dora at first declared that life out of London was impossible, but later she saw the point of the idea and even found it rather exciting').[18]

It became usual to assume that the most profound literature deals with such issues of spiritual alienation from the modern world. In *The Struggle of the Modern* (1963) Stephen Spender (editor of *Encounter* and professor of English) distinguished 'contemporaries', who engage in a direct, rational way with social and political conditions, often looking for improvement; and 'moderns', who dislike twentieth-century society so much that they cannot envisage any improvement, and therefore tend to locate significance in the act of communication itself, seeking to expose the individual sensibility, which they regard as typical of the 'human condition'. The latter outlook increasingly became the touchstone of serious literary purpose, especially in the rapidly growing university departments of English, where it displaced the nineteenth-century tradition of realism and its twentieth-century continuation in liberal, Leavisite criticism. In terms of reception, the fifties and sixties were actually the decades of Eliot, Lawrence, Joyce, Yeats, Woolf, Conrad and Pound. With certain exceptions (especially Joyce) and in different ways, these writers were right-wing and preoccupied with topics associated with religion.

The crisis of secularism

The decreasing legitimative power of religion ran parallel with a failure of confidence in the secularist goals of science and politics. Secularism has sometimes cohered into a purposeful world-view with the legitimating power of religion (Enlightenment rationalism, nineteenth-century liberalism). In modern times the humanist and biologist Julian Huxley looked for an evolutionary religion which will 'sanctify the higher manifestations of human nature, in art and love, in intellectual comprehension and aspiring adoration, and will emphasize the fuller realization of life's possibilities as a sacred trust'.[19] Arthur Koestler's account of communism is in similar terms: 'Nothing henceforth can disturb the convert's inner peace and serenity – except the occasional fear of losing faith again, losing thereby what alone makes life worth living, and falling back into the outer darkness.'[20]

The religious language in these commitments indicates inability to relinquish the idea of a grand, transcendental scheme. Such intense hopes faltered in the face of revelations of Nazi atrocities, the corruption of the Russian revolution and the atomic bomb. In *The Impact of Science on Society* (1952) Bertrand Russell restated the advantages of rationalism, but with a new irony: 'We were told that faith could remove mountains, but no one believed it; we are now told that the atomic bomb can remove mountains, and everyone believes it.'[21] Science and politics were the dominant discourses of secular society, but both had taken horrifying directions and neither offered a substitute for religion.

The influence of George Orwell, as a leftist intellectual disillusioned with Stalinism, is established in Chapter 2. In *Nineteen Eighty-Four* (1949) his critique takes in not just a particular political system but human nature and politics in general. Tyranny is made to seem inevitable. The proles are presented as happily benighted – 'Until they become conscious they will never rebel, and until after they have rebelled they cannot become conscious'[22] – though it is unclear why they should not be alerted by contradictions in their experience, as Winston is. And Winston's crippling move occurs in his first meeting with O'Brien, where he agrees without hesitation to cause the deaths of hundreds of innocent people and sets up Goldstein as a replacement Big Brother. Thus he forfeits his moral position, though this is surprising, since he sees and concedes the point at once when O'Brien later uses it against him.[23] Orwell means to render pointless all political aspiration.

This reading differs from that offered in Chapter 2, where the authors argue that Orwell believed that a genuine socialism was possible, though it had not been achieved. In any event, *Nineteen Eighty-Four* was often taken in the fifties as an anti-socialist representation of the immediate and probable future of English society. The continuing need to absorb the facts of the Third Reich and Stalinism, the persistence of armed conflict in many parts of the world, including the British Empire, the suppression of the Hungarian revolt and the threat of nuclear war did not afford the conditions for a revival of secularist optimism.

Even the achievements of the period were felt to be disappointing. The welfare state seemed about to realize the hopes of a century of liberal reformers: there was full employment, national insurance provided a safety net against at least the extremes of poverty, everyone was at school until 15, and medical treatment was available and free (by 1956 deaths of mothers in childbirth were one-sixth of the pre-war figure). But this was found to afford no basis for a continuing commitment. On the Right, George Scott in his autobiography *Time and Place* (1956) regarded the welfare state as 'something I do not wish to see wholly undone'. But in so far as the aspirations of the Attlee administration had been socialist – which Scott held they had been – it had tended to create 'not a universal brotherhood but a clogging spreading weed of bureaucracy, leading logically perhaps to an authoritarian state'.[24] Colin Wilson in his *Declaration* essay affirmed, 'There must be greater aims than short-sighted social aims to fight for.' He needed to despise the 'stupidity' of ordinary people who 'flock to the films and football matches, or to hear the latest crooner or evangelist at Harringay' in order to set up his lonely Nietzschean hero. He believed that 'we have seen enough of "humanism" and scientific "progress" to know how much they are worth'.[25] The Left too, unable to think of a vision to rival 'You've never had it so good', fell back on quasi-religious complaints that 'material improvements' were causing 'the body of working-people to accept a mean form of materialism' while their leaders hardly realized 'the dangers of spiritual deterioration'.[26] Somewhere in the middle but moving fast towards the Right was Kingsley Amis, who in his brilliant Fabian pamphlet *Socialism and the Intellectuals* (1956) attributed the current defection of intellectuals from political commitment to several factors: self-interest, the influence of Orwell, affluence, scepticism about nationalization, a preference for non-political issues, and above all the romanticism of intellectuals which, Amis felt, demands grand issues.

The difficulty of sustaining secularist faith under these conditions, and of directing it purposefully, are the themes of C. P. Snow, Doris Lessing and Arnold Wesker; hence Jimmy Porter's inability to perceive a cause (see Chapter 2). And, throughout, there is a tendency to find compensating value in personal relationships. Comprehensiveness, as in religion, gives way to privatization. Assaults upon secularist pretensions asserted either our existential pointlessness or our innate depravity. Both approaches are liable to bounce back into religion.

The human sciences demanded attention, for the problem was less that we can make atomic weapons than that we had used them and were preparing to do so again. Humanity seemed programmed to behave selfishly and violently, and evidence of our natural depravity was drawn from psychology and ethology. Psychology suggested that violence is deeply embedded in our nature. So Orwell posits 'power' as the motivation for tyranny, and generalizes the analysis: 'The German Nazis and the Russian Communists came very close to us in their methods, but they never had the courage to recognize their own motives.'[27] In the introduction to *The New Poetry* (1962; discussed also in Chapter 7) A. Alvarez insisted that depth psychology requires us to acknowledge as 'libido' what theologians call 'evil', and to locate in ourselves the sources of genocide and the nuclear threat: 'the forceable recognition of a mass evil outside us has developed precisely parallel with psychoanalysis; that is, with our recognition of the ways in which the same forces are at work within us.'[28] He attacked 'gentility' in English poetry, epitomized by Larkin taking off his 'cycle-clips in awkward reverence' ('Church Going'). Alvarez admired the desperately vivid fantasies of Sylvia Plath – evocations of personal breakdown in the languages of psychoanalysis, Nazi atrocities and a resentful Christianity.

In Pinter's plays psychological determination even transforms characters physically into their fantasy terror (*The Room*, 1957; *A Slight Ache*, 1959). Pinter also picks up the undermining of rationality by our reported susceptibility to psychological 'brainwashing'. This Cold War fear was accommodated in Koestler's *Darkness at Noon* (1940) and in the psychologist William Sargent's proposal that the west and the churches sustain themselves by adopting 'Soviet' methods of 'thought control' (*Battle for the Mind*, 1957). In *Nineteen Eighty-Four* there is no limit to O'Brien's success: 'Men are infinitely malleable.'[29] Pinter presents breakdown under interrogation, expressing and producing paranoid violence, as psychologically fundamental in *The Birthday Party* (1958), *The Caretaker* and *The Dumb Waiter* (1960). That breakdown is not just the consequence of pressure, for the characters anticipate and acknowledge it; it appears as the development of intrinsic inadequacies.

Ethology links animal and human behaviour. Sargent used Pavlov's experiments with the 'conditioned reflexes' of dogs. Popular studies by Konrad Lorenz and Desmond Morris suggested that people are really naked (hairless) apes, except that we are more cruel and we lack animals' techniques of avoiding conflict. The deduction in 1953 of the double-helix structure of the DNA molecule seemed to emphasize our determination by genetic coding. Some sought comfort in Teilhard de Chardin's *Phenomenon of Man* (trans. 1959), which claimed to reconcile Christianity and evolution, though experts in neither field were convinced. Edward Bond identified generally a survival of 'original sin' – 'not the old religious version of it, but the new doctrine of natural aggression'. Science fiction explored this theme as much as the potential of technology; other worlds often revealed either analogues or contrasts to humanoid aggression. When men landed on the moon in 1969 J. G. Ballard remarked, 'If I were a Martian I'd start running now!'

The horror in Pinter's plays derives from this conception. People, like animals, fight for 'territory': 'You're in my blasted house, on my territory, drinking my wine, eating my duck' (*A Slight Ache*). The difference, according to ethologists, is that animals use signals so that the weaker withdraws unhurt, whereas people fight to the death, physically or psychologically. In Pinter's plays the defeated character is destroyed: in his view the human investment in territory is not just for material support, it involves consciousness, the self. Pinter proposes as the particular site of our agony the inner resources where Christians locate the soul and secularists our humanity.

Ted Hughes's use of animals is based on the same proposition: we are like them but suffer the additional burden of consciousness. His thrushes experience

No indolent procrastinations and no yawning stares,
No sighs or head-scratchings. Nothing but bounce and stab
And a ravening second. . . .

With a man it is otherwise.

('Thrushes', 1960)

The bull seems to know 'nothing / Of the ages and continents of his fathers', but the boy who peers into the byre takes 'a sudden shut-eyed look / Backward into the head.' The creature comes gradually into focus, 'as onto the mind's eye' ('The Bull Moses', 1960). The animal recalls the primeval impulses that are imprinted in our minds and also – because it is observed (the observer is crucial in Hughes's strategy) – exposes our consciousness. We imagine ourselves mentally superior to animals, but are driven by the same forces and only deluded by our minds. In 'To Paint a Water Lily' (1960) the surface/depths dichotomy that supports psychoanalysis and other theories of underlying corruption is applied to a lily in a pond and given evolutionary justification. The surface is, in actuality, violent enough, but on the pond-bed, at the 'root',

Prehistoric bedraggoned times
Crawl that darkness with Latin names,

Have evolved no improvements there . . .

'Whatever horror nudge her root' appears to be grounded in science with its 'Latin names'.

Crow's conscious scrutiny is his most sinister attribute, for to him the terrors of the universe are significant and therefore intrinsic: 'Crow went on laughing', 'Crow flew guiltily off', 'He stared at the evidence', 'Crow walked and mused' (*Crow*, 1970, 1972). Hughes blames secularism for our troubles: we depend upon a limiting, scientific outlook, repressing 'archaic energies of instinct and feeling'; we should recover a mythopoeic imagination.[30] *Crow* seems intended to do that, but Hughes's projection of our disasters on to a supposedly universal perspective through myths of psychoanalysis and a bitter, blackened Christianity tries so hard for the comprehensiveness of a reversed legitimation that it becomes indiscriminate. In 'Magical Dangers' Crow thinks of a palace, a fast car, 'the wind's freedom', a wage, 'the soft and warm', intelligence and 'nature's stupor': it is proposed that these diverse enticements, deprived of all social location, are related genetically through the myth of Crow. The genuinely horrifying poem is the closest to a human action, 'Crow's Account of St George', in which a man kills his family while hallucinating them as predatory beasts. His monstrosity is illuminated by the humanity of the people he distorts and kills; thus this poem does not, like most of *Crow*, present the human and the monstrous as if they are the same.

The intimations of religion which we keep noticing sometimes emerge as a grim Christianity. In Golding's *Lord of the Flies* (1954) a religious perspective is placed upon innate depravity so that we may interpret it as 'original sin'. By focusing upon children, Golding appears to uncover our fundamental determination. The 'beast' is first discovered in the nightmare of a small child; it is pre-social, and the pretext for regression to a tyranny: 'There isn't a snake-thing. But if there was a snake we'd hunt it and kill it.' Piggy the secularist denies the beast, ''Cos things wouldn't make sense. Houses an' streets, an' TV – they wouldn't work.' But Simon the seer says, 'maybe there is a beast . . . maybe it's only us.'[31] The analysis seems ratified by the adult war: the children, left to themselves, have 'naturally' re-created adult society. In Anthony Burgess's novels hopes of a decent society founder in apparently congenital violence. This is presented with a disconcerting glee, presumably reflecting what in *The Wanting Seed* (1962) is called an Augustinian 'gloomy pleasure in observing the depths to which human behaviour can sink'.[32] The approach rebounded on Burgess in the early seventies when the film of his novel *A Clockwork Orange* was said to 'glamorize evil' (Mary Whitehouse).

Existentialism

The limitations of secularism were conceptualized also within existentialism, which repudiates all the absolute categories, religious and secular, through which we have claimed significance for ourselves. 'Man first of all exists, encounters himself, surges up in the world – and defines himself afterwards.'[33] Meaning is made by us, there is no essence or absolute, either within or beyond us – neither God nor the soul nor human nature. The only unethical action is that which is 'inauthentic', in 'bad faith' with oneself.

This philosophy gave intellectual support to privatization: to the tendency to abandon the broad legitimation traditionally afforded by religion – historically the most prominent and ambitious essentialism – and to locate transcendent significance instead in the self (see also the discussion of liberalism in Chapter 2). As we shall see, existentialist preoccupation with religion sometimes represented a persistence of the religious sensibility, and it proved vulnerable to religious recuperation. Existentialism became extremely influential in the fifties, especially through attention to Camus and Dostoevsky. Colin Wilson rose to sudden fame with his version of it in *The Outsider* (1956).

Psychology and ethology threaten us with determinism, existentialism with a free will so total that life becomes arbitrary. Both tend to appeal to extreme situations, for the theory of human depravity assumes that our 'true' selves are revealed under stress, and existentialists claim that we define ourselves through crucial choices. Neither admits that circumstances limit significance – that behaviour under pressure is what people do under pressure, and cannot logically implicate behaviour in other circumstances. Both tend to discredit the significance of secular activity in the reality of everyday life.

There are three principal developments of existentialism: anguish at our meaninglessness, affirmation of human responsibility, and recuperation of religion. The anguish of pointless existence, burdened again by consciousness, is reproduced in Beckett's readers and audiences. We can assume nothing – not that yesterday's boots will fit today, certainly not that Godot will come to give meaning to existence. Attempts to theorize are represented by Lucky's speech; in the second act he is silenced. Characters tell themselves endless stories to explain who they are, but they always break down; the agony of consciousness remains. Pinter's plays also thwart all attempts to discover significance. Stanley in *The Birthday Party* has no coherent biography. We may seek to explain Goldberg and McCann by their ethnic origins, as gangsters or as medical attendants, but it can't be done; they control the situation but have no special access to meaning ('Because I believe that the world . . .'). The deluded Meg is the maker of meanings, lurching into defensive social and linguistic clichés.

'Absurdist' writing is basically a complaint at the absence of God.

'The bastard! He doesn't exist!' (*Endgame*): even Beckett's atheistic joke on Christ's parenthood depends on theological expertise. It all witnesses to a difficulty in abandoning supernatural explanations. In Pinter's early plays human interaction is precisely observed, but our attention is referred beyond that to a mysterious force (Monty, the Matchseller, the person controlling the dumb waiter, the Buddha).

The second development of existentialism despises this harking back to God. Sartre declares that release from essentialist delusions creates the possibility of genuine human existence: 'this theory alone is compatible with the dignity of man, it is the only one which does not make man into an object'; it makes man 'responsible for what he is'.[34]

John Fowles deals with reluctance to relinquish God as a means of evading responsibility in *The Magus* (1966, 1977). Fowles explains: 'I did intend Conchis to exhibit a series of masks representing human notions of God, from the supernatural to the jargon-ridden scientific; that is, a series of human illusions about something that does not exist in fact, absolute knowledge and absolute power' (Foreword, 1977). The reader is mystified and tempted into crediting other-worldly explanations (Timothy Leary called this 'the first great psychedelic novel'). But in the end we see that it has all been caused by human manipulation. Nicholas falls for the illusions Conchis creates because he lives in radical bad faith – 'always I had acted as if a third person was watching and listening and giving me marks for good or bad behaviour'.[35] Thus he elides his aloneness and his responsibility. He is obliged to face Dostoevsky's observation (often quoted by existentialists), 'If God did not exist, everything would be permitted', and to conclude that the only authentic morality, pursued for itself rather than for a supposed absolute, is not hurting people.

There are two problems here. First, there is the danger of reasserting an absolute – humanity itself. Sartre denies that his 'humanism' is of this kind, but the implication is difficult to resist. Second, the moral perspective proposed by Sartre and Fowles is, typically, privatized, part of the relocation of post-religious significance in personal integrity and relationships. They choose public issues – in *Existentialism and Humanism* whether a youth should stay with his mother or join the Free French; in *The Magus* whether Conchis should execute captured guerrillas or allow hostages to die. But each choice is designed as an 'impossible' one whose significance can therefore be referred back to the authenticity of the chooser. Thus political issues are dissolved into private ones. Fowles wants to show the disasters of twentieth-century history as of a piece with Nicholas's inauthenticity. He suggests through Conchis – profoundly, I think – that the problem is not the collapse of absolute values but the attempt to maintain them:

> I saw that this cataclysm must be an expiation for some bar-barous crime of civilization, some terrible human lie. . . . it was our believing that we were fulfilling some end, serving some plan – that all would come out well in the end, because there was some great plan over all. Instead of the reality. There is no plan. All is hazard. And the only thing that will preserve us is ourselves.[36]

But the novel develops only an interpersonal ethic. Though this may be continuous with the responsibility of political decisions, it hardly engages with the public dangers we face. (See also the discussion of *The Golden Notebook* in Chapter 3.)

Religious existentialism performed an important function in the period, for it made religion seem intellectually respectable. It informed Auden's Christianity and received popular formulation in Colin Wilson's *The Outsider* and John Robinson's *Honest to God*. It discovers a frame of reference beyond the immediate existential fact of being. Heidegger posits 'Being' of which all 'beings' are a part. Buber says that every '*I*' develops through 'a personal meeting' with a '*Thou*' and that the common ground of such meeting is the 'final *Thou*' (*I and Thou*; *Eclipse of God*). For Karl Jaspers, 'boundary situations' – death, suffering, struggle and guilt – are 'the font from which we draw the assurance of being' and the possibility of transcendence. This is the flip-over from the assumption that breakdown under pressure indicates our true nature: extreme situations lift us into 'absolute con-sciousness'.[37] Kierkegaard's existentialism is explicitly Christian: the experience of anguish is taken, in a leap of faith, as evidence of separ-ation from God. Paul Tillich develops this through an apparent allusion to *Godot*: 'We are stronger when we wait than when we possess'; 'The condition of man's relation to God is first of all one of *not* having, *not* seeing, *not* knowing, and *not* grasping.'[38]

Graham Greene explored spiritual extremes in *The Power and the Glory* (1940) and *The Heart of the Matter* (1948). *A Burnt-Out Case* (1961) focuses (through the missionaries) the failings of the insti-tutional church and (in the humanist Doctor Colin) the claims of secularism. Leprosy is the image for spiritual extremity: Querry is mutilated because, in his love of women and his work as an architect, he has lacked any faith that would transcend self. His development, from the depths of his indifference, of an unexploitative concern for others is given a religious interpretation by Colin: 'With suffering we become part of the Christian myth.'[39] This is perhaps a strange sentiment for a 'humanist' dedicated to evolutionary progress and the eradication of disease, but Greene has designed Colin to set up Quarry's spiritual experience. Querry thinks, like Kierkegaard, that his aridity might be evidence not of God's absence but of his existence: 'there were moments when he wondered if his unbelief were not after all a final and conclusive proof of the King's existence.'[40] Crude and uncomprehending characters assert that Querry is in receipt of special grace, but there seems to be truth in the idea. His last words – 'this is absurd or else . . .'[41] – recognize the power of the absurdist view but also correct it, for it is Querry's humility that prevents him declaring that his life and death are part of a divine purpose. Religion seems to force its way through secularism: despair bespeaks God's goodness, and scepticism and corruption witness to spiritual truth. The public world – politically aware blacks from the coast – enters near the end as an unabsorbable threat to the personalized work of the mission.

In *Pincher Martin* (1956) Golding's view that neglect of God and moral absolutes makes us pointless, inauthentic and predatory becomes apparent. In *Free Fall* (1959) his perspective is aggressively clear at the start: 'I have seen people crowned with a double crown, holding in either hand the crook and flail, the power and the glory.'[42] Sammy's enquiry into the loss of his freedom exposes the shortcomings of established Christianity (the church has been seduced by liberalism and only Miss Pringle's sadistic legalism is effective) and of secularism (Nick Shales is good but preaches 'a most drearily rationalistic universe'; p. 161). With the failure of these guides, Sammy is left without moral bearings. His prison-camp interrogation exposes the loathsome thing at the core of his own being – 'this was the human nature I found inhabiting the centre of my own awareness' (p. 144). Breakdown triggers the Kierkegaardian flip-over: Sammy is 'visited by a flake of fire, miraculous and pentecostal; and fire transmuted me, once and forever' (p. 142). He discovers 'a kind of vital morality' (privatized, of course) – 'the relationship of individual man to individual man' (pp. 143–4). So he sees, finally, that he lost his freedom when he realized that he could get what he wanted with 'the appropriate sacrifice' (p. 178), that he wanted Beatrice and was prepared to sacrifice her.

The principle of responsibility for others is like Fowles's. Golding

adds a conviction of essential guilt which renders rational moral purpose of little avail. Guilt is inevitable, as for Karl Jaspers: 'It is not a
matter of guiltlessness any more, but of really avoiding whatever guilt I
can avoid, so as to come to the profound, intrinsic, unavoidable guilt';
and this experience gives us 'our chance at a revelation of intrinsic
being'.[43] In *Free Fall* Golding concludes: 'We are the guilty. We fall
down. We crawl on hands and knees. We weep and tear each other'
(p. 190). And this guilt is the condition of transcendence: 'the spirit
. . . touches only the dark things, held prisoner, incommunicado,
touches, judges, sentences and passes on' (p. 192). So the climax of the
novel is Sammy's responsibility for Beatrice's cataleptic degradation:
'Beatrice pissed over her skirt and her legs and her shoes and my shoes.
The pool splashed and spread' (p. 184). She is the focus of Sammy's
guilt and hence the condition of his spiritual awareness. We may feel
an unintended suspicion that he is *still* using her – that her degradation is needed to set up his 'revelation of intrinsic being'.

Honest to God

Existential Christianity, in the work of Greene and Golding, despises
rather than legitimates society. Some churchmen sought to regain
contemporary authority by 'modernizing', meeting the contemporary
world on its own ground. In one aspect this produced important contributions to radical campaigns like CND and anti-apartheid, and
support for causes like Third World aid and community service. In
another aspect it produced the 'trendy vicar', who was mocked in
Beyond the Fringe and in Michael Frayn's dialogue between Rock Richmond and the Bishop of Twicester (say it 'Twister'):

> You see, religion's not just a narrow set of do's and don'ts, or
> a lot of abstract doctrine and long-winded ritual. It's your
> whole way of life. It's – well, it's taking a girl to the pictures.
> It's doing the ton on your motor-bike. It's rocking and rolling.
> (*The Guardian*, 1962)

There were moves, also, to modernize doctrine. 'Radical theologians'
suggested that church institutions were moribund, that other sects and
religions are equally true, that moral rules are socially derived and
provisional, that love is above the law. Most scandalously, they proposed that sexual experience outside marriage may not always be sinful.
The profoundest disturbance was in the Roman Catholic Church,

which until the accession of Pope John XXIII in 1958 refused to compromise its ancient 'truths'. When John called the Second Vatican Council (1962–5) to 'look to the present, to new conditions and new forms of life' many English Catholics seized the opportunity for critical discussion (Evelyn Waugh was horrified). Birth control was especially controversial: David Lodge's novel *The British Museum is Falling Down* (1965) evoked the ludicrous but distressing plight of hard-up Catholics whose 'sexual relations were forced into a curious pattern: three weeks of patient graph-plotting, followed by a few nights of frantic love-making, which rapidly petered out in exhaustion and renewed suspense. This behaviour was known as Rhythm and was in accordance with the Natural Law.'[44] But the expectation of change was largely frustrated by the election of Pope Paul VI in 1963. The English Cardinal Heenan asserted, 'the strength of the Catholic Church has always been authority. . . . We *know* what to believe.'

The contradictions besetting attempts to 'modernize' Anglicanism are exposed in *Honest to God* by John Robinson, Bishop of Woolwich (1963; preceded by an *Observer* article headlined 'Our image of God must go'). Robinson sought to align Christianity with the key contemporary concepts of existentialism and personal relationships. The *Church Times* declared, 'It is not every day that a bishop goes on record as apparently denying almost every Christian doctrine of the Church in which he holds office.' Robinson proposed 'the end of theism' because the popular idea of God as a person 'out there' – 'a sort of celestial Big Brother'[45] – is now incredible. Hence we must also abandon the absolute, supranaturalist ethic which, anyway, is discrediting Christianity by tying it to 'the old, traditional morality'.

Criticism was contradictory, reflecting the divide between traditional and modern which the book tried to bridge. As Bernard Levin put it,

> the bishop's attack on the concept of a God 'out there' was both a cruel theft of a comforting image from those who had held it all their lives, and a laughable work of supererogation, since nobody had believed anything of the kind for many years.[46]

But people like to be told that contradictions can be resolved. The book sold 300,000 copies by 1965, and in 1968 three-quarters of ordinands leaving college agreed or strongly agreed with it.

Robinson was avowedly following the existential Christianity of Rudolph Bultmann, Dietrich Bonhoeffer and Paul Tillich (one of the complaints was that he had got his ideas from foreigners). Bultmann held it 'impossible to use electric light and the wireless . . . and at the same time to believe in the New Testament world of spirits and miracles' (compare Golding's Piggy). He dismissed biblical 'mythology' as the product of a pre-scientific culture, the Holy Spirit and sacraments as incomprehensible, sin punished by death as abhorrent and Christ's atonement for our sin as primitive.[47] Bonhoeffer wrote, from the Nazi prison where he was to die, that not only in science and ethics but also in religion we now 'cope with all questions of importance without recourse to God as a working hypothesis', that religion itself was 'a historically conditioned and transient form of human self-expression', and that in becoming 'radically religionless' mankind has 'come of age'.[48]

These arguments leave little of Christianity intact, and Robinson drew back from their implications. He took his positive proposal mainly from *The Shaking of the Foundations* by Tillich, who declared (calling psychoanalysis and Nazism to witness) that we know existentially of 'a deeper level of our being'. Robinson says 'God' is not 'another Being *at all*' but 'the depths of your life . . . what you take seriously without any reservation'.[49] Julian Huxley pointed out that by retaining the word 'God', with its inevitable supernatural and personalist aura, Robinson tries 'to keep his cake and eat it'[50] – to retain the terminology and hence, apparently, the continuity of Christianity while denying its traditional content. Robinson does not conceal his recuperative purpose: 'If Christianity is to survive, let alone to recapture "secular" man, there is no time to lose.'[51]

Robinson glosses 'what you take seriously without any reservation' as 'love', which sounds traditional enough; and that is glossed as 'the *ultimacy* of personal relationships'.[52] So he neatly incorporates the dominant value of the period. He can then abandon moral absolutes, holding that 'love' has a 'built-in moral compass'. Following Buber, he projects the value of personal relationships on to 'ultimate reality'. So as a defence witness in the *Chatterley* trial Robinson declared that Lawrence tried to portray the sexual relation as 'something sacred, as in a real sense an act of holy communion' (see Chapter 3 above). Thus Robinson tries to install the church in the region where many contemporaries located ultimate significance. By promoting privatized values, however, he furthered the marginalization of Christianity from the wider social order.

Iris Murdoch treated these issues in *The Time of the Angels* (1966).

The novel has even a genial Robinsonian bishop; his blandness worries Marcus, who wants to retrieve absolute morality after the loss of its foundation in God. Marcus's brother, Carel, convinces him that this is 'the lie of modern theology', masking the true situation: 'With or without the illusion of God, goodness is impossible to us. We have been made too low in the order of things.' Following Heidegger (who, Murdoch remarks in *The Sovereignty of Good*, is possibly 'Lucifer in person'), Carel declares, 'nothing is real for us except the uncanny womb of Being into which we shall return'.[53] Thus Carel deploys both the natural depravity and the existentialist repudiations of secularist pretensions. Philosophers have all taught 'a facile optimism', that 'goodness is there at the centre of things radiating its pattern'.

In her essays, collected as *The Sovereignty of Good* (1970), Murdoch acknowledges a dangerous degree of truth in Carel's argument: Freud has shown us 'a realistic and detailed picture of the fallen man'[54] (the psychoanalytic reference and the recuperated Christian language we have seen before). She has two main proposals. First, we should recognize that moral life is possible through a steady, decent attention to reality, which imperceptibly 'builds up structures of value round about us'. It is not, as existentialists assert, a matter of crucial choices in extreme conditions, but 'a small piecemeal business which goes on all the time'[55] (this is a significant criticism of existentialism). Marcus tries to say this to Carel; more important, he is shown as living it – he seems to have Robinson's 'built-in moral compass'. He is rewarded eventually with the opportunity of a positive relationship with an old friend, though only its possibilities are indicated. *The Nice and the Good* (1968) and *A Fairly Honourable Defeat* (1970; see Chapter 3 above) show more of how such goodness may work.

Murdoch's second proposal is that we should 'attempt to look right away from self towards a distant transcendent perfection, a source of uncontaminated energy, a source of *new* and quite undreamt-of virtue'. She admits that this sounds like 'the old concept of God in a thin disguise' but nevertheless finds a value in prayer and sacraments.[56] Hence the persistent recuperation of religious categories in these novels. Marcus's friend is a psychiatric social worker (a secular specialist in personal relationships), but she has been employed by the bishop (almost a Prospero figure) and disguised as a church organizer; she is 'a sort of Buddhist now really'.[57] In *The Nice and the Good* we read: 'All power is sin and all law is frailty. Love is the only justice. Forgiveness, reconciliation, not law.'[58] With a writer whose thought is so independent, it is disappointing to be asked to pick up these concepts again as if they had never been criticized.

All this debate did not help the Church of England. Confirmations of boys aged 12–20 fell steadily during the sixties. From 1911 to 1961 they had varied between 2.5 and 3.5 per cent, but by 1970 they were 1.5 per cent. In 1964 one person in seventeen said they had no church, in 1968 more than one in five.

Doing your own thing

In the mid-sixties, frustration among young people combined with economic buoyancy to form what amounted to a 'counter-culture'. 'Young people are not correcting society. They are regurgitating it.'[59] The movement was dispersed and confused, but at its most ambitious it aspired to replace the dominant ideology by projecting existential and personal values with new urgency into the public, political domain. The key move was a repudiation of theories of innate depravity and existential pointlessness. The latter was perceived as the consequence of the former, and the former was perceived as wrong.

Freud had indicated that repression enables people to live together in society. Norman O. Brown (*Life Against Death*), Herbert Marcuse (*Eros and Civilization*), Wilhelm Reich (*The Function of the Orgasm*) and R. D. Laing (*The Politics of Experience*) declared (in different ways) that repression, especially of sexuality, is the instrument of a bad (capitalist) society and that we would come closer to our natural potential, in a better society, if released from it. (See the analysis in Chapter 3 of the idea of the subversive power of sexuality.) Suddenly legitimation of the dominant values in society was looked at from the other end. It is not that we are lost without authoritative meaning, but that too much 'meaning' is imposed on us through socialization – which Laing redefined as 'getting each new recruit to the human race to behave and experience in substantially the same way as those who have already got here'. We feel existential pointlessness because the 'real' person is submerged beneath the structures of bureaucracy and technology:

> In order to get back to what the ego is and what actual reality it most nearly relates to, we have to desegregate it, de-depersonalize it, de-extrapolate, de-abstract, de-objectify, de-reify, and we get back to you and me, to our particular idioms or styles of relating to each other in social context.[60]

So 'madness' does not constitute a 'failure of adaptation' but the struggle to cope with a socially mystified reality (the theme of *Morgan – A Suitable Case for Treatment* and other work by David Mercer). Psychology reveals not innate depravity but, in its techniques of confinement, electro-convulsive and drug treatments, an oppressive society (compare Aston in *The Caretaker*).

Psychedelic drugs were regarded by some as a way of breaking through to the true self. Thom Gunn said *Moly* (1971) could be seen as 'a history of San Francisco from 1965–9'. The title poem represents humanity as Ulysses' sailors when turned to pigs by Circe – 'Buried in swine'. The obvious comparison is with Hughes's 'View of a Pig' (1960), where the animal is observed with awed and pointed detachment. Gunn's concern with the animal is different, for real humanity is inside and waiting to be released: we dream of moly – in Gunn's terms, LSD – which turned Ulysses' pigs back into humans; through this we become plants in 'The Garden of the Gods'. (The terms are sourly reversed in Auden's 'Circe' (1969), where 'Make love not war' is written over the gate to the deceiver's garden: 'She does not brutalize Her victims (beasts could / bite or bolt), She simplifies them to flowers.')

Notice the persisting wish to project one's values, religiously, on to a transcendental plane. These writers appeal to existentialism to disqualify undesirable attitudes as social mystifications, but then to an essential human nature to ratify their own idea of the good life. Correspondingly, drugs are said to oppress personality when used by psychologists, but also to be the means of liberating the true self. Timothy Leary exploited these paradoxes by claiming that LSD tunes us in to the genetic DNA code which is 'the language of God'.[61] The outcome was a disabling underestimation of the obstacles to change in modern society.

Sometimes this movement was hedonist, sometimes nihilist. But there was also an attempt to feed personal values back into the world as political analysis and intervention. Laing called his approach 'both existential and social', requiring understanding of 'the *political* order, of the way persons exercise control and power over one another'.[62] Private values were extended radically to legitimate an alternative society ('make positive changes wherever you are, right in front of your nose'; *International Times*, 1967). From this perspective the main problem seemed to be the scale and impersonality of modern societies. The ways business and government were abusing technology were declared contrary to personal needs and therefore to nature and humanity. The power of modern armaments was demonstrated in Vietnam; Rachel Carson's *Silent Spring* (1962) argued that we are poisoning ourselves with chemicals; there seemed to be no end to the growth of traffic and urban sprawl; even disease control was causing overpopulation, and it was proposed to produce out of test-tubes people suitable for such an environment. Even the BBC Reith lecturer, Edmund Leach, noting that 'the young are just appalled at the way science is being used', asserted: 'The real danger here is not the sophistication of the technology, it is the antediluvian mentality of the military advisers, and of those whom they advise.'[63]

One answer that was widely proposed in the counter-culture was a new respect for the ecological balance in nature and for ourselves as part of nature, expressed in a simpler way of life (perhaps 'dropping out'). Another answer, especially in 1968, was political demonstration – happy in the sense of release, angry when confronted. The third answer, once more, was recuperated religion. Jeff Nuttall declared, 'a religion must be instituted which each individual may enfuel and conduct from his own utterly unique sensibility'.[64] The difficulty of 'instituting' something entirely 'individual' is germane, for, while spirituality was intended by some to legitimate an alternative world-view, often it was just the extreme of personal reaction against the 'dehumanization' of bureaucracy and technology. History and geography were ransacked for likely modes – Zen Buddhism, yoga, transcendental meditation, Sufism, Krishna Consciousness, astrology, spiritualism, witchcraft, Satanism, Druidism, black and white magic – anything that was not, like conventional Christianity, part of 'the system'. But Christianity persisted as a reference point. Timothy Leary remarked:

> The Old Testament is exactly that. Old. The garbled trip diary
> of a goofy bunch of flipped-out visionaries. Don't you know
> that God's revelation comes to us today clearer and more
> directly than it did to Elijah, Abraham, Isaiah, Jeremiah?[65]

The counter-culture's 'literary' effects (the idea of the literary was scorned) were dispersed and often ephemeral; the generally sour reaction of the literary establishment is described in Chapters 2 and 5. But, as Richard Neville proclaimed, the subversive impact depended on its being 'alive, exciting, fun, ephemeral, disposable, unified, unpredictable, uncontrollable, lateral, organic and popular'.[66] Poetry was suddenly important among students and likeminded people. It was performed (with or without music) in pubs, on the seashore, in

Hyde Park and the Albert Hall. Editing *Children of Albion: Poetry of the Underground in Britain* (1969), Michael Horovitz said it represented a network of poets 'at work and play in their own gardens of love, where only "Thou Shalt Not" is taboo – in an atmosphere of finer awareness, radiating a sense of community & a more open, humane and practical way of life.'[67] Adrian Mitchell's 'To Whom it May Concern' seemed central:

> Every time I shut my eyes all I see is flames.
> Made a marble phone book, carved all the names
> > So coat my eyes with butter
> > Fill my ears with silver
> > Stick my legs in plaster
> > Tell me lies about Vietnam.

The poem is incremental: personal sensation and understanding, which would enable us naturally to perceive the truth, are systematically blocked by the government machine. 'You put your bombers in, you put your conscience out, / You take the human being and you twist it all about'; the physical mutilation of the Vietnamese and the psychological mutilation of the imperialist countries are the same process. Establishment critics thought it crude and self-indulgent, but Mitchell said he wanted to 'talk directly and honestly to people about the things which matter most to us'.

The counter-culture did not displace the dominant ideology, though it did force a widening of acceptable thought and behaviour. The main problems were, first, that it was too smoothly reactive – 'Policemen will be beaten up by poets / Trade Unions will be taken over by workers' (Adrian Henri, 'Don't Worry / Everything's Going to be All Right'). Playful irony was intended to undercut the solemnity of the system, but it was also a substitute for hard thinking. Second, as it was reactive, so it was dependent upon the technological society it deplored. Neville's *Playpower* envisaged a world with machines doing most of the work; 'dropping out' was financed by parents or social security; light shows and LSD used high technology; the poetry followed the styles of advertising copy, was on the fringes of the pop music industry, and was itself a 'media phenomenon'. Third, its positive base was too narrow: it tried to construct a world-view (like an inverted pyramid) upon personal impulse. It developed no adequate social analysis; 'the personal is the political' too easily slides back to privatism.

We are liable, now, to regard the aspirations of the sixties counter-culture with, at best, ambivalence. Certainly the sexual politics of the seventies needed to repudiate its complacent views of sexuality (see Chapter 3). But its excesses were necessary if it was to make any impact at all upon a system so deeply entrenched. The crucial failure, perhaps, was not in the sixties but in the seventies, when the insights and opportunities that had been created – albeit extravagantly, imprecisely and insecurely – were not followed up.

The difficulties were registered by Aldous Huxley, who had been writing of psychedelic experience since the war. *Island* (1962) creates a 'happy', non-technological community founded on human responsiveness and mystical awareness. But the paradoxes of social control do not disappear, for the community depends on drugs and careful socialization: 'Pavlov purely for a good purpose. Pavlov for friendliness and trust and compassion. Whereas you prefer to use Pavlov for brain washing, Pavlov for selling cigarettes and vodka and patriotism. Pavlov for the benefit of dictators, generals, and tycoons.'[68] This is bold, but it hardly allays the fear of the age, which is of being manipulated and determined, however benignly. Either way, the generals and tycoons don't disappear, for invasion, inspired by an oil company, threatens throughout and is accomplished at the end, supported by the legitimative slogan 'Progress, Values, Oil, True Spirituality'. The society is destroyed because it has rejected the principle of resistance. Huxley does not expect personal values to challenge the system successfully.

The end of the period coincided with increasing economic anxiety and scepticism about euphoric intellectual adventuring – the mood is described more fully at the end of Chapter 2. The traditional-minded tried to reassert themselves. This is how Mary Whitehouse saw it all:

> Throughout the 1960s Britain was punch drunk. On the one hand, a continual stream of advocacy in favour of pre-marital sex, abortion on demand, homosexuality. On the other, abuse of the monarchy, moral values, law and order and religion. Intellectuals without faith, middle-aged entrepreneurs still hankering after their lost youth, careerist clerics more concerned with publicity than with the Gospel, combined to seduce a whole generation into accepting sex as the great liberator, and self-control and self-denial as the only sins.[69]

Some of Whitehouse's allies – the Charismatics in the churches, the Jesus People, the Festival of Light – adopted methods associated with the counter-culture. For radicals, violence in Northern Ireland, the confrontational stance of the Heath government and the challenge of feminism indicated that social injustice would not be dispelled by legalizing marijuana and, anyway, it wasn't going to be legalized. Attention turned back to traditional politics and especially Marxism. Most people, as they had throughout, did their best to make sense of their private and working lives more or less within society's norms. But these had changed. In the credibility of the churches, Christian doctrine and the supernatural, in the scope of sexual attitudes and practices, and in the valuation of innovation and tolerance against tradition and authority, secularist developments would not easily be reversed.

Notes

1 John Wain, *Sprightly Running* (London: Macmillan, 1962), p. 143.
2 Quoted in Humphrey Carpenter, *The Inklings* (London: Allen & Unwin, 1978), pp. 206, 64.
3 John Lehmann (ed.), *The Craft of Letters in England* (London: Cresset Press, 1956), pp. 153–4, 217.
4 Helen Gardner, *The Art of T. S. Eliot* (London: Cresset Press, 1949), p. 7; see also p. 9.
5 T. S. Eliot, *Notes towards the Definition of Culture* (London: Faber, 1948), p. 108.
6 Evelyn Waugh, *Unconditional Surrender* (Harmondsworth: Penguin, 1964), pp. 141, 238.
7 In Tom Maschler (ed.), *Declaration* (London: MacGibbon & Kee, 1957), pp. 75–6.
8 Peter L. Berger, *The Social Reality of Religion* (London: Faber, 1969), p. 108.
9 Bryan R. Wilson, *Religion in Secular Society* (Harmondsworth: Penguin, 1969), pp. 11, 10.
10 Berger, op. cit., p. 29.
11 Mass Observation, *Puzzled People* (London: Gollancz, 1947).
12 Richard Hoggart, *The Uses of Literacy* (Harmondsworth: Penguin, 1958), p. 113.
13 Berger, op. cit., p. 133.
14 Billy Graham, *Peace with God* (Kingswood: The World's Work, 1954), p. 186.
15 In Maschler (ed.), op. cit., p. 41.
16 Iris Murdoch, *The Bell* (Harmondsworth: Penguin, 1962), p. 131.
17 Ibid., pp. 302, 191.
18 Ibid., p. 302.
19 Julian Huxley, *Essays of a Humanist* (London: Chatto & Windus, 1964), p. 88.

20 Arthur Koestler, *The God that Failed* (London: Right Book Club, 1949), p. 32.
21 Bertrand Russell, *The Impact of Science on Society* (London: Allen & Unwin, 1952), p. 25.
22 George Orwell, *Nineteen Eighty-Four* (Harmondsworth: Penguin, 1954), p. 60.
23 Ibid., pp. 140, 217.
24 George Scott, *Time and Place* (London: Staples Press, 1956); in Gene Feldman and Max Gartenberg (eds), *Protest* (St Albans: Panther, 1960), pp. 242, 246.
25 In Maschler (ed.), op. cit., pp. 42, 41.
26 Hoggart, op. cit., p. 323.
27 Orwell, op. cit., p. 216.
28 A. Alvarez, *The New Poetry* (Harmondsworth: Penguin, 1962), p. 27.
29 Orwell, op. cit., p. 216.
30 Ted Hughes, 'Myth and Education', in Geoff Fox *et al.* (eds), *Writers, Critics and Children* (London: Heinemann, 1976).
31 William Golding, *Lord of the Flies* (Harmondsworth: Penguin, 1960), pp. 36, 88, 85.
32 Anthony Burgess, *The Wanting Seed* (London: Heinemann, 1962), p. 11.
33 Jean-Paul Sartre, *Existentialism and Humanism*, trans. Philip Mairet (London: Methuen, 1948), p. 28.
34 Ibid., pp. 44–5, 29.
35 John Fowles, *The Magus* (St Albans: Triad/Granada, 1977), p. 495.
36 Ibid., p. 120.
37 Karl Jaspers, *Philosophy*, vol. 2, trans. E. B. Ashton (Chicago, Ill., and London: University of Chicago Press, 1970), p. 199.
38 Paul Tillich, *The Shaking of the Foundations* (Harmondsworth: Penguin, 1962), p. 151.
39 Graham Greene, *A Burnt-Out Case* (Harmondsworth: Penguin, 1975), p. 122.
40 Ibid., p. 158.
41 Ibid., p. 196.
42 William Golding, *Free Fall* (Harmondsworth: Penguin, 1963), p. 5; page references to this edition are subsequently given in the text.
43 Jaspers, op. cit., p. 217.
44 David Lodge, *The British Museum is Falling Down* (St Albans: Panther, 1967), p. 11.
45 John Robinson, *Honest to God* (London: SCM Press, 1963), p. 57.
46 Bernard Levin, *The Pendulum Years* (London: Cape, 1970), p. 107.
47 Rudolph Bultmann, 'New Testament and Mythology', in *Kerygma and Myth*, ed. Hans Werner Bartsch, trans. Reginald H. Fuller, 2nd edn, vol. 1 (London: SPCK, 1964), pp. 5–7.
48 Dietrich Bonhoeffer, *Letters and Papers from Prison*, ed. Eberhard Bethge (London: SCM Press, 1971); quoted in Robinson, op. cit., pp. 36–7, 122.
49 Robinson, op. cit., ch. 3.

50 Huxley, op. cit., p. 222.
51 Robinson, op. cit., p. 43.
52 Ibid., p. 49.
53 Iris Murdoch, *The Time of the Angels* (St Albans: Triad/Panther, 1978), p. 165.
54 Iris Murdoch, *The Sovereignty of Good* (London: Routledge & Kegan Paul, 1970, p. 51.
55 Ibid., p. 37.
56 Ibid., pp. 101, 72, 69.
57 Murdoch, *The Time of the Angels*, p. 219.
58 Iris Murdoch, *The Nice and the Good* (London: Chatto & Windus, 1968), pp. 276–7.
59 Jeff Nuttall, *Bomb Culture* (St Albans: Paladin, 1970), preface.
60 R. D. Laing, *The Politics of Experience* (New York: Ballantine Books, 1968), p. 67.
61 Timothy Leary, *The Politics of Ecstasy* (St Albans: Paladin, 1970).
62 Laing, op. cit., p. 123.
63 Edmund Leach, *A Runaway World?* (London: BBC Publications, 1968).
64 Nuttall, op. cit.
65 Leary, op. cit., p. 300.
66 Richard Neville, 'Carry on Motherfuckers', in *Playpower* (St Albans: Paladin, 1970), p. 52.
67 Michael Horovitz, *Children of Albion* (Harmondsworth: Penguin, 1969), p. 371.
68 Aldous Huxley, *Island* (Harmondsworth: Penguin, 1964), p. 197.
69 Mary Whitehouse, *Whatever Happened to Sex?* (Hove: Wayland, 1977), pp. 8–9.

Further reading

Alvarez, A. *The Savage God*. London: Weidenfeld & Nicolson, 1971. Harmondsworth: Penguin, 1974.
Berger, Peter L. *The Social Reality of Religion*. London: Faber, 1969. (Published in New York by Doubleday as *The Sacred Cosmos*, 1967.)
Ferris, Paul. *The Church of England*. Rev. edn. Harmondsworth: Penguin, 1964.
Geertz, Clifford. *The Interpretation of Cultures*. New York: Basic Books, 1973. London: Hutchinson, 1975.
Hebblethwaite, Peter. *The Runaway Church*. London: Collins, 1975.
Leach, Edmund. *A Runaway World?* London: BBC, 1968.
Leech, Kenneth. *Youthquake*. London: Sheldon Press, 1973.
Luckmann, Thomas. *The Invisible Religion*. London: Macmillan, 1967.
MacIntyre, Alasdair. *Secularization and Moral Change*. London: Oxford University Press, 1967.
Macquarrie, John. *Studies in Christian Existentialism*. London: SCM Press, 1966.

Martin, Bernice, *A Sociology of Contemporary Cultural Change*. Oxford: Blackwells, 1981.

Perman, David, *Change and the Churches*. London: Bodley Head, 1977.

Roszak, Theodore. *The Making of a Counter Culture*. London: Faber, 1970.

van Buren, Paul M. *The Secular Meaning of the Gospel*. London: SCM Press, 1963.

Wilson, Bryan R. *Contemporary Transformations of Religion*. London: Oxford University Press, 1976.

Wilson, Bryan R. *Religion in Secular Society*. London: Watts, 1966. Harmondsworth: Penguin, 1969.

Part II
Literature in society

5 The production of literature

STUART LAING

There are two senses in which literature is produced, and this chapter is about both of them. On the one hand, it is produced materially: books are published, plays are produced. This requires natural resources, capital and labour, and their deployment involves commercial institutions and reference to market forces (this is true even of a poets' co-operative). It is affected by developments in adjacent areas of production (other communications media, for instance) and, finally, by the structure and condition of the economy at large. On the other hand, literature is produced as a concept. Writing is continuously sorted and classified by various institutions, including publishers, journals, libraries, the Arts Council and the education system. Aspects of these two kinds of production are discussed in Chapter 1; this chapter specifies their historical operation in the post-war period.

Like 'culture', 'literature' can be a descriptive or an evaluative concept; it can be inclusive or selective. At one extreme, literature means printed matter of any kind (for instance, advertising or political handouts, 'campaign literature'). The wider selective meaning includes all 'good' or 'quality' books, as in the title *The Times Literary Supplement*. In a more specialized usage literature means 'imaginative' writing – the Arts Council declares: 'our involvement is necessarily with literature as an art and not with the entire range of general subjects dealt with in printed books' (*Annual Report*, 1970–1). The most restrictive use of all is embodied in phrases like 'the literary tradition' and 'English literature' ('Eng. lit.'). Here the idea is to discriminate those works which are to be most highly valued, thus identifying the 'canon' of English, European or world literature as the embodiment, usually, of transcendent human values.[1] In this chapter all these conceptions of literature are relevant, for they interact both as concepts (often they are defined in opposition to each other) and in the material production of literature (often publishers are involved with many kinds of book).

In practical analysis, the two kinds of production identified here are hardly separable. The decisions a publisher takes about costs and marketing often involve a sense of the potential of a book within one or another of the conceptions of literature (this may be as specific as aiming a textbook at an A-level course). Conversely, the fact that a book reaches the market through a certain publisher and in a certain packaging will influence its chances of being perceived as literature in one of the selective meanings of the term. Intermediaries like reviewing journals, libraries, the Arts Council and educational institutions, which seem at first sight to be working mainly at the conceptual level of production, cannot finally be separated from economic and political considerations; and their effects on the market may be very direct.

The initial topics, therefore, are the market and the public sector – reflecting the fact that writing, like other activities in the mixed economy of Britain, is subject to market forces and also to intervention from governmental institutions. Then separate consideration is given to education (the most influential part of the public sector), which developed specialized conceptions of literature with particular vigour in the period; and to the mass media, which have been perceived influentially as the main institutions opposing and subverting education and literature. The final section considers the opportunities for alternative forms.

Books in the market

A consideration of books as commodities in the market immediately undermines one common assumption about literature: that the individual author simply submits his or her creative work to the judgement of the individual reader. Literary work is made available through the publishing industry which, with all its individual characteristics, is ultimately like other industries: it is subject to similar pressures and responds with similar policies of organization and marketing.

During the war, publishing experienced the same kinds of restrictions as other non-essential industries. In 1939 14,904 titles were published in Britain; by 1945 this had shrunk to 6747. The main reason was paper rationing. It was introduced in March 1940, and publishers were restricted to a percentage of the paper used in the twelve months up to August 1939. The initial figure was 60 per cent but it fluctuated considerably and during 1942 and 1943 was only 37 per cent. Other constraining factors were a compulsory war-risk insurance scheme, the increased cost of materials, the bombing of London warehouses (more than 20 million books were destroyed in London in the winter of 1940–1) and of paper stocks, and the loss of skilled personnel (e.g. bookbinders) to war service. Fiction titles were halved and then quartered, from 4687 in 1938 to 2342 in 1941 and 1246 in 1945. And it took longer for a manuscript to be printed and published: in 1946 one printer reported that his firm had a year's waiting list of publishers' manuscripts for printing.

At the same time, as supply dried up, demand expanded, both in the civilian population and, particularly later in the war, in the organized supply of reading matter to the forces. The situation was such that by June 1944 the Publishers' Association reported that 'nine new books out of ten are oversubscribed before publication'; in August 1943 *The Times Literary Supplement* had suggested that 'any paper that anyone can contrive to obtain to bind up into a book can be sold at any price'. One consequence of the sum of these factors was that despite many individual publishers' commitments to publishing new work there were neither the resources nor the economic pressures to take risks on new authors. Nevertheless, poetry flourished (see Chapter 7).

The continuing austerity of the post-war period brought little improvement. The paper quota was increased to 65 per cent but then reduced again in the economic crisis of 1947, which saw also the collapse of the high level of wartime demand. Paper rationing was abolished in 1948, and in 1949 the 17,034 titles outstripped the 1939 figure by 2000. Then in the fifties books shared in the general boom in consumer durables. The number of new titles rose to 25,000 by 1961 and 33,000 by 1970. Perhaps more striking was the rise in spending on books. In 1939 £7 million was spent in the home market. By 1949 this had risen to £24 million and by 1970 to £85 million. If publishing for export is included, then the increase was even sharper – from £10 million in 1939 to £34 million in 1949 and over £150 million in 1970. Taking into account the fourfold rise in the cost of living between 1939 and 1970, this still indicates an expansion in turnover of around 375 per cent.

As books shared the general economic conditions, so they experienced the particular economic pressures of the time. Publishing, like other industries, responded to growth and enhanced competition with the mergers, takeovers, development of multinational corporations and tendencies to horizontal and vertical monopoly which characterized this aggressively confident phase of late capitalism. By 1970 many of the older, smaller publishing houses had been absorbed by bigger ones or indeed by large corporations, sometimes American, sometimes involved mainly in non-publishing fields. Secker and Warburg had become part of Heinemann in 1951 and by 1970 Heinemann itself was controlled by Tillings, a transport company. Hogarth Press moved under the wing of Chatto and Windus in 1945 and in 1969 Chatto and Jonathan Cape merged as a defence against possible takeover by a big corporation. The Thomson newspaper group moved into book publishing by taking over Michael Joseph in 1962 as well as Thomas Nelson and Hamish Hamilton; they also controlled Sphere paperbacks. Granada controlled a number of hardback firms as well as Panther and Paladin paperbacks. Again as a defence against such control a number of smaller houses (including Methuen, Tavistock, Eyre and Spottiswoode, and Chapman and Hall) combined into Associated Book Publishers. In 1967 ABP were one of the six largest publishers, taking 20 per cent of the market. Another was Hamlyn, controlled by IPC (the country's leading newspaper publisher); IPC were themselves taken over by an international corporation, the Reed Group, in 1970. Penguin were also among the six; they were taken over, on the death of Allen Lane in 1970, by Longman Pearson, a company with banking, industrial, television and publishing interests.

In a number of these corporations book publishing was no longer the main concern. In 1972 only 5 per cent of Granada's turnover came from books (it also controlled commercial television in Lancashire, cinemas and bingo clubs); and less than 25 per cent of Thomson's came from books and magazines (it had major interests in air travel, package holidays, television and hotels). This kind of organization was far removed from the small publishing houses of the inter-war period, when a significant number of firms could be identified as the creation and, in terms of policy, the reflection of specific individuals: Hogarth Press (the Woolfs), Secker and Warburg, Jonathan Cape, Victor Gollancz, Penguin (the Lanes, particularly Allen Lane). Within economic constraints, specific cultural or political aims could be pursued – in the Left Book Club, in Frederic Warburg's preference for the 'radical, anticonservative and unorthodox', or Sir Geoffrey Faber's more traditional wish to 'raise the standard of public taste'.

The increase in the scale of post-war publishing did not altogether eradicate these concerns. Many publishing editors retained high-cultural ideals in the sixties, and some new houses (e.g. Calder and Boyars) continued the independent tradition. Nevertheless Michael Lane in *Books and Publishers* (1980) reports one publisher as describing the pre-war period as the age of the editors, 1947–60 as the era of the sales staff and post-1960 as the age of the accountants. It is certainly clear that traditional publishing ideals – of editorial freedom, publishing potentially unprofitable books for cultural or prestige reasons, and developing a backlist – came under scrutiny as more immediate financial criteria of success and failure were applied. The problems posed by these developments were somewhat cushioned in the sixties by the continuing expansion of the market (they became much more severe in the seventies – as exemplified by the major retrenchment within Penguin Books in 1974–5).

The most overt sign of the expansion and competitiveness of the book trade was the so-called paperback revolution, which sought and found a mass market. By 1968–9 nearly 90 million copies of paperbacks were being sold by British publishers (with up to 40 per cent of these for export). Cheap reprints of novels dated back to the yellow-back 'railway' novels of the mid-nineteenth century. The post-war boom was rooted in the initiative and successes of Allen Lane's Penguins (from 1935 on). At 6*d.* a copy they were much cheaper than most other reprint libraries, and depended on high sales with a first printing of at least 25,000 copies. Their high-cultural status began with the topical Penguin Special series (from 1938); its initial success placed Penguin very well in the allocation of paper and this, together with the unusual wartime conditions (which removed, if only temporarily, many hardback publishers' traditional objections to paperbacks), established Penguin, along with other centre-left cultural ventures such as *Picture Post* and the *Daily Mirror*, as one of the successes of the 'people's war'.

During the late forties the name of Penguin became virtually synonymous with paperbacks (upgrading the cultural status of both in the process); in 1948, for example, they negotiated first-refusal rights of all titles with many of the leading hardback publishers. Their dominance continued through the fifties and, despite increasingly vigorous challenges from Pan, Fontana, Corgi and Panther, through the sixties too. Their sales rose from 12 million copies in 1959 to 29 million in

1968, and between 1960 and 1970 the total number of paperback titles in print rose from under 6000 to over 37,000. In 1967–8 they were taking nearly one-third of the paperback sales (27 million). Among

5 John Osborne and Mary Ure in 'Ban the "H" Bomb Campaign' march in Whitehall (1959). Mary Ure acted the part of Alison in the first production of *Look Back in Anger* and was John Osborne's wife.

Penguins that had sold over a million by the late sixties were *Lady Chat-terley's Lover* (over 3.5 million), *The Odyssey*, *Animal Farm* and *Room at the Top*. By the late sixties the chief rival to Penguin was Pan (jointly controlled by Macmillan and Heinemann), with 17 million

6 London students meet West Indian immigrants at Waterloo (1961)

copies in 1967–8; among their million-sellers in the early sixties were *Saturday Night and Sunday Morning* and a number of Ian Fleming's James Bond novels. By 1970 paperbacks accounted for approximately 40 per cent of sales revenue in book publishing.

Much paperback publishing was concerned with reprints, and the field of completely new titles was almost solely non-fiction. As regards novels, a pattern became established whereby the paperback publisher would select some novels from the range of hardback publication and publish them after a gap of a few years. Through the fifties this gap, in the case of potentially good sellers, gradually narrowed to about two years and by the late sixties, as marketing became ever more aggressive, in some cases to one year. Periods of six or seven years elapsed between the initial publication in 1954 of *Lucky Jim* and *Lord of the Flies* and paperback publication. For *Room at the Top* (1957) and *Saturday Night and Sunday Morning* (1958) the gap was two years. For *Kes* (1968) and *The French Lieutenant's Woman* (1969) paperback versions were available in 1969 and 1970 respectively. By 1970 (and beyond) there was, however, no sign that the gap would be closed completely. Paperback publishers, almost without exception, were unwilling or unable to publish completely new fiction. The economic risk was generally too great, given the large print-run needed to keep the price low enough to attract an adequate readership. Paperback publication of novels relied on the heavy sellers, titles whose initial impact on the market (including advertising and reviewing) and first-copy costs (including the major editorial expenses and author payment, much of it in advance) had been sustained by the much higher prices of the hardback edition.

The consumers at which all this production was aimed were by no means homogeneous. A study by Michael Young and Peter Wilmott in the London area in 1970 reported that only 46 per cent of married men read books with any regularity (defined as twelve or more times a year), as opposed to figures of 64 per cent for gardening and 97 per cent for watching television. Perhaps of more significance was the difference between social classes, which was more marked than for any other leisure activity: 67 per cent of professional and managerial groups read books regularly as against 33 per cent of skilled manual workers and 28 per cent of unskilled or semi-skilled manual workers.[2] Even without details of which books were read, these figures suggest that book reading was one of the most pronounced indicators of social class in postwar Britain. The proportions of these figures were in fact little different from those of a Mass Observation survey in Tottenham in 1946.

Peter Mann in *Books, Buyers and Borrowers* (1971) reports on a series of studies carried out mainly in Sheffield. He confirms the general emphasis of the London figures, while suggesting some modifications. Mann found that 26 per cent of those using the public library and 38 per cent of those using a general bookshop were students (the figure for Dillon's in London was 60 per cent). This indicates one area in which the 46 per cent London figure (based on men in work) needs revision. Class analysis of Mann's figures reinforces the conclusions drawn above, with a sharp differentiation between white-collar and manual workers: 72 per cent of the bookshop customers came from white-collar occupations as against 14 per cent from manual (in the population as a whole the proportions are 32 per cent white-collar and 60 per cent manual). In addition, there were notable differences between library and bookshop users: the lower grades of white-collar workers used the library more than professional and managerial groups (for the bookshop this was reversed); and library borrowing was especially important to retired people.[3]

Paralleling the expansion of the book market was that for other, more popular forms of reading material. Expenditure on magazines in the period was almost exactly the same as on books. Between 1957 and 1967 it increased from £46 million to £80 million (an increase in real terms of just over 30 per cent). Many of these magazines were aimed specifically at one age group, sex or sub-cultural group (from *My Weekly* to *Playboy* and *Farmer's Weekly* to *Fish Trades Gazette*). The most general market penetration here was achieved by the women's magazines: by 1970 the leading four had a combined circulation of 7 million per week. Any full account of popular literary forms in the period would have to take account of the close relationship between the stories and serials in such magazines and the successes of Mills and Boon formulaic light romantic fiction in the late sixties (in 1967 Mills and Boon had a mailing list of 9000, of whom two were men).

Expenditure on newspapers exceeded that on books and magazines put together (over £200 million a year by 1967 as against less than £170 million on books and magazines). It is here that printed material was most pervasive and reading skills most exercised and reinforced. The national press had already achieved virtually total coverage of the population: in 1938 the circulation of the nine national dailies had risen to 10.7 million and that of the twelve Sundays to 14.9 million. This means that in the case of dailies 95 copies were bought for every 100 households. The total daily sale (including London evening papers and all provincial dailies) was 19.25 million. This level was sustained and improved through the 1940s, to a total of nearly 29 million in 1948. The peak year was 1956, with just under 30 million, although already (taking into account population growth) a proportionate decline was beginning. By 1971 the total was 23.2 million, national dailies having lost 2.5 million between 1956 and 1971. There can be little doubt that the growth in both television ownership and news coverage constituted a major challenge to the dominance of print.

The pressures of writing in a market economy were more obvious and spectacular in newspapers. Here again, ownership became more concentrated, and there was also a decrease in the number of titles. The *News Chronicle* and the *Daily Herald*, which could not command sufficient advertising, closed in 1960 and 1964 respectively, despite circulations of over a million. Advertisers, above all, demanded a clearly defined group of readers (class particularly, age and sex if possible) to ensure that their messages were reaching the right people. Papers such as those mentioned which cut across class boundaries or whose readership was not composed of potential consumers were starved of the advertising funds essential to maintain a competitive price. The most notorious instance of this dominance by advertising was the attempt by Lord Thomson to increase *The Times'* s overall circulation after 1965. It was successful, but only at the expense of economic failure, for advertisers disapproved of the resulting lower percentage of A/B-class (higher managerial, administrative and professional) readers. The paper returned to its older policy of seeking a more selective readership in 1969.

The national press (in the era of the so-called 'classless' society) helped to maintain and indeed further cultural stratification during the period, especially through the distinction between 'popular' and 'quality' papers. The 'qualities' were *The Times*, the *Guardian* and the *Daily Telegraph*; and *The Sunday Times*, the *Observer* and the *Sunday Telegraph* (this last was the only entirely new national newspaper launched in the period, in 1961). They improved both their relative and absolute circulation figures during the late fifties and sixties. While total sales of dailies fell from 15.8 million to 14.2 million between 1961 and 1971, 'quality' sales rose from 1.9 million to 2.3 million – a rise from 12 to 16 per cent of the market. Two aspects of this shift anticipate further sections of this chapter. One is that only the 'quality' papers regularly concerned themselves with book reviews, literary news and articles and, therefore, attracted literary advertising.

The other is that the shift correlates with the expansion of higher education in the period.

Literature in the market

The production of books as commodities is to some extent in the same hands as the production of the concept 'literature'. Two levels in the ascription of literary value may be distinguished: the maintenance and reordering of the inherited 'literary tradition', the great works of the past; and the valuation of new work. The latter especially begins with publishers: their rejection of 99 out of 100 manuscripts is the primary stage of valuation.

According to a crude idealist model, it is here that the cause of true literary values is hindered by the dead hand of the market-place. It seems obvious that, since publishing is a business, publishers will choose books to make a profit rather than on their literary merit. The true position is more complex. Michael Lane's study, *Books and Publishers*, suggests that, even within the new conglomerate corporations, many editors still saw themselves as committed to the cause of promoting cultural standards. Many books (including most first novels and much poetry) were published without the expectation of making a profit or even a reasonable certainty of covering costs. This may be attributed to historical traces of the gentleman-publisher, or to the wish of many publishers to see themselves as professional rather than business people. Lane reports that publishers tend 'to define book publishing houses as comparable with museums, universities and other places of higher learning'.[4]

In fact, this apparently altruistic attitude was compatible with a publishing policy that made economic sense. First, it has proved impossible to predict which books will be heavy sellers, particularly over a long period. A publisher may have to reckon on only one in five books making a profit (although the extent of that profit will outweigh the losses on the other four, if the house is to survive). This 'shotgun' approach (as Lane terms it) parallels the 'Mud-on-the-wall' tactics of the pop record singles industry in the later fifties and sixties (if you throw enough singles at the public, then some are bound to stick). Second, there may be a need to publish some unprofitable books for public relations or promotional reasons.

Finally, the key to a stable publishing house is the creation of a successful backlist, a collection of books that will sell steadily over a number of years rather than simply be ephemeral bestsellers. Although the readership for 'serious' literature is limited, it is generally affluent. The search for a 'classic' of lasting value provides a meeting-ground for cultural advancement and economic stability. In 1969 John Calder illustrated the compatibility of an 'idealistic' and a 'commercial' view of publishing by citing Beckett:

> When we first took on Beckett he was completely unsaleable. Today Beckett is taught in universities. We've made a very nice revenue purely out of allowing people to quote from him in their own books. . . . Beckett is somebody who helps us to live these days.[5]

Calder's comment also alludes to the expansion of the market for 'serious' literature, especially through the growth of sixth forms and higher education. Even poetry could be popular when well packaged. The Penguin Modern Poets series in the sixties proved this; by 1965 the first volume had sold over 50,000 copies.

There was also a range of journals that sought to construct a specifically literary milieu. At one end of the scale were small, occasional and shortlived magazines, often with local circulation by hand or word of mouth; at the other were the literary journals, the political weeklies and the 'quality' national press. It is hardly possible to produce a systematic account of the former. The variety and transience through the whole post-war period were considerable. In 1945 Denys Val Baker's *Little Reviews Anthology* listed twenty-one 'little reviews' including the 'Apocalyptic' *Kingdom Come*, the pacifist *New Vision* and *Now*, the communist *Our Time*, *Seven* ('a magazine of people's writing'), the Catholic *Wind and the Rain* and *Oasis* ('intended as the domestic literary quarterly publication of a group of members of an Army Bomb Disposal Unit') – as well as the better-known *Poetry (London)*, *Horizon* and *Penguin New Writing*. By 1947–8 Baker was listing over seventy magazines, although already some of those listed in 1945 had ceased publication; by the beginning of the fifties nearly all had disappeared. At the other end of the period, a survey in the late sixties would produce an equally numerous list of completely different titles (including *Stand*, *The Review*, *Agenda*, *Ambit*, *Listen*, *Northern House*, *Outposts*, *Phoenix*, *Resuscitator*, *Cleft* and *King Ida's Watch-Chain*), some of which were to have equally shortlived careers.

Even the most established literary periodicals have, in the mid-twentieth century, tended to have a strictly limited life. Many seem almost to have defined an aspect of the literary climate of a decade – as did Eliot's *Criterion*, or *Left Review* in the thirties. Under war conditions, after 1940, the opening of new magazines was theoretically illegal (to aid paper rationing), although in practice it was possible, particularly if the magazine was disguised as a series of anthologies or miscellanies. Two journals – representing different attitudes and climates of opinion – proved especially successful in the forties. *Penguin New Writing* began in January 1941, although it was effectively a continuation of John Lehmann's *New Writing* journal founded in 1935. Lehmann managed to persuade Allen Lane to print about 75,000 copies a month (equivalent to the Hogarth Press entitlement for a year); the magazine became a quarterly in 1942 but continued to sell up to 100,000 per number until the end of the war. The format was a mixture of reportage, short stories, poems and critical articles. In wartime, however, Lehmann felt the need for a shift of emphasis from the thirties; he explains in *I am my Brother*: 'If *New Writing* was to go on, it must avoid the political, yes, but emphasize the human, be committed to the human scene even more completely.'[6] *Penguin New Writing* continued until 1950 (by which time its circulation was under 20,000) and, with the pressures against new work experienced in book publishing, it provided a valuable and widely read vehicle for many writers. Cyril Connolly's *Horizon* began in January 1940. It had a much smaller circulation (under 10,000) and was more concerned with upholding artistic standards, mainly through critical articles, although it also published poetry and imaginative prose, including Angus Wilson's first short stories. It was inaugurated with the declaration, 'our standards are aesthetic and our politics in abeyance'.

Non-academic literary journals were less successful in the period after 1950, although in 1954 John Lehmann founded the *London Magazine* (modelled partly on *New Writing*), which survives in 1983. A new magazine perhaps more attuned to the fifties was *Encounter*, begun in 1953, a transatlantic monthly, ideologically and economically a child of the Cold War (it was eventually revealed to be dependent on finance from the United States Central Intelligence Agency). Its concerns were not exclusively literary; it was, rather, a cultural and political journal with a consistently anti-communist line. By 1969 its circulation was 37,000, of which 10,000 went to America. But it seemed that the age of the general literary journal was over – that its functions were split between small poetry magazines, academic journals and the literary sections of the weeklies or 'quality' national press.

Poetry was especially dependent on small magazines which, although often ephemeral and localized, proved remarkably resilient as a general form. Often these were inspired and managed by one man, as in the case of Jon Silkin's *Stand* which had a circulation of 3000 in 1957 and (with a short break in the late fifties) was still prominent in 1974 with a circulation of 4500. Ian Hamilton's *The Review*, founded in 1962, was designed as 'a magazine of poetry and criticism', but as its size and price increased, with Arts Council support, the criticism was more in evidence than the poetry. New poetry could also find a place in *Critical Quarterly* (founded in 1959), and their annual poetry pamphlets were selling between 10,000 and 12,000 by 1968. Occasional poems were published in the political weeklies or even, more rarely, in the 'quality' national press. Blake Morrison in *The Movement* records that the *New Statesman* published over forty Movement poems between 1949 and 1953 while the *Spectator*, between 1953 and 1956, published 240 Movement contributions, mostly poems. The *Listener* also remained (as it had been in the thirties) a regular publisher of new poems; its circulation averaged 140,000 between 1945 and 1955. Poetry showed itself to be a far more flexible form than prose fiction, especially the novel, whose conventional minimum of about 50,000 words required a relatively high level of capital investment.

More significant, in most cases, than the actual new creative writing in journals was their construction of a distinctive literary ambiance which contributed importantly to the continued specialization of 'literature' in the period. Through this agency readers identified themselves as literary and producers identified the readers as a market. Specifically, journals and the 'quality' press mediated literature by reviewing new publications and commenting on the literary scene. This is the second stage in the production of literary value: a whole process of filtering of knowledge and opinion. To some extent this was assisted by radio (though hardly at all by television) through programmes such as *New Soundings* and *First Reading*, which helped promote Movement writing in the early fifties, and *The Critics* and *The World of Books* later in the period. This secondary sifting may be viewed simply as a further quantitative selection: publishers choose from the range of novels they receive which ones to publish, and then a 'quality' paper receiving perhaps 20–25 new novels each week for review will discuss probably only four or five. The production most readers are likely to notice is further narrowed down.

The most consistent, influential and successful literary journal in the period and throughout the century was *The Times Literary Supplement*. It gave coverage to the general world of books and, as a weekly, was able to carry news as other less frequent journals could not (excepting, perhaps, a trade paper like the *Bookseller*). Sustained by the status of *The Times* itself, the *TLS* pretended, particularly through the use of anonymous reviewers, to impartiality and objectivity. Like *The Times*, it helped to develop an establishment. A librarian remarked in 1968:

> Half one's spare time may be taken up by reading reviews, and no reviewing source should be neglected. *The Times Literary Supplement* is, of course, one of the few sources of real literary criticism left in Britain. It reviews few novels, but anything noticed is worth one's attention. Occasionally it will give a novel the full 'middle-page' treatment; if *this* particular book isn't already in circulation, your book selection is at fault.[7]

The good librarian is supposed not just to follow the *TLS* but actually to anticipate its judgements.

The selections made by libraries constitute, with bookshops, book clubs and education, a third stage in the valuation, and hence the production, of 'literature'. The private-sector wholesaling of books through shops and clubs exhibited in the period the same tendencies towards larger organizations and more aggressive marketing that we saw in publishing. Libraries and education take us into the public sector.

The public sector

Since the sixteenth century the financing of literature has moved from individual patronage to the market, though with a continuous overlap (and patronage has remained important in painting, sculpture and architecture). Apart from the sponsoring of specific state occasions, the principal concern of government has been censorship – the prevention of subversive references to government policy and to the basic structure of society as it is expressed in the persons of the royal family and the orthodoxies of religion and sexuality. The post-war period witnessed a major shift towards the positive promotion of literature and the other arts by government, reflecting an assumption that the definition and maintenance of literary values are matters of public interest. In 1967, it has been estimated, £51 million was spent by individuals in the

7 Anti-Vietnam demonstration outside the American Embassy in Grosvenor Square (21 July 1968)

136

8 Struggles between police and demonstrators trying to storm the American Embassy in Grosvenor Square (17 March 1968)

purchase of books; public libraries spent £11 million; and expenditure by educational institutions and for use in them amounted to £21 million.[8] Government grants to the Arts Council were £235,000 in 1946, £820,000 in 1955–6, £3,205,000 in 1964–5, £9,300,000 in 1970–1.

State involvement in literature developed precisely alongside its involvement in welfare and education, and it has connections with the development of state intervention in industry and commerce. The positive theory of cultural and welfare intervention is that certain human needs are so fundamental that provision for them should be made, as of right, by the community before it satisfies merely personal desires. The negative theory is that certain activities need protection against the direct operation of market conditions which must normally prevail. The concern of the state with literature was justified through both theories, and generally in the period, as in public policy at large, there was an air of consensual satisfaction that a 'mixed economy' was the right answer.

The belief that literature is in and of itself beneficial brought the traditional state function of censorship under increasing pressure. A 'purge' in 1954 on a number of novels led to a campaign and the passing of the Obscene Publications Act in 1959. This provided that a person shall not be convicted of publishing an obscene article if it is 'justified as being for the public good on the ground that it is in the interests of science, literature, art or learning'. This formulation allows the interesting possibility that a work may be obscene *and*, through its literary value, 'for the public good'. Two ideological inconsistencies are apparent here, manifesting change in society. One concerns attitudes to sexual morality (this is discussed in Chapter 3 in relation to the *Lady Chatterley* trial of 1960 in which the Act was first tested, and in Chapter 6 in relation to similar controversy and change in the theatre). The other concerns the status of literature, which here comes to rival morality as a self-evident public good.

The issue was contested in the courts during the sixties, notoriously in the case of *Last Exit to Brooklyn*, by the American Hubert Selby, Jr, in 1967, where a conviction was quashed on the grounds of misdirection by the trial judge, leaving the interpretation of the Act in some disarray. In practice, the liberal implications of the Act were often circumvented through the use of section 3, which was designed to hinder the pornography trade and did not admit a defence on the grounds of literary merit. It was used, for instance, to prosecute Bill Butler's 'alternative' Unicorn Bookshop in Brighton in August 1968.

The magistrates condemned issues of the American avant-garde *Evergreen Review*, objecting specifically to work by Samuel Beckett, J. G. Ballard, William Burroughs, Gregory Corso, LeRoi Jones and Michael McClure. Far from accepting that an argument from literary merit might be relevant, the magistrate (Mr Ripper) declared himself appalled 'that responsible people, including members of the university faculty, have come here to defend . . . something which is completely indefensible from our point of view. We hope these remarks will be conveyed to the university authorities.'[9] The status, or at least the definition, of 'literature' was by no means unquestioned.

At the same time as the state, though with decreasing confidence, sustained its surveillance over unacceptable literature, it also sought to promote desirable books. The consequence was often amusingly inconsistent, witnessing to the cultural instability of the time. Authors who were on university syllabuses were proceeded against (Beckett has just been mentioned), theatres were subsidized to produce plays which were banned, *Ulysses* was acceptable as a book but not as a film, and at the time of the Unicorn Bookshop case de Sade's *Justine*, one of the books objected to, was available in Brighton Public Library to borrowers who gave reason for wanting it.

The public library service continued its growth from 247 million issues in 1939 to 312 million in 1949, 397 million in 1959 and over 600 million by 1970. During the mid-sixties, library provision benefited from the Public Libraries and Museums Act of 1964 which for the first time required the government to ensure that every library authority should provide 'a comprehensive and efficient service'. Between 1960 and 1968 expenditure on public libraries doubled.

This expansion of the public sector was at the expense of commercial lending libraries. In the inter-war period these had been a major factor in the economics of publishing, particularly in such areas as popular biographies and novels. Orwell in 1936 referred to the lending libraries as 'the novelist's foster-mother'.[10] The public libraries of the period, with relatively low budgets and no statutory obligations, were in some ways the poor relations; for example, the Board of Education Kenyon Report of 1927 advised librarians to take their time over choosing fiction, since 'the needs of those who require the newest books while they are new are sufficiently catered for by the subscription libraries'. The commercial libraries still appeared to be flourishing in the fifties. Boots had nearly a million subscribers during the war, and total circulating loans have been estimated at 150 million a year for the late forties.[11] However, the closure and sale of Mudie's (the oldest circulating library, founded in 1842) in 1937 proved a more accurate omen.

The major commercial libraries could not, or chose not to, compete with the twin threats of cheap paperbacks and free public libraries. W. H. Smith's closed in 1961 and Boots' in 1966, by which time only 140,000 subscribers remained and less than one-third the number of pre-war branches. For both these companies, the option was open to concentrate on the sale of paperbacks as their main involvement in books (for Boots in any case the lending library was often a loss leader, the book stock being positioned so that the customer had to walk through the rest of the shop to reach it). The extent of the shift from commercial to public was such that, whereas in 1936 Rowntree found that in York lending was equally split between public and commercial, by 1953 a Derby study found the proportion was two to one in favour of public libraries; by 1967 it was over twenty-five to one (over 500 million public loans to 20 million commercial loans).[12]

One effect of the shift to public libraries was that their clientele went somewhat up-market; the public library was no longer seen as a form of late Victorian 'rational recreation' for the lower classes. Another consequence was the new importance of public libraries (and librarians) for hardback fiction publishing, particularly where novels by little-known authors were concerned. Squeezed between the growth of paperback quality fiction and the greatly enlarged role of public libraries in meeting demand for new hardback fiction, the market for the sale of hardback novels direct to the public shrank rapidly. In fact, public libraries in the post-war period constituted the main market for new writing, crucially determining the shape of 'literature' as it was available to much of the public. Two statements by publishers in the late sixties illustrate this. Michael Dempsey of Hutchinson's subsidiary, New Authors Limited, reported that one novel – chosen by the *Guardian* as the most important novel of 1967 – had sold 2243 copies in its first year of publication, 2050 of which were bought by public libraries. In 1969 Tom Maschler of Cape echoed the implications of this, estimating that 90 per cent of sales of the average first novel went to public libraries.

Since it has been established that one library book may be borrowed somewhere between forty and eighty times before it has to be taken out of stock, it is clear that well over 90 per cent of the readership of hardback fiction were library users. Not surprisingly, there were demands throughout the period, particularly from the Society of Authors, for a public-lending right, which would somehow reward authors in proportion to the number of actual readers. However, despite near successes in the late sixties, no government action was taken until 1981–2.

Literary standards were not the sole concern of libraries; they were also committed to providing books for recreation, entertainment and practical information. But the concern with high culture was much plainer in the one completely new institution involved in creating artistic values – the Arts Council. It was founded in 1946 as the successor to the wartime Council for the Encouragement of Music and the Arts (which was intended as a morale builder) with a mandate to develop 'a greater knowledge, understanding and practice of the fine arts exclusively, and in particular to increase the accessibility of the fine arts to the public'. In 1967 this was amended to exclude the word 'fine', reflecting, among other changes, the greater role that literature had come to play in the Council's operations. From the beginning, its major commitments were to the performing arts (music and drama) and, to a much smaller extent, the visual arts. Indeed, during the forties literature was generally held not to be a concern of the Arts Council; for drama, however, it was crucial (see Chapter 6).

The slight attention to literature perhaps occurred because another public-sector institution – libraries – was performing the major role. Until the mid-sixties, novel writing received no support at all and even by 1964–5 the amount of help for poetry was only just over £5000 (about 2 per cent of the Council's budget). Among the forms of support provided in the fifties were the Festival of Britain poetry competition in 1951, grants to poetry-reading societies and, after 1955, subsidies to poetry magazines (for periods of up to three years). By 1965–6 the number of magazines supported (for about £150 each) had grown to sixteen. From 1953 the Council also provided funds to establish the Poetry Book Society, one of whose functions was to help readers 'sift out and discover the best English poetry being written today'.

In the sixties the support for literature increased both absolutely and relatively. In February 1965 the new Labour government produced a White Paper (*A Policy for the Arts*) which proposed both a large increase in the Arts Council budget and a more active encouragement of individual artists, including writers. Between 1964 and 1968 the amount spent on literature increased from £5000 to over £80,000. This was still only 1 per cent of the total budget (which rose from £3 million to £7 million); nevertheless, with the establishment of a separate Literature Panel in 1966, it allowed new forms of support. Emphasis shifted to aiding individual writers directly (56 per cent of the 1968 literature expenditure as opposed to 9 per cent in 1964), and for the first time fiction was recognized as eligible for support. Among over 150 authors helped by Arts Council bursaries in 1966–70 were the poets Basil Bunting, Vernon Scannell, Peter Redgrove and Tom Pickard, and the novelists B. S. Johnson, V. S. Naipaul, Christine Brooke-Rose, A. S. Byatt and Susan Hill. However, during the seventies there were hints of a reversion to a policy of supporting institutions rather than individuals (by the mid-seventies the Poetry Society, the New Fiction Society and the *New Review* were each receiving well over £20,000 a year, while expenditure on direct grants to writers was more or less pegged).

Writers and literary enterprises might also find some support from the regional arts associations which came into existence through the sixties and early seventies. These had their origins in responses to the Arts Council's closure of its ten regional offices between 1952 and 1956 as part of a policy of redirecting funds towards grant giving rather than direct promotions. The South West Arts Association (1956) and the Midlands Arts Association (1958) were among the earliest to be organized, but during the sixties the largest and most prominent became the Northern Arts Association, founded originally as the North East Arts Association in 1961 after initiatives from the Gulbenkian Foundation and local authorities (particularly Newcastle).

While patterns of funding varied among RAAs, the budget of the Northern Arts Association for 1966–7 provides some exemplification. Out of a total income of £130,000, £60,000 came from the Arts Council, £57,000 from local authorities and £13,000 from other sources, including industry, commerce and membership subscriptions. In the same year, however, only £3085 was allocated by the Northern Arts Association for the 'spoken and written word'; the pattern of activities supported (including poetry readings, small magazines, poetry and prose competitions) was not strikingly different from that of the Arts Council, and generally literature did not tend to figure significantly higher in regional than in national priorities. Over all, by 1969–70 the Arts Council was allocating £300,000 out of a total budget of £6.3 million to the nine English RAAs then in existence. During the seventies RAAs were to become of some considerable importance in literary funding, but even by the end of the sixties many of them were still in a formative (and under-financed) stage.

The impact of the Arts Council varied. It made little intervention in the novel before 1970. In the case of theatre, it gave essential finance and the status of its imprimatur to new work which, at the time at least, seemed daring and innovative. It was probably of considerable importance to poetry through its aid to small magazines: here relatively small sums of money could have large effects at the point where other avenues of publication were not available – the point where a poet sought his or her initial readership. In more general terms the Council's commitment to maintaining artistic standards provided, particularly after 1965, a point of reference for defining the social value of good literature.

In the Council's 1965–6 report, Cecil Day Lewis (the chairman of the new Literature Panel) discussed why literature should be subsidized:

> The answer is surely simple enough. It is through its literature more than any other feature of its life that an age is remembered and judged: and, more urgent still, writers have the duty to preserve our language, to affirm civilized values, and to enlarge the imagination of their contemporaries.

Despite the self-proclaimed simplicity of this declaration, there is scope for dispute about what is the literature of the age, what is its language, what are civilized values, and which contemporaries have their imaginations enlarged. There was a broad consensus in the period that the Arts Council was a good thing; but there were also persistent anxieties about the details of its operations. It was rarely recognized that these problems were in fact linked to fundamental incoherences in the concepts of 'art' and 'literature' in that diverse and changing society.

One related group of issues concerned élitism, centralization and conservatism. Opera and ballet took 58.5 per cent of the Council's expenditure in 1959. This could be seen (quite reasonably) as manifesting a bias towards London at the expense of the provinces, towards a wealthy élite at the expense of the wider potential audience, towards established prestige institutions at the expense of promising new ventures, towards (by and large) established classics at the expense of new and experimental work, towards high accomplishment at the expense, perhaps, of the only live professional work in a whole region, towards the conservative at the expense of the questioning or radical. Subsequently more resources were directed to the provinces and to experimentation, but in the final years of the period a third of the budget was going to Covent Garden, Sadler's Wells, the National Theatre, the Royal Shakespeare Company and the Welsh National Opera. But, then, how *could* these issues be settled? – how much comparison is there between *Giselle* and The People Show?

A second group of issues concerned the political independence of the Arts Council and its relations with the private sector – how far it should support anti-establishment work, how far it should offend popular taste, how far it should collaborate with commercial interests. And then there were questions of judgement and control. In provincial theatres there was a sequence of disputes between artistic directors and public representatives (the resemblance to the relationship between the manager of a Football League club and his directors was uncanny). Nationally, it seemed that decisions were made by self-perpetuating committees, all too many of whose members were involved with the institutions whose finances they were deciding.

All this struggle, ultimately, was about who was to control the key concepts, 'art', 'literature' and 'culture', and hence the resources and influence that accompanied them. The final anxiety that we should note is, once more, cognate with perceptions of the mixed economy at large. Until the mid-sixties, approximately, state assistance was courted by many cultural producers as the essential means by which to evade the crippling effects of commercial values. Increasingly, however, the state was perceived not as a refuge from capitalism but as its crucial institution. Radical cultural workers especially (and the point may be extended to include radical teachers and students) found themselves dependent upon a suspect source of funding – and exposing its contradictions inevitably threatened their own continuance. The problem was hardly to be resolved.

Education

The remarkable expansion of education in the period affected the production of literature in both the senses pursued here. As regards school education, textbook production expanded substantially as publishers specializing in educational provision developed new markets resulting from the 1944 Education Act. Between 1945 and 1965 the number of secondary school pupils rose from $1\frac{3}{4}$ million to over 3 million, and this, together with a general improvement in the quantity and quality of provision, constituted a quickly growing market which, in publishing terms, was very predictable in its demands. In higher education there was a gradual increase in numbers during the fifties and then a sharp rise in the mid-sixties, from 217,000 in 1962 to 376,000 in 1967 – an increase greater than that over the whole of the previous twenty-five years. New universities opened, others expanded, but even more striking were increases in the colleges of further education and, in particular, teacher-training colleges (from 42,200 in 1962 to 105,600 in 1968). An increase in the proportion of 18-year-olds achieving two or more A-levels (from 4.5 per cent in 1955 to 10.9 per cent in 1967) combined with the effects of the post-war bulge in birth-rate (peaking, for 18-year-olds, in 1965), and a less tangible growth in educational aspirations, to generate sufficient demand to fill these places. It was no coincidence that Penguin formed their first educational division in 1964 as a means of extending their foothold in this newly profitable market.

The importance of literature in education was repeatedly reasserted. The Newsom Report (*Half Our Future*, 1963), dealing with 'average and below-average pupils', contains a humane and thoughtful section on 'English', but the belief in the value of literature is expressed with more firmness than coherence. First we are told that 'teachers of English tend to think of their subject from three different but related points of view: as a medium of communication, as a means of creative expression, and as a literature embodying the vision of greatness.'[13] The problems here are apparent enough: how 'creative expression' differs from 'communication' (imagination versus facts?); how a child is to pursue seriously his or her 'creative expression' in the shadow of 'the vision of greatness'; what 'the vision of greatness' might be. But then, within a few pages, further accounts of the supposed effects of literature are given. Is the 'sympathetic insight into human relationships gained through literature' an integral part of 'the vision of greatness' or is it a fortunate by-product? And we read also of 'the civilizing experience of contact with great literature'.[14] Does this mean something more or less than 'sympathetic insight into human relationships'? Is it about ideas of how society might be organized (dangerous) or good manners (trivial)? An anxiety that, supposing these claims for literature to be true, its actual modes may baffle most pupils emerges hesitantly: they 'can respond to its universality, although they will depend heavily on the skill of the teacher as an interpreter' (but surely the universal, by definition, is that which does not need an interpreter); and 'How far the great poetry of earlier ages can be introduced with advantage only the teacher can say.'[15] 'Greatness' and 'universality' may not, after all, be accessible to everyone.

These issues were argued out in several specialized academic-literary journals – another instance of public-sector policy and investment promoting certain kinds of publishing and understanding of literature.

Pre-eminent in influence among these was *Scrutiny*, even though it was already in decline by the late forties. The journal (founded in 1932) had emerged out of debates and institutional developments within the Cambridge English School in the twenties to stand as a major intellectual force arguing not merely for the supreme value of great literature but even more for the necessity of a rigorously evaluative literary criticism. *Scrutiny* concerned itself with a range of art forms (including music and cinema) and also with social analysis (both past and present), although characteristically the assumption here was of an inevitable link between literary achievement and general cultural health. The opening number referred to 'a necessary relationship between the quality of the individual's response to art and his general fitness for a humane existence'. The values embodied in the best literature were seen as particularly precarious in a modern world which had been deprived by industrialization and mass society of the order and wholeness that had allegedly sustained pre-industrial 'organic' society.

F. R. Leavis was the major figure at the heart of the *Scrutiny* project, but, as Francis Mulhern has demonstrated in *The Moment of 'Scrutiny'* (1979), the journal was never the mouthpiece of one man. Other central figures were Q. D. Leavis, L. C. Knights, Boris Ford, Denys Thompson and Wilfred Mellers. By 1945 the original group had dispersed, but its members continued to spread its point of view. *Scrutiny* closed in 1953 (its circulation was always small – 1400 in 1950). In retrospect this closure appears not so much as a failure but as a recognition that the issues and social practices in question were now too considerable to be focused in a single academic journal.

During the fifties and sixties *Scrutiny*'s legacy was apparent in every field of literary criticism and education. The whole journal was reissued in a twenty-volume set by Cambridge University Press in 1963, and Leavis's *Selections* appeared in two volumes in 1968. The presence of Leavis was felt both through his published criticism (his major study of Lawrence appeared in 1955) and through his appetite for controversy – most notably in the 'Two Cultures' debate with C. P. Snow in the early sixties. Snow deplored the divide between scientists who have 'the future in their bones' and administrators bred in 'the traditional culture'. He advocated more general education in science. Leavis replied by asserting that the 'creation of the human world, including language', was a prior human achievement 'without which the triumphant erection of the scientific edifice would not have been possible'. The study of literature was the means of recognizing the 'nature and priority' of this achievement.

Scrutiny's influence was also substantial through the seven-volume *Pelican Guide to English Literature* (completed in 1961), edited by Boris Ford and written in the main by former *Scrutiny* contributors. The paperback marketing of this comprehensive literary guide broke new ground in providing inexpensive access to an authoritative framework of historical knowledge and critical judgements for an expanding readership (and in the early sixties Ford contributed to the intellectual direction of the first of the 'new universities' at Sussex). By 1967 the last volume of the *Pelican Guide*, *The Modern Age*, had been reprinted four times.

Scrutiny was influential in other areas. The journal *The Use of English*, founded in 1949 (but based on the earlier *English in Schools*, begun in 1939), was clearly traceable as an offshoot of *Scrutiny*; it flourished into the sixties and beyond (its significance is discussed below). *Politics and Letters* (1947–8) was short-lived, but one of its aims – to relate Leavisite literary criticism and socialism – became the long-term concern of Raymond Williams who, together with Richard Hoggart, was a key figure in a move away from literary analysis towards cultural studies in the late fifties. Over all, while there can be no simple correlation between *Scrutiny* and the development of post-war English literary criticism, *Scrutiny*'s areas of concern set much of the agenda for any debate over the status, value and proper sphere of literary criticism, and for wider debates about literature and culture.

Certainly no new academic journal could afford to ignore its example. In 1951 *Essays in Criticism* was founded by F. W. Bateson, with the defensive comment that it was 'not intended to be the organ of a new "Oxford" school of criticism, which might challenge the so-called "Cambridge" school of Dr F. R. Leavis, Professor L. C. Knights and their associates'. By 1970 the circulation had grown to 2400. In a dispute with Leavis in 1953 Bateson insisted on historical scholarship on the grounds that interpretation of texts without it is likely to be self-indulgent. This position might seem to call in question the comprehensibility and relevance of literature, but Bateson asserted nevertheless the central importance of the traditional canon: 'The values of the modern world seem to the layman to be embodied in literature to a far greater degree than they are in modern religion or philosophy.'[16]

The most successful academic journal of the period was the *Critical Quarterly*, founded in 1959; by 1968 it had a circulation of 5000. Changes in its editorial policy through the sixties amount to a brief guide to the rapidly altering mood in higher education; the confident moment of the journal's foundation gives way to alarm about the role of literature in higher education and the state of high culture generally. In the first number C. B. Cox (who with A. E. Dyson has jointly edited the journal from the beginning) announced that *Critical Quarterly* had 'no new critical manifesto' although it would be particularly concerned to discuss twentiety-century (especially post-1950) writers. It believed that one of criticism's main functions was 'to assist rather than oppose the powerful and dangerous immaturities out of which truly creative writing grows'. The generosity and breadth of this approach were reflected in the view that on the subject of culture Hoggart and Williams could be grouped with Arnold as 'current classics' (autumn 1960). Raymond Williams, especially, was a frequent contributor to *Critical Quarterly* in the early sixties. Leavisite narrowness was rejected: Dyson felt that Leavis's inability to do justice to anything but 'the very best' was his major flaw (spring 1960). The *Pelican Guide* volume *The Modern Age* was criticized by Cox as an example of how 'The myth of a culture in decline has dominated much *Scrutiny* thinking and blinded many of its writers to the riches of their own period' (winter 1961).

In the mid-sixties *Critical Quarterly* felt itself, correctly, to be an important influence in the expansion of English studies in higher education. An editorial in spring 1964 asked, 'Have we reached a crisis in the state of literary criticism?' It answered, No. But by the late sixties the crisis was at hand and the language of the editorials became increasingly strident and dramatic. Arnold now stood alone. In the spring 1969 issue Dyson announced:

> If Arnold were to return in 1969 . . . he would be horrified to discover anarchy subverting the temple of culture itself. What would he make of the Jacobinism rampant in our educational theory, or of the spectacle of universities becoming the new home of the mob? What would he make of the inroads made by romantic egotism upon disciplined learning, or of the theory that 'self-fulfilment' is the chief end for which education exists?

In literary terms this 'anarchy' was manifesting itself (according to Cox) both in 'pop' writers who 'compose their often self-indulgent and sentimental verses about slums, civil rights or Vietnam' (summer 1969) and 'neo-modernists' with their 'lack of moral purpose, their contempt for traditional wisdom and civilized order' (winter 1969). The central issue, however, was less contemporary literary practice than contemporary educational practice. 'Rebellious students' were part of the problem. They 'arrive at our universities without the body of knowledge, or the critical intelligence, or the scholarly and moral ideals, or the commitment to learning, or the capacity or the will for self-discipline, which a real university must require' (summer 1970). Equally at fault were 'progressive education' and the Labour government's commitment to comprehensive schools. In the same article (entitled 'Culture in Decline' – this being no longer a *Scrutiny* 'myth') Dyson implied a recantation of earlier liberal beliefs:

> Certainly, the liberal era of the 1950s is now over: the era of apparent consensus, where cultivated men felt guilt about their own education and cultural attainments, felt doubt about their own moral or even professional authority, felt a moral duty even to encourage – in trends like pop culture – inferior forms of speech, writing, behaviour, taste and knowledge to their own.

These outbursts reflected genuine shock at the unexpected source of this 'anarchy': it was not from cynical commercial interests or a defensive establishment (as in the heroic days of *Scrutiny*) but, often, from socially concerned literary critics and from students experiencing the benefit of a literary education. Cox feared that literary criticism might be superseded by newer concerns. In autumn 1971 he observed:

> As high culture has become increasingly the expression of despair, so the young have turned to 'pop' for life and energy. These trends are now influencing curriculum development in schools and colleges. 'Cultural studies' is being put forward as a substitute for the traditional study of English literature.

Here Cox correctly signalled important areas of development and debate for the seventies; within higher education, these involved particularly the new kinds of humanities degrees offered by many CNAA-validated public-sector colleges. His comment also registers an anxiety that the ground may be cut away from 'traditional' English studies by changes in English as a subject in schools.

English teaching in schools was equally controversial. During the whole post-war period it experienced two sharply conflicting pressures. On the one hand there was a continuing attempt to improve educational standards and to give evidence of this by enabling a greater number of pupils to pass formal examinations. On the other hand,

English as a subject was regarded increasingly as valuable not so much for its teaching of correctness in language as for its general humanizing properties. From the thirties there had been concern about how to reconcile these two pressures in relation to examinations in literature. In 1933 L. C. Knights in *Scrutiny* argued that standardization in the marking of literature papers was damaging the proper purpose of literary education. His call to abolish external examinations in English literature was echoed by the Spens Report of 1938 (on grammar schools): 'prescribed books do more to injure the growth of a budding sentiment for literature than to encourage it, and therefore [we] recommend that books should no longer be prescribed in the School Certificate Examination.'

Such a proposal was not implemented, partly because within the *Scrutiny*, literature-as-humanizing school there were opposite tendencies too. In *Mass Civilization and Minority Culture* (1930) Leavis had argued that there were 'in any period' only a 'very small minority' capable of appreciating the greatest literature – Shakespeare, Donne and Conrad were cited as instances of 'the finest human experiences of the past'. The implications of this were to endorse set syllabuses and examinations, which were aimed at recognizing the élite minority and ensuring that ability to discriminate between works was upheld. Whether these ideas were well founded or not, a consequence was the involvement of 'literature' in the process by which society establishes its hierarchy of class and meritocratic privilege.

The debate continued in the forties. In the first number of *The Use of English* in 1949 Robin Pedley discussed the state of English examinations:

> It is the literature paper, perhaps, which especially suffers from the inescapable conditions of mass marking. The kind of question which will genuinely test the child's reading capacity or awareness of literature cannot be set, because it cannot be marked to a standard marking scheme.

Pedley's proposal sought to mediate between extreme positions. He argued that under the new GCE system (then in preparation) fewer candidates should be entered, especially for A-level, so that proper teaching and examining of the 'best' literature and the 'best' candidates could take place. For the remainder, a more open and flexible literature syllabus should provide 'a stimulus and a profit the present mass-production methods based on unworthy incentives make impossible'.

These comments proved an accurate prediction of the two-tier approach to literary education (embodied in the GCE/CSE split; see below) which subsequently came about, particularly in the sixties. As the educational system developed, the contradictory pressures grew stronger. The introduction of the GCE in 1951–3 made little difference to examining procedures. D. Shayer in *The Teaching of English in Schools 1900–70* remarks:

> An 'O' level English candidate of the early sixties would find the papers for the twenties almost unremarkable in their familiarity. He might find . . . the questions on set books tending to the biographical-historical rather than to the critical, but the general pattern, content, and feel of the papers would be the same.[17]

The number of candidates continued to increase; but the pressure for more creative English teaching also increased. The cause was crucial to *The Use of English*. Its editor, Denys Thompson, was a supporter both of 'creative' approaches to English teaching and of Leavisite critical principles. Its circulation increased from 1400 in 1953 to 4000 in 1964 and 5000 in 1969, and it claimed a much larger readership through school, college of education and university libraries. The National Association of Teachers of English was founded in 1963 around *The Use of English* and the London ATE. The Crowther Report (1960) and more particularly the Newsom (1963) and Plowden (1967) Reports gave support to the idea of English as a 'creative' subject. In the early sixties a range of books supported a more flexible approach – notably David Holbrook's *English for Maturity* (1961) and *English for the Rejected* (1964), and works by other *Use of English* contributors including Denys Thompson, Brian Jackson and Frank Whitehead. Brian Jackson in *English versus Examinations* (1965) invoked a double enemy when he described *The Use of English* as 'the centre for twenty-five years where teachers of English have done what they could to resist the increasing power of examinations within schools and of mass media without'. He stated clearly why English teaching and examinations were inevitably opposed: 'examinations are necessarily the terrain of the measurable and our *prime* concern is with the play of the sensibility.'[18]

During the mid-sixties, however, there was one area where these two aims seemed partly reconcilable. Much of the energy of the creative English movement went into secondary modern (or lower-stream) syllabuses and, in particular, into those of the new CSE examination (begun in 1964). The CSE Mode 3 (which gave individual schools considerable control over syllabus and assessment) seemed to offer new possibilities in examinable literature teaching. Set books could now be chosen much more to suit the needs of particular groups of pupils. There was, however, some hostile comment from the more traditional wing of the Leavisite philosophy, which had opposed the extension of secondary education and the Butler Act of 1944. In 1966 an article appeared in *The Use of English* entitled 'Second Rate Books for Second Rate Children'. Denis Butts argued:

> the compromises over set books have been dangerous because they are of principle. If we believe in the civilizing influence of great literature, then we must present great literature in our schools as skilfully as we can, and great literature does mean books by Shakespeare, Jane Austen and Dickens.

The debate continued about whether literary education was essentially a matter of what was read or how it was read. In retrospect, it appears that, while so much energy and argument was expended on CSE and lower-stream English, the continuing expansion of a barely changed GCE went almost unnoticed and unassessed. The general rise in the proportion of 18-year-olds taking A-levels has been noted; there was also a relative swing towards humanities subjects. Between 1961 and 1967 there was a 114 per cent growth in numbers of school leavers with two or more A-levels in arts subjects as against only a 52 per cent growth for science subjects.[19] On one board alone (the Joint Matriculation Board) the number of English literature A-level candidates rose from 7730 in 1963 to 11,036 in 1965. At the same time, in 1963, the measurement aspect of the examination was made more important by the introduction in all boards of A to E grades – predominantly to help universities select their students.

The syllabuses remained firm in their commitment to 'great literature'. In their spring 1966 issue *Use of English* published an analysis by W. H. Mittins of GCE texts over the period 1955–65. The texts that had appeared on all nine GCE board syllabuses through the period were two Chaucer 'Tales', Shaw's *St Joan*, Milton, Keats, Hazlitt's essays and seven Shakespeare plays. Mittins commented, 'it is hardly necessary to say that Shakespeare heads all lists of this kind'. Texts that had appeared on all but one of the boards were twelve Shakespeare plays, three Chaucer 'Tales' and additionally three Jane Austen novels,

Arnold's poems, Spenser's *Faerie Queene*, Swift's *Gulliver's Travels*, Pope's *Rape of the Lock* and Dryden's *Absalom and Achitophel*. Dickens, Hardy and Conrad would also appear in this list if it considered authors rather than individual works. If these lists are put together, they form (with the possible exceptions of Shaw and Hazlitt) a skeleton of the English literary tradition as taught in most universities in the period. This was, of course, no accident. Universities exercised a determining and largely conservative influence over GCE syllabuses (particularly A-level) during the period up to 1970 and beyond.

Within higher education there were many new developments in critical method and emphasis of approach through the fifties and sixties. The sixties especially, with the development of interdisciplinary work in new universities and the questioning of received notions of academic standards towards the end of the decade, contained many moments at which the traditional forms of literary study seemed about to be superseded. But, crucially, whatever methods were employed (whether Leavisite, New Critical or archetypal in the fifties, or sociological, linguistic or Marxist in the sixties), the texts to be studied remained substantially the same – and this was largely true for both Marxist and structuralist criticism in the seventies. As long as the central core of texts persisted, then, as far as definitions of literary value were concerned, critical method (however political or interdisciplinary in character) was of secondary importance. By 1970, despite new attitudes in schoolteaching, course criticism in higher education and, on the other side, *Critical Quarterly*'s 'Black Papers' lamenting a decline in standards, the O-level, A-level and BA interlocking triumvirate continued to provide a firm, well-capitalized institutional base for transmitting and maintaining literary values and the literary tradition.

The mass media

If education was literature's prime support, then, as Brian Jackson's comment illustrates, the 'mass media' were frequently seen as its major enemies. This perception was partly a consequence of the technology itself. By definition, the electric media (cinema, radio and television) are not producers of literature (printed matter). Indeed, it was precisely their emphasis upon oral delivery (usually, unlike serious drama, with no definitive repeatable written text) that was seen by many (and most stridently by Marshall McLuhan in *Understanding Media*, 1964) as marking the inauguration of a new cultural era. Certainly the cultural centrality of these media, particularly television, was a decisive influence on literary production and consumption in the period.

Cinema and radio, of course, were both prominent elements in inter-war society. Cinema had received a new charge of energy after the introduction of talkies at the beginning of the thirties. By 1939 there were just under 1000 million visits per year to the cinema – 19 million per week; on average every man, woman and child visited the cinema 22 times a year. The peak year of cinema attendance was 1946, with 1635 million visits, and after that a gradual decline set in, although in 1956 the figure still stood at 1101 million. The sharp decline came in the late fifties, as television penetrated working-class homes. Attendances slumped to 501 million by 1960 and the number of cinemas fell from 4349 to 3034. By 1965 another 1000 cinemas had closed and attendances were 328 million. The fall continued into the early seventies – 182 million in 1972. This, given the increase in population, represents a tenth of the 1946 figure and about a seventh of the 1956 figure – a decline from a mass to a minority entertainment paralleled possibly only by cinema's own replacement of live theatre, variety and music hall in the early years of the century.

Radio, beginning in the early twenties, developed steadily through the period – the number of sets reached 9 million in 1939, 73 per cent of all households. By the end of the war, coverage was virtually total, with 10.7 million sets in 1946. During the thirties and forties radio and cinema complemented rather than competed with each other. Radio catered for home, family, casual listening and information, while cinema, with the extra visual element, was a collective experience, an evening or afternoon out in a more luxurious environment. After the war the structure of radio programming was altered: the Reithian assumption of cultural unity was abandoned and a deliberate three-tier system introduced, with the Light Programme, the Home Service and the Third Programme. This change, unintentionally, prepared radio for the new supporting role it was to play in the television age.

Television had begun in 1936 with reception confined, except for the odd freak occurrence, to within about 50 miles of London. By 1939 there were only 20,000 sets and service was suspended for the duration of the war. The service resumed in 1946 but initially growth was slow. By 1951 there were still only 650,000 sets in Britain; one problem here for the BBC was that, compared to radio, TV programmes and production units were expensive. Licence money was needed to make TV viable, but a sufficient quality and quantity of programmes were needed first to persuade the public to buy sets.

The turning-point was in 1953, when the fifties consumer boom got fully under way. Between 1952 and 1953 expenditure on consumer durables rose from £531 million to £678 million (in the decade as a whole such expenditure doubled, as against a 25 per cent rise in spending on food). The number of new cars sold rose from 300,000 to 500,000 and the number of new TV sets from 700,000 to 1.1 million. Sales of sets were boosted by the coronation of June 1953, which was watched on TV by an estimated 20 million people (many neighbours and friends gathered round the 2 million or so sets then in use); this helped to establish the medium as an acceptable component of national life. Throughout the fifties the number of sets increased by just over a million each year, until by 1964 there were 13 million sets in use and virtually total coverage had been achieved. (The number of sets continued to increase, to 15 million in 1968, 17.7 million in 1975 and nearly 19 million in 1980). Television, in short, became a necessity rather than a luxury. The opening of the ITV commercial service in 1955 and BBC2 in 1964 provided, in theory at least, a greater range of programmes. There can be no doubt of the quantitative domination of television watching as a leisure activity in the sixties. In 1970 Young and Wilmott found 97 per cent of adults to be regular viewers with an average watching time of nearly twelve hours a week (the figure grew further through the seventies). There proved to be few differences between the social classes in the amount of viewing, although an analysis of the viewing pattern of individual programme types would have produced more differentiated results.

More difficult to assess were the cultural consequences. Television clearly had an effect on the established media. It supplanted radio as the medium for home entertainment in the evening, although radio retained most of its daytime functions even after the extension of TV hours into the afternoon. With the swift expansion of the recorded music market from the late fifties, radio became important as the major medium through which its goods were displayed. The success of the commercial 'pirate' radio stations between 1964 and 1967 forced the BBC to accommodate this need (and in the early seventies generated legal commercial stations in Britain). In other areas too, radio, in response to TV expansion, developed specialist and subcultural functions (including that of helping to construct and reinforce the 'literary' world). Cinema proved much less flexible. The growth of television was part of a general shift towards home-based leisure, and the cinema industry was forced to contract considerably to survive (it was not until the seventies that alternative strategies were devised to maintain at least some cinema presence in the popular market). The closure of cinema newsreels during this period (Paramount in 1957, Gaumont British/ Universal in 1959 and Pathé, after an attempt to readjust, in 1970) indicates how cinema lost its place as a central cultural institution.

As television took that place, it provided new impetus to (and new raw material for) the debate about cultural levels and the protection of standards which had been continuing since at least the early nineteenth century and especially since Arnold's *Culture and Anarchy* (1869). Particularly with the growth of commercial TV, in which (it was alleged) advertising and programmes were difficult to distinguish, TV became the prime instance of 'mass culture' where, according to G. H. Bantock, writing in 1961 in the *Pelican Guide to English Literature* volume *The Modern Age*, 'night after night a selection of programmes of inane triviality sterilize the emotions and standardize the outlook of millions of people'.[20]

The 'mass culture' thesis discovered threats both to the authentic culture of the people (a culture based on active participation rather than passive consumption) and also to traditional high culture, often as represented by education and educational standards. The most articulate expression of the former threat was Richard Hoggart's *The Uses of Literacy* (1957), a book which, although mainly dealing with pre-television material was seen as a summary of the effects of the 'telly age'. Hoggart argued:

> at present the older, more narrow but also more genuine class culture is being eroded in favour of the mass opinion, the mass recreational product and the generalized emotional response. The world of club-singing is being gradually replaced by that of typical radio dance-music and crooning, television cabaret and commercial-radio variety. The uniform national type which the popular papers help to produce is writ ever larger in the uniform international type which the film-studios of Hollywood present.[21]

Denys Thompson's *Discrimination and Popular Culture* (1964) had some similar emphases, but also used high-cultural standards as a reference point (the Leavisite belief in cultural discrimination was powerful here). Many of these arguments came together in the Pilkington

Report (1962) on television, which was particularly critical of commercial television for (allegedly) simply meeting public demand. The report had little effect on broadcasting practices.

The mass culture debate continued through the sixties, although increasingly the concept was found too simple to explain the new cultural situation. In *Culture and Society* (1958) Raymond Williams had remarked that when the term 'mass' was used it never referred to the user, his 'relatives, friends, neighbours, colleagues', but always to 'the others, whom we don't know and can't know'. According to Williams, 'There are in fact no masses; there are only ways of seeing people as masses.'[22] It also became clear that class (particularly the working class) had not disappeared as a result of the 'age of affluence' and the uniform fact of television ownership. More fundamental social influences – family, education, peer group, income level, work experience – remained the key determinants of attitudes and beliefs.

In the Introduction to the 1964 edition of *Discrimination and Popular Culture* Thompson claimed:

> It is in leisure, not in work, that most people nowadays really live and find themselves. More and more what we do with our leisure decides the quality of our living. If this is correct, the mass media matter a great deal; they may well be altering the aims and character of the nation.[23]

The 'if' was a necessary proviso: repeated attempts to demonstrate the 'effects' of television through social-scientific research were largely fruitless. What the research did reveal was a degree of variation in audience response to television, which indicated that viewers were not passive recipients of media messages but, rather, active participants in a process of interpretation. In the revised 1973 edition of *Discrimination and Popular Culture* Thompson's bold claim had disappeared. The mass media were manifestly important, but the very extensiveness of their operations and the degree of their interpenetration with other social institutions were such that it proved impossible to isolate a separate set of media effects.

Equally, the blanket opposition set up between the mass media and literature (even in its most selective sense) is unhelpful in understanding the substantial degree of interaction and transference of material that took place. This can be considered in three areas: the ways the new media provided of transmitting (or adapting) existing literary material; the new opportunities for contemporary writers to work directly for broadcasting; and the production, within film and broadcasting, of new kinds of cultural work (much of it collective) which staked a claim to the cultural space previously reserved for printed work. The transference of stories from one medium to another was not innovatory in itself. Much Elizabethan and Jacobean drama adapted earlier prose works (romances or histories), and the same process was common in Victorian popular theatre. Early cinema was a direct inheritor of this tradition; classic and contemporary material from *Hamlet* to *East Lynne* and *Love on the Dole* was reworked.

Radio provided new possibilities. Written work could now be communicated without adaptation. A novel could be read out, in serial form, straight from the page, or, more usually, poetry could be presented in a way (orally) arguably more suitable to its nature than the printed page. During the war and more particularly after the opening of the Third Programme in 1946, contemporary poetry was a regular item in broadcasting. Existing novels and plays were treated by radio more in the manner of the cinema, but generally remaining closer to the original texts. From the beginning, radio drama relied on the classic canon for material: it began in 1922 and 1923 with scenes from *Julius Caesar*, *Henry VIII* and *Much Ado about Nothing*. From 1925 novels were adapted, beginning with *Westward Ho!* and *Lord Jim*. As with poetry, the introduction of the Third Programme allowed a wider range of work; among new novels adapted for radio drama was *Lord of the Flies* in 1955 (five years before the paperback and seven before the film). The balance with the classics was retained. In 1971 Martin Esslin (Head of Radio Drama from 1963) reported:

> It is the stated policy of the BBC's radio drama department to enable each generation growing up to hear the bulk of classical drama, from the Greek tragedians and Aristophanes to the Elizabethans, Restoration comedy, the great nineteenth century realists, Ibsen, Chekhov, Strindberg, Shaw, right down to Brecht and Beckett; this means that the standard masterpieces are regularly revived in a recurring cycle of about ten years' duration.[24]

The BBC stood squarely alongside the Arts Council and formal education as a public-service institution committed to upholding literary standards and possessing the resources to do so.

From the mid-fifties, television rivalled radio and cinema as the major medium for adaptation of literary material. Nevertheless, British cinema played a key part in the transmission of the new literary movement of the late fifties. Precisely at the time when cinema as a mass entertainment was being superseded, the British film industry capitalized on the 'social realism' of post-1956 drama and novels to produce a sequence of films that combined box-office success and (so it was regarded) serious social comment. The plays of John Osborne and Shelagh Delaney (*A Taste of Honey*) and the novels of Kingsley Amis, John Braine, Alan Sillitoe, Keith Waterhouse, Stan Barstow and David Storey were all filmed between 1957 and 1964. During the sixties many other contemporary novelists had their work adapted for film, including William Golding, John Fowles, Muriel Spark and Margaret Drabble. These adaptations increasingly stimulated a new kind of marketing for literature – in which the paperback version would appear as the book of the film with the front cover using stills from the film as a selling-point. By the end of the sixties this practice had extended to TV serializations – including classic novels, where a new market (for Jane Austen and, most successfully, Galsworthy's *Forsyte Saga*) was generated. With contemporary work the chain of adaptations could be substantial. Braine's *Room at the Top* was a hardback and newspaper serial in 1957, a film and paperback in 1959, a sequel (*Life at the Top*) in 1962 (itself later filmed and marketed in paperback) and a TV series, *Man at the Top*, in the late sixties. The paperback thrived off each new development and was in its nineteenth reprint in 1970. Meanwhile Braine's second novel, *The Vodi* (1959), was adapted as a radio play. This is an exceptional case, but much new literary material had an extended cultural presence in various media.

Television played an increasingly important part in this dissemination of classic and contemporary literature, mainly through serialization of novels (most regularly Dickens's early novels) and classic plays. The dramatization of Orwell's *Nineteen Eighty-Four* in 1954 gave an early indication of the major impact possible through a medium that could command a simultaneous audience of millions. Also, it was a BBC screening of part of *Look Back in Anger* in October 1956 which helped the play towards commercial success. However, television was generally more significant as a presenter of original material than as a means of extending the audience for contemporary stage plays.

From the beginnings of the cinema and particularly after the advent of talkies, novelists and dramatists were tempted into scriptwriting. But as film developed it became the director who controlled the finished product, in so far as any single mind did; the scriptwriter was merely a (frequently minor) member of a team of employees. In broadcasting the writer came to be identified much more closely as the key creator. In 1947 Louis MacNeice (then working for the BBC) claimed that in radio 'the author . . . has far more say about the performance of his piece than in any other medium which involves teamwork'.[25] Since the twenties, radio drama had provided an additional medium and market. In the immediate post-war period writers such as Stevie Smith, Laurie Lee, Angus Wilson, Henry Reed and David Gascoyne all wrote plays specifically for radio. Verse drama was extensively promoted, including plays by MacNeice and, most notably, Dylan Thomas's *Under Milk Wood* (1954). Pinter and Arden both found radio a valuable base for their early work; from the late fifties Beckett began to write plays specifically for the Third Programme.

Original TV drama developed slowly. As few as four original plays for television were broadcast before the war and virtually none between 1946 and 1952. BBC policy altered from 1953 with the attempt to attract a nucleus of contracted writers, but TV drama did not gain an independent identity until after the 1956 theatrical watershed and the opening of commercial TV. ATV's *Armchair Theatre* series began in September 1956 and, after the arrival of Canadian Sidney Newman in April 1958, developed a positive policy of seeking new plays with contemporary settings. Between 1959 and 1961 *Armchair Theatre* produced plays by Harold Pinter, Angus Wilson, Clive Exton and Alun Owen. Audiences were numbered in millions – at times as high as 10 million. Pinter estimated that it would take a thirty-year run of *The Caretaker* to equal the 6.3 million audience which his play *A Night Out* received through one showing in April 1960.

In April 1963 Newman moved to the BBC and split the drama department into three sections: series, serials and individual plays. The individual play spots he initiated included (notoriously) *The Wednesday Play*, beginning in October 1964. This again attracted work from writers already established elsewhere (Christopher Logue, William Sansom, John Betjeman, Peter Terson) but also provided a space for TV specialists (Alun Owen, David Mercer, Dennis Potter), and for the dramatized documentaries of Tony Parker and Jeremy Sandford, author of *Cathy Come Home* (1966). During the sixties TV drama afforded both a crucial economic base and a genuine opportunity for writers with serious social and aesthetic purposes in search of a mass audience.

Despite this, it proved (then and subsequently) very difficult to

recognize TV drama as a medium of contemporary literary achievement. Part of the problem was its ephemeral nature. An individual
play would be shown once or at most two or three times. Video equip-
ment was rare, certainly not generally in use by individuals or, even,
many educational institutions. Play scripts might be published (as
Dennis Potter's *Nigel Barton* scripts were by Penguin), but they did not
have the same authority as the text of a theatre play. For a TV play the
definitive version (normally the only version) was the finished visual
and aural product. The script was essentially a reminder of it. This
situation intensified as increasing use was made of location film as
opposed to studio scenes.

As a literary text, then, the TV play was unstable, unavailable and
possibly (if the company kept only partial archives) completely lost. It is
hardly surprising that literary criticism, with its emphasis on works of
permanent value, has had almost nothing to say about TV drama. A
further set of problems arises when a cultural product neither fits into
accepted literary forms nor appears as the work of a single originating
author. Cinema provided the earliest instances here, although both the
stability of its texts (made to be shown repeatedly and to exist in
multiple reprints) and the possibility of reinstating an author (or
'auteur') through emphasis on individual directors, from Eisenstein to
Lindsay Anderson, allowed the general framework of literary criticism
to be applied (with the aid of techniques for analysing visual images).
Film, in fact, could increasingly be handled as a new branch of literary
and dramatic development.

Broadcasting posed further, even wider problems, because of the
special diversity in kinds of programming. Louis MacNeice wrote his
radio plays within the Features Department; simultaneously he worked
on scripts for dramatized documentaries and historical reconstructions.
The McColl/Seeger/Parker 'Radio Ballads' of the late fifties and early
sixties were an amalgam of documentary material and original songs
and writing. They constituted an important element in the widespread
attempts to transgress accepted boundaries of cultural levels within
novels, film and theatre, and they stand as considerable achievements
in their own right, but it is inconceivable that they could figure in the
'literary history' of the period.

Television inherited and equalled radio's diversity of programming.
Newman's splitting of BBC drama into three sections was one recognition of this. The TV series, in particular, was radically different from
accepted models of literary creation. Esslin has argued that the series is 'a

new genre different in *kind* and obeying different aesthetic laws. If the single play is a product of *craftsmanship*, the series is an *industrial product*, mass-produced.'[26] Esslin designates the series, rather desperately, as the 'modern folk epic', the 'collective dream material of a given culture'.

The reality is more mundane and various. The most innovatory form of broadcast drama was the radio daily 'slice of life' chronicle, begun before the war with *The English Family Robinson* (1938) and institutionalized in the fifties with *Mrs Dale's Diary* and *The Archers*. Formally this combined elements of both serial (a connected story-line from one episode to the next, often with a cliffhanger to retain audience interest) and series (a major emphasis on construction of character and a potentially unlimited number of programmes). BBC TV versions (*The Grove Family*, *The Appleyards*) were shortlived, particularly compared to Granada's *Coronation Street*, begun in 1960 and by the mid-sixties viewed in 8 million homes twice a week. More limited series (runs of, usually, thirteen weeks) permitted greater authorial control, particularly in situation comedy, where Hancock (an early translation from radio), Steptoe and Alf Garnett were the direct creation of one or two writers. Certainly the series format had its own formal requirements, including the potential restrictions of stability and continuity in character and setting. These did not necessarily signify 'mass production'; they may equally plausibly be seen as the conventions of the particular dramatic form and, as such, hardly unique in the history of literary forms.

The suggestion is not that all this kind of work should have been regarded (within the terms, say, of the Arts Council) as of literary merit. The point is, rather, that within literary criticism there was no possibility of beginning such a debate. Consequently, in so far as television watching was supposed to be supplanting literary reception (novel reading, theatre-going), it was perceived negatively. In reality, the new media's relationship with existing literary institutions and practices occurred along a wide spectrum of response, from affirmation to translation to challenge and replacement. So, even as writers were attracted away from novels and plays to radio and television, so broadcasting's new opportunities allowed writers to subsidize their less profitable endeavours in the more traditional literary forms, and many of the traditional objectives were attempted within the new media.

Alternative literature

By the mid-sixties, literary institutions and practitioners were learning to live with television. The economic support it provided (directly and indirectly) was accepted and its more radical challenges were consigned to the areas of mass or popular culture. The undeniable difference between a book and a TV set was, in the end, a critical weapon in securing the specificity of literature. It was when alternatives were developed (albeit on a smaller scale) within accepted literary forms themselves that insecurities were revealed – particularly in the position of poetry. In the sixties a new generation of 'pop' and 'underground' poets seemed to threaten poetic norms and standards which had been protected, hitherto, by a combination of educational centrality and social marginality. The challenge was felt along several related dimensions – notably, the mixing of poetry with other art forms (including improvised theatre and non-classical music), an emphasis on poetry as spoken rather than written, an explicit openness to American influences (poetic and social), and a new sense of the potentialities of audience involvement.

The immediate roots of this challenge can be located in the late fifties. In 1959 *Protest*, a transatlantic anthology edited by Gene Feldman and Max Gartenberg, combined extracts from English 'Angries' and American 'Beats' in a way which (despite the claims of its editors) revealed major differences in styles of 'protest'. Allen Ginsberg, Jack Kerouac and William Burroughs were clearly worlds apart from Kingsley Amis and John Braine, and their apocalyptic, neo-romantic language and concerns signalled different possibilities for contemporary writing. Within British culture the late fifties saw also the rise of CND, whose Easter marches combined an eclectic, informal and unofficial cultural style (including 'trad' jazz, folk music and poetry) with the experience of a celebratory event lasting for days at a time and felt to be of political significance.

The 'poetry and jazz' formula became very familiar in the sixties and by no means always signalled a break with traditional ideas of poetry. Several hundred programmes of 'Poetry and Jazz in Concert' were organized between 1961 and 1969 with an average audience of 400. The structure here, Jeremy Robson explained, was 'generally four poets reading, two in each half, with specially written interludes of jazz played as "bridges" between readers – also a few poems read with jazz'. Jazz was essentially used to attract a bigger audience, not to modify the poetry; at least, that is how Robson saw it in 1969:

Poetry readings are an introduction to the written word . . . not an end in themselves. Despite the many readings I cannot

believe in a 'public' or 'pop' poetry – only in poetry written
for the page, in isolation, with the life and discipline and
complexity which good poetry has always possessed.[27]

The tone of this disclaimer indicates Robson's wish to dissociate
respectable 'poetry and jazz', in the late sixties, from 'pop' poetry.
Nevertheless, there had been alternative lines of development from the
late fifties. Robson's jazz (which, he proudly recorded, surprised a
college principal by its resemblance to 'chamber music') was always
quite distinct from Mike Horovitz's jazz – 'underground movement,
living mythology and international language'.[28]

In 1959 Horovitz with, among others, Cornelius Cardew (musician)
and John McGrath (playwright) had founded the magazine *New
Departures*. Horovitz (who invoked Blake as his spiritual mentor)
recorded in 1968 that the review seemed only

> half-alive on the pages. Its travelling circus incarnation –
> '*Live* New Departures' – soon came naturally. . . . In eight
> years we've mounted some 1,500 shows – involving spoken
> poetry with jazz, plays, mime, new music, electronics,
> speeches, film light/sound projections, sculpture, dance –
> and with all manner of people and places, many of them
> hitherto barren of arts.[29]

On 11 June 1965 the massive Poetry International at the Albert Hall
was conducted within this kind of framework. Particularly prominent
were the Americans Gregory Corso, Lawrence Ferlinghetti and Allen
Ginsberg, and the atmosphere, as recalled by Jeff Nuttall in *Bomb
Culture* (1968), was manifestly American-inspired – being one of
'pot, impromptu solo acid dances, of incredible barbaric colour, of face
and body painting, of flowers and flowers and flowers, of a common
dreaminess in which all was permissive and benign'.[30] Robson had this
in mind when he complained that 'Orgies of exhibitionism – in or
outside the Albert Hall – only do poetry a disservice'.[31] But there was
also something traditional to be recognized in the image of the
bohemian romantic poet appealing to transcendent and authentic
values, as in the favourite hero Blake (of Ginsberg, Horovitz, Adrian
Mitchell and others), and in Robert Gittings's poem celebrating the
event and invoking the spirits of Keats, Shelley, Wordsworth and
Coleridge ('measuring his opium against modern mescalin').[32] This
movement was reactivating, in a new context, a possibility for poetry
that had existed intermittently since the Romantics.

Children of Albion, published by Penguin, was subtitled 'Poetry of the "Underground" in Britain'. Horovitz sought in his 'Afterwords' to distinguish this poetry from conventional 'words on the page' poetry ('verbal critics are going to get left farther & farther behind in understanding poets for whom the reading IS the thing'). At the same time, he distanced this work from commercialized 'pop' poetry: 'the most publicized sector of the "breakthrough" – the Merseyside Blow Up – has been marketed via the guillotine channels of the pop industry – at the expense of what really happened.'[33]

The pop industry was not as one-dimensional as Horovitz implied. By the mid-sixties the emergence of both Bob Dylan (with his mix of folk/blues roots, complex extended lyrics and rock instrumentation) and the Beatles (whom Wilfred Mellers, music critic of *The Times* and a former editor of *Scrutiny*, celebrated as serious composers) exemplified the case for the artistic achievement of the rock, singer-songwriter side of the pop business. The fashion for Liverpool-based rock groups was at its height between 1963 and 1966, and on the coat tails of the Beatles (in publicity and marketing terms at least) came the 'Liverpool Poets' – Roger McGough, Adrian Henri, Brian Patten and Pete Brown. Brown was less involved with 'Liverpool'. As early as 1960 he had worked with Horovitz and others in poetry and jazz events and 'fringe' poetry readings. In the mid-sixties he wrote lyrics for the most innovative rock band of the period, Cream, as well as touring with his own group, the Battered Ornaments. He did appear in Edward Lucie-Smith's anthology *The Liverpool Scene* (1967),[34] but most of the poems included were by Patten, McGough, and Henri. These three were grouped together again in 1967 in Penguin Modern Poets No. 10, entitled *The Mersey Sound* (the only one of the whole series to be given its own title).

McGough and Henri, particularly, were committed to the idea of poetry as performance. McGough's work was often read as part of the act of the Scaffold, which combined sketches, satire, music and poetry (and Paul McCartney's brother was among their members). Henri, a former art student, claimed to have organized the first 'happenings' in England in Liverpool in 1962 after reading a piece by the American painter Allan Kaprow. From the mid-sixties he was part of a poetry-rock group, the Liverpool Scene. He was fully prepared to alter his poems to suit oral delivery ('If you can't say it, don't write it'), and to allow the form of a poem to be determined by what 'seems to go down well'.[35]

By the late sixties these developments had become part of the more general threat to the literary establishment. *Critical Quarterly* was initially patronizing and genial, noting in autumn 1968 that 'This new "pop" verse often has a slight lyric grace, some humour and a pleasing simplicity of diction. There is no doubt, however, that so far its poetic achievement is small, and its notoriety largely a result of publicity gimmicks.' But the challenge intensified with the increase in sophistication (and pretension) of progressive rock and underground culture generally, and the publication of *Children of Albion* (there was also the 'pop' poetry paperback anthology from Corgi, *Love, Love, Love*, edited by Pete Roche in 1967). A growing politicization was exemplified especially by Adrian Mitchell in poems such as 'You Get Used to It' ('hell or Alabama') and 'To Whom It May Concern' ('Tell me lies about Vietnam' – see Chapter 4). By autumn 1971 *Critical Quarterly* was more defensive, condemning the fact that 'the confusion of high culture with "pop" values, so that the Beatles can be called major poets, is a characteristic of present times.' A symptomatic document is Jeremy Robson's anthology *The Young British Poets* (1971) – young being defined as born after 1935. Robson included twenty-three poets, while *Children of Albion* had included over forty poets born after 1935; there is not one poet who appears in both books. Robson's Introduction is almost wholly concerned with the dangers of the current 'remarkable' popularity of poetry. Among these dangers were: writing specifically for the audience, equating pop-song lyrics with poetry, finding that 'readings have grossly inflated the reputations of certain showmen', forgetting that a poem finally belongs 'on the page', throwing together 'catchy advertising slogans . . . for instant appeal', writing about 'the Bomb, Vietnam and so on, in the safety of Hampstead, Liverpool or wherever' and being 'overwhelmed by American influences'.[36] The multiplicity of these threats reflected the fear that by the end of the sixties the secure, if small, world of serious poetry, as taught in formal education or funded by the Arts Council, was being completely swamped by ersatz poetry, as performed or sung irresponsibly and uncontrollably in a variety of subcultural and commercialized settings.

The new emphasis on poetry in performance created links with theatre. Jeff Nuttall's description of The People Show, a theatre group founded in 1965 with Nuttall as scriptwriter, sounds very like Horovitz's *New Directions* – combining 'techniques from music hall, happening, straight drama, cabaret, funhouse and children's party'.[37]

Both the technical requirements of theatre and particular developments since 1956 meant, however, that an 'alternative' drama was less
striking in its impact, for the issues of audience participation, collective
creation and political statement had already been worked through,
certainly in the subsidized theatre. The late sixties saw a continuation
of this, rather than a decisive break into new areas, with the dissolution
of the stable text, the extension of places of performance and styles of
staging, and more intensive efforts to incite audience response.

The visits to London in 1967 of the American Open Theatre and
Café La Mama companies and the opening of the Arts Lab in 1968 provided examples and spaces for this development. Ed Berman's Inter-
Action group concentrated on the physical settings of the audience/
actor relationship; the 'Come Together' twenty-day festival at the
Royal Court in autumn 1969 included the burial of fish, the spreading
of chocolate cake over the laps of the audience and a one-man vomiting
act. Such extreme instances were difficult to recuperate, but generally,
as is argued in Chapter 6, it was difficult to find a form that could not
quite quickly become acceptable to the official subsidized theatre.
More radical possibilities lay in moving outside theatre buildings,
although the considerable development in lunchtime pub theatre did
not necessarily involve plays of radical form or content. And there were
substantial differences between the work of John McGrath's 7:84 political theatre and that of John Fox's Welfare State, which in 1973
staged a two-week drama of the fight between Lancelot Quail and the
Fire King on a council rubbish tip near Burnley.

If theatre was often too flexible to allow 'alternatives', then fiction,
especially the novel, was too rigid. All the devices of the post-Sterne,
post-modernist novel did not alter the basic social relation of a published book, sold as a commodity, and an individual reader. B. S. Johnson was working at the edges of this problem with *The Unfortunates*
(1969), published in a box with the middle sections loose and available
to be rearranged by individual readers. It was Johnson who proposed in
New Society (9 January 1969) that writers should form a co-operative to
publish their own books and sell directly to the public by mail order.
The aim, however, was not so much any ideological subversion of
literary categories as greater financial rewards for authors. It was not
until the seventies that alternative ideas and practices of prose writing
began to develop. There was then a broadening of the concept of literature to include oral history and autobiography (as well as fiction and
poetry); and, more importantly, a localizing and diversifying of the

institutions and participants in literary production and consumption –
writers, publishers and readers. The Federation of Worker Writers and
Community Publishers was set up in 1976 to link a number of locally
based groups (in Brighton, London, Liverpool, Manchester, Birmingham and other urban centres), most of which had been founded in the
early seventies and were 'engaged in the publishing of local histories,
poetry and autobiographies'.[38] The roots of this movement were diverse
– in 'community politics', in oral history, in dissatisfaction with the
middle-class base of the sixties attempts at alternative literature, and in
the spin-off from 'creative' English teaching, for instance in the
Penguin anthology of children's poetry *Stepney Words*, edited by
Chris Searle (1971).

The FWWCP sought funding from the Arts Council Literature
Panel, and a complex debate developed about the work of the Federation's groups and the nature of literature. According to the Panel (in
1979), 'on a community level the work is of sound value'; but 'they
considered the whole corpus of little, if any, solid literary merit'.[39]
Because of this the FWWCP were asked to apply to the Community
Arts Committee rather than the Literature Panel. In an already
notorious letter Charles Osborne, the Literature Director, replied to
one FWWCP member's criticisms:

> It may seem unfair to you that some people are more talented
> than others, and indeed it is unfair; however it remains a fact
> that talent in the arts has not been handed out equally by
> some impeccable heavenly democrat. . . . It is important that
> we do all we can to increase audiences for today's writers, not
> that we increase the number of writers. There are already too
> many writers chasing too few readers. Although the real writer
> will always emerge without coaxing, it is not easy to encourage
> new readers into existence.[40]

This unusually explicit debate about the nature of literature takes us
beyond the period under consideration here. The seventies saw various
new developments – in the responses of publishers and libraries to
economic crisis, in the sudden importance of literary prizes (particularly the Booker Prize), in Arts Council policy, in the continuing
expansion of higher education (especially the Open University, the
polytechnics and the conversion of many teacher-training colleges into
degree-awarding colleges of higher education). But the Arts Council/
FWWCP debate demonstrates that the material production of literature

and its production as a concept remain closely and inevitably linked; it is, indeed, impossible that it could be otherwise.

Notes

1 The history and relationship of these usages is studied by Raymond Williams, *Marxism and Literature* (London: Oxford University Press, 1977), pp. 45–54.
2 Michael Young and Peter Wilmott, *The Symmetrical Family* (London: Routledge & Kegan Paul, 1973), ch. 8.
3 Peter Mann, *Books, Buyers and Borrowers* (London: Deutsch, 1971).
4 Michael Lane, *Books and Publishers* (London: Heath, 1980), pp. 107–8.
5 Quoted in Peter Firchow (ed.), *The Writer's Place* (Minneapolis, Minn.: University of Minnesota Press, 1974), p. 71.
6 John Lehmann, *I am my Brother* (London: Longman, 1960), p. 42.
7 R. Astbury (ed.), *The Writer in the Market Place* (London: Bingley, 1969), p. 146.
8 See ibid., p. 163.
9 *Guardian*, 2 September 1968.
10 *The Collected Essays, Journalism and Letters of George Orwell*, vol. 1 (Harmondsworth: Penguin, 1970), p. 191.
11 *The Times Literary Supplement*, 3 February 1966.
12 Cited in Bryan Luckham, 'The Market for Books', in Astbury (ed.), op. cit.
13 Ministry of Education, *Half Our Future* (the Newsom Report) (London: HMSO, 1963), p. 152.
14 Ibid., pp. 159, 155.
15 Ibid., pp. 155, 156.
16 *Essays in Criticism*, 3, 1 (1953), p. 21.
17 D. Shayer, *The Teaching of English in Schools 1900–1970* (London: Routledge & Kegan Paul, 1972), p. 112.
18 Brian Jackson, *English versus Examinations* (London: Chatto & Windus, 1965), pp. 9, 11.
19 R. Layard *et al.*, *The Impact of Robbins* (Harmondsworth: Penguin, 1969), p. 45.
20 G. H. Bantock, in *The Pelican Guide to English Literature, The Modern Age* (Harmondsworth: Pelican, 1961), p. 38.
21 Richard Hoggart, *The Uses of Literacy* (London: Chatto & Windus, 1957), p. 280.
22 Raymond Williams, *Culture and Society* (Harmondsworth: Penguin, 1961), p. 289.
23 Denis Thompson (ed.), *Discrimination and Popular Culture* (Harmondsworth: Penguin, 1964), p. 21.
24 Martin Esslin, *Mediations* (London: Eyre Methuen, 1980), p. 174.
25 Louis MacNeice, 'Scripts Wanted', *BBC Year Book* (1947), p. 26.
26 Esslin, op. cit., p. 204.

170   *Society and Literature 1945–1970*

27 Jeremy Robson, *Poems from Poetry and Jazz in Concert* (London: Souvenir Press, 1969), p. 11.
28 Michael Horovitz, *Children of Albion* (Harmondsworth: Penguin, 1969), p. 328.
29 Ibid., p. 321.
30 Jeff Nuttall, *Bomb Culture* (London: MacGibbon & Kee, 1968), p. 192.
31 Robson, op. cit., p. 14.
32 Horovitz, op. cit., p. 340.
33 Ibid., p. 328.
34 Edward Lucie-Smith (ed.), *The Liverpool Scene* (London: Donald Carroll, 1967).
35 Adrian Henri, *Tonight at Noon* (London: Rapp & Whiting, 1968).
36 Jeremy Robson, *The Young British Poets* (London: Chatto & Windus, 1971), Introduction.
37 Nuttall, op. cit., p. 210.
38 Dave Morley and Ken Worpole (eds), *The Republic of Letters* (London: Comedia/Minority Press Group, 1982), p. 2.
39 Ibid., p. 132.
40 Ibid., p. 136.

Further reading

Wolff, Janet. *The Social Production of Art*. London: Macmillan, 1982.

Publishing and the literary industry
Astbury, R. (ed.). *Libraries and the Book Trade*. London: Bingley, 1968.
Astbury, R. (ed.). *The Writer in the Market Place*. London: Bingley, 1969.
Bradbury, Malcolm. *The Social Context of Modern English Literature*. Oxford: Blackwell, 1971.
Firchow, Peter (ed.). *The Writer's Place*. Minneapolis, Minn.: University of Minnesota Press, 1974.
Hewison, Robert. *In Anger*. London: Weidenfeld & Nicolson, 1981.
Hewison, Robert. *Under Siege*. London: Weidenfeld & Nicolson, 1977.
Hutchison, Robert. *The Politics of the Arts Council*. London: Sinclair Browne, 1982.
Lane, Michael. *Books and Publishers*. London: Heath, 1980.
Mann, Peter. *Books, Buyers and Borrowers*. London: Deutsch, 1971.
Sutherland, J. A. *Fiction and the Fiction Industry*. London: Athlone Press, 1978.

Literature in education
Jackson, Brian. *English versus Examinations*. London: Chatto & Windus, 1965.
Mulhern, Francis. *The Moment of 'Scrutiny'*. London: New Left Books, 1979.
Shayer, D. *The Teaching of English in Schools 1900–1970*. London: Routledge & Kegan Paul, 1972.
Widdowson, Peter (ed.). *Re-Reading English*. London: Methuen, 1982.

Literature and the mass media
Curran, James, and Seaton, Jean. *Power without Responsibility*. London: Fontana, 1981.
Drakakis, John (ed.). *British Radio Drama*. Cambridge: Cambridge University Press, 1981.
Esslin, Martin. *Mediations*. London: Eyre Methuen, 1980.
Fiske, John, and Hartley, John. *Reading Television*. London: Methuen, 1978.
Shubik, Irene. *Play for Today*. London: Davis-Poynter, 1975.
Thompson, Denys (ed.). *Discrimination and Popular Culture*. Harmondsworth: Penguin, 1964; rev. edn, 1973.
Williams, Raymond. *Communications*. Harmondsworth: Penguin, 1962. Rev. edn, London: Chatto & Windus, 1966; Harmondsworth: Penguin, 1968.
Williams, Raymond. *Television: Technology and Cultural Form*. London: Fontana, 1974.

Alternative literature
Ansorge, Peter. *Disrupting the Spectacle*. London: Pitman, 1975.
Horovitz, Michael. *Children of Albion*. Harmondsworth: Penguin, 1969.
Melly, George. *Revolt into Style*. Harmondsworth: Penguin, 1970.
Morley, Dave, and Worpole, Ken (eds). *The Republic of Letters*. London: Comedia/Minority Press Group, 1982.
Nuttall, Jeff. *Bomb Culture*. London: MacGibbon & Kee, 1968. St Albans: Paladin, 1970.

6 The theatre and its audiences

ALAN SINFIELD

Did *Look Back in Anger* signify a revolution in the English theatre in 1956? – the question is often asked. The play is formally old-fashioned and its amalgam of sex and class was anticipated by Tennessee Williams and, indeed, Strindberg. Yet it was perceived as the trigger of a new movement.

Such a question, about significant change in the arts, cannot be taken very far without discussion of those changes in society which were its preconditions and, in some respects at least, its determinants. Chapter 5 relates the production of literature, materially and as a concept, to relevant markets and institutions in particular social conditions; the remaining chapters, on theatre, poetry and novels, are premised upon this analysis, and draw attention to the active construction of ideas about those genres in the period. Theatre is the most social of literary forms, for in its modern urban manifestation a play needs good initial audiences to survive. The question of change in the drama must be considered in relation to changes in audiences – in economic, social and institutional relationships, both in society at large and as they impinge upon the theatre. There was no revolution in post-war Britain, but there has been significant change.

Of course, the principal development in drama in the period concerns television, which is discussed in Chapter 5. But theatre justifies particular treatment, for although it is patronized by only about 2 per cent of the population it was in this period the particular form within which a new, growing and ultimately influential section of the middle class discovered itself. In the terms developed by Raymond Williams in *Culture* (1981), *Look Back in Anger* was associated with the development by a 'class fraction' of an independent set of attitudes within the dominant culture.[1]

Loamshire

The harbinger of new developments was Kenneth Tynan, who became drama critic of the *Observer* in 1954 at the age of 27. He asserted that 'apart from revivals and imports, there is nothing in the London theatre that one dares discuss with an intelligent man for more than five minutes', and identified as the prevalent genre the play set in

> a country house in what used to be called Loamshire but is now, as a heroic tribute to realism, sometimes called Berkshire. Except when someone must sneeze, or be murdered, the sun invariably shines. The inhabitants belong to a social class derived partly from romantic novels and partly from the playwright's vision of the leisured life he will lead after the play is a success – this being the only effort of imagination he is called on to make. Joys and sorrows are giggles and whimpers: the crash of denunciation dwindles into 'Oh, stuff, Mummy!' and 'Oh, really, Daddy!' And so grim is the continuity of these things that the foregoing paragraph might have been written at any time during the last thirty years.[2]

This pattern had been disrupted by controversial London productions of Tennessee Williams and Arthur Miller – *A Streetcar Named Desire* provoked parliamentary questions in 1949 and the *Daily Express* critic found in it 'the progress of a prostitute, the flight of a nymphomaniac, the ravings of a sexual neurotic'. But Tynan's stereotype was broadly true of English writing. *Look Back in Anger* could have been designed to challenge it. The upper-middle-class daydream is confronted by Jimmy's lifestyle and attacked in the reported behaviour of Alison's mother; its obsolescence is confessed by her father. Jimmy's main conviction is of the value of emotional intensity. Osborne adds a comment that Tynan did not make – that the Loamshire fantasy obscures power relationships: 'you've never heard so many well-bred commonplaces come from beneath the same bowler hat. . . . But somewhere at the back of that mind is the vague knowledge that he and his pals have been plundering and fooling everybody for generations.'

The tyranny of Tynan's stereotype is apparent even in plays that tried to extend its range. *The Burning Glass*, by Charles Morgan, was produced in February 1954. A scientist who discovers how to focus the sun as a weapon is captured by Russian agents; the play is about the circumstances in which one might use such a weapon, and how to deal with such an international crisis. Ivor Brown in the *Observer* declared it 'a rare pleasure to have in our theatre a play whose matter invites argument'.[3] The treatment of the moral issue is quite sophisticated, but the language and attitudes given to the rulers of England are pure Loamshire. The prime minister speaks of his responsibilities:

> Decision, decision, decision – the hardest of all currencies.
> Courage – to be blamed by cowards for being ruthless. The
> courage to move – and not to move. The courage to reject
> whatever has become valueless: our prides, our ideals – even
> our friends; to let them go; to bury the dead. We must do that
> – we Prime Ministers, we Christians.

This is a fantasy of English upper-class reason, determination and inevitable rightness; the one unstable character kills himself from fear that he might one day let the side down. The inadequacy of the genre for the issues Morgan is raising appears in the symbols it offers for western civilization and Russian barbarism: a game of chess and a bad preparatory school. However, *The Times* considered that 'the theatrical impression is that a crisis of immense consequence has been excitingly resolved'.[4]

T. S. Eliot wrote in verse to widen the scope of the drama so that it could deal with religious experience, but in successive plays he compromises increasingly with the dominant manner. In *The Cocktail Party* (1950) language and action are so close to West End norms as to undermine the stature both of his spiritual leaders ('Guardians') and of the ordinary people who 'make the best of a bad job'. The Guardians suggest Eliot's ideal 'community of Christians'; he said they are not 'merely the nicest, most intelligent and public-spirited of the upper-middle class', but their presentation mainly through cocktail party chitchat makes them appear rather less than that. Eliot allows them only the thinnest and vaguest of liturgical languages:

> Protect her from the Voices
> Protect her from the Visions
> Protect her in the tumult
> Protect her in the silence.

The final triviality of Edward and Lavinia, who are supposed to represent the best of ordinary experience, is not just due to a played-out stage language. Their initial attempts to develop some emotional intensity in their lives are disqualified by Eliot as selfish delusion, and their eventual reduction to the social norm is offered as a truer mode of behaviour. Eliot believes in Loamshire.

Terence Rattigan in *The Deep Blue Sea* (1952) anticipates Osborne by lowering the income of the characters, giving them urgent sexual and emotional needs, and making them less able to cope. But Freddie is hard-up and a cad not because he is lower-class and reluctant to join the system but because he had been damaged by his experience as a fighter pilot (the same excuse occurs in *The Burning Glass*: only the strain of saving the country can explain why a gentleman fails to behave like one). Hence Rattigan does not develop a new idiom. Harold Hobson thought this 'one of the frankest plays ever seen on a London stage', but he indicated its limitations by admiring Rattigan's ability to 'keep his dialogue entirely free from offensiveness'.[5] The language anaesthetizes the experience by restraining it within the bounds of Loamshire decency.

The Deep Blue Sea intersects precisely with *Look Back* when the suicidal Hester is asked, 'Why should you accept the world's view of you as a weak-willed neurotic – better dead than alive? . . . You alone know how you have felt. And you alone know how unequal the battle has always been that your will has had to fight.' This comes close to Jimmy Porter's question, 'That voice that cries out doesn't *have* to be a weakling's, does it?' But Rattigan's version is reasonable, whereas Jimmy speaks out of his anguish. Furthermore, the Rattigan speech has amazing consequences for it seems to resolve the whole problem by inspiring Hester with calm dignity so that she does not kill herself. Osborne denies that profound emotions can be so easily managed. Jimmy and Alison slip back into their game of cuddly toys with only slightly improved chances of making it work; in Rattigan's play a few words of good sense and a stiff upper-lip save the day.

The complacent claim that disagreeables can always be brought under control annoyed Tynan and Osborne above all. This was the fantasy of the middle class as it liked to see itself and England in the theatre: that traditional decency and reticence are not only best, they are also adequate to the post-war world. This belief inspires Edward and Lavinia, and the only alternative Eliot can envisage is crucifixion on an ant-hill. Morgan's prime minister plans the third world war as if it

were the Oxford and Cambridge Boat Race, and there is no trace of the
tottering and deluded Churchill of 1954 or of the deceitful and fum-
bling Eden of 1956. That is why Jimmy Porter's violent attack on
complacency in personal and public life constituted a significant
development.

A non-U intelligentsia

Traditionally minded reviewers found Jimmy to be in bad taste: the
Daily Mail called him an 'oaf', the *Manchester Guardian* a 'boor', the
Financial Times 'blatantly loutish', the *Birmingham Post* 'self-pitying,
uncouth, cheaply vulgar'; the *Daily Mirror* found the play 'neurotic,
exaggerated and more than slightly distasteful'.[6] But, as Lindsay
Anderson pointed out, the public who came to the play saw something
else:

> Not merely, it is obvious, the hysterical boor which is all the
> central character could seem to the middle-aged, unperceptive
> eye; but a tremendously forceful expression of their own
> disgust with contemporary hypocrisies, and at the same time a
> reflection of their own sense of confusion and lack of focus.[7]

David Jones, who went on to work for the BBC arts programme,
Monitor, and as a director with the Royal Shakespeare Company, was
'excited, because I thought this was the way my generation talked and
felt and it was actually happening on the stage – there was an identification with the way we used to talk at the university'.[8]

The importance of Tynan's review is that he recognized not 'a good
play' but a new potential audience, eager to see issues that exercised
them treated in terms of their own lifestyle. He began by quoting
Somerset Maugham, a distinguished practitioner of the Loamshire
play, on grant-aided students: 'They are scum.' The post-war extension
of state education produced a new, growing and articulate group. By
1955 the numbers of sixth-formers and of university students had
doubled since 1939, and three-quarters of the students received grants.
These people did not share the Loamshire fantasy. Their relatively
lower-class origins left them with quite different ways of thinking, feeling and speaking, which they could not shed if they wished to. Tynan
identified this 'non-U intelligentsia' as the audience for *Look Back*.
They derived their confidence – and their opportunities for relatively
well-paid employment – not from social background but from

educational attainment. They had every reason to welcome an attack on the ethos and credentials of the established middle class, which seemed to be sustaining extremes of wealth and poverty, stifling creativity by despising those without the right accent, and endangering the world by obscuring the reality of the international situation.

All surveys suggest that this educated and upwardly mobile fraction of the middle class was hugely overrepresented at new plays in the sixties. At the National Theatre, the Glasgow Citizens, and the West End production of *The Man in the Glass Booth* (about the trial of a Nazi for crimes against Jews), between 55 and 80 per cent of the audience were under 35. Between 18 and 35 per cent were students; and between 23 and 48 per cent had completed higher education (this latter group amounted to 3.7 per cent of the population as a whole). Before 1956 the public school was a favoured setting; by 1970 it was replaced by the university.

Between 1956 and 1958 productions at the Royal Court of plays by John Osborne, Nigel Dennis, John Arden, Ann Jellicoe and Arnold Wesker, together with the introduction of Brendan Behan and Shelagh Delaney by Joan Littlewood's East End Theatre Workshop, were generally taken to signify the growth of a new, radical theatre. The common feature was disrespect for traditional middle-class attitudes, expressed directly and through aggressive presentation of other lifestyles. Theatre Workshop developed a boisterous, irreverent, improvisatory, music-hall technique which seemed an affront to 'good form'. Reviewers were forced into explicit political or social comment. *The Times* declared of Wesker's *Roots* (1959), 'since all its characters are inarticulate they are not, for the most part, given anything interesting to say';[9] and of Arden's *Live Like Pigs* (1958) that 'the spectacle of human beings behaving as uninhibited animals is, after all, of limited interest'.[10] Hobson asserted, apropos of *Serjeant Musgrave's Dance* (1959), 'It is the duty of the theatre, not to make men better, but to render them harmlessly happy';[11] and of *The Hostage* (1959), 'Much of what Mr Behan says about British rule in Cyprus, Kenya, and elsewhere, seems to me childish.'[12]

But the new drama was not characterized by coherent political thought. The reason was partly pressure from the existing system – a need to cover costs while the anticipated new audience formed. In 1959 *Serjeant Musgrave's Dance* played to 21 per cent of box office for twenty-eight performances covering only three-quarters of its immediate costs. Some Royal Court productions (like Noël Coward's *Look after Lulu*, 1959) were frankly intended to make money, and transfers to the

West End broke up the 'permanent company' which was supposed to stimulate new standards of production. Theatre Workshop also was in danger of compromise. *The Times* complained of Behan's *The Quare Fellow* (1956), which is about tensions in a prison on the eve of a hanging, that 'the play was not turned into an entertainment'.[13] But their reviewer admired *The Hostage*, where the entertainment virtually overwhelms the issue of an English soldier seized by Irish nationalists. The hostage is killed by police trying to rescue him, but *The Times* saw this as 'only Mr Behan's fun. . . . the main substance of the rollicking entertainment is the outrageous fun poked at Irish types'.[14] Even *Oh What a Lovely War!* (1963) became relatively sentimental after transferring to the West End. Somehow the alternation of comedy and stark horror was unbalanced, so that the former predominated; the explicit comparison with atomic warfare which concluded the original production was cut.

The uncertain political stance of the new drama should be traced mainly to its producers and its audiences. Some major figures had lower-class roots (Shelagh Delaney, Peter Hall, Arnold Wesker, Harold Pinter, Edward Bond), but, of a sample of prominent writers and directors that I took, only a quarter had not studied at university and of that quarter a half had been at public schools. Of the whole sample, almost half had attended public schools (including Osborne, though he was expelled) and over half had been at Oxford or Cambridge. Many of these people could have followed their parents into traditional middle-class occupations, but they used their education as the means to creative and influential work in the theatre and other communications media. They tended, perhaps, to welcome the opportunity to display their contempt for conventional mores, but their critique was often limited.

The Royal Court company avowed no political position, and it was not looking especially for left-wing plays. As well as Brecht, Arden and Wesker it sponsored Beckett, Ionesco and N. F. Simpson, so that, over all, its political impetus was quite indeterminate. George Devine, its director, remarked in 1962 that, although it was outside the West End, 'it could draw on a large residential area of Chelsea (rapidly becoming the new Mayfair) and Kensington'.[15] These weren't the places to find the working-class audiences Osborne and Wesker said they wanted. Jonathan Miller suggested that the censor tolerated *Beyond the Fringe* (1961) because the cast were men with the 'right background', university wits, 'us' rather than 'them'.[16] The satire boom which followed

Beyond the Fringe was characterized by an almost random choice of targets.

The audiences were likely to have been from predominantly grammar school and redbrick backgrounds (15 per cent of the writers and directors sampled had this background). But though they were less privileged they were probably upwardly mobile and shared some of the aspirations of the public school and Oxbridge people, at a lower level of income and attainment. Such an audience felt its exclusion from power, but its educational attainment promised dividends without radical change. By the mid-sixties, surveys were revealing, as well as youthfulness and education, that 70–80 per cent of the London audiences for serious drama had executive, managerial or professional occupations. Of the audience at the National Theatre, 96 per cent earned over £500 per annum (only 78 per cent of the population had that income); 47 per cent earned over £1750 (only 14 per cent of the population earned as much); and 29 per cent earned more than £2500 (national figure: 5 per cent). These people might be capable of revolutionary gestures, but we might expect the fundamental impetus to be more diffuse.

A key issue was the Lord Chamberlain's power to censor plays that he thought irreverent, indecent or subversive. As long as the makers and audiences of theatre were broadly at one with the dominant values in society, this caused little problem, and 'advanced' work could always be produced in theatre clubs where the censor did not interfere. But the new movement perceived at once that censorship tended to privilege and legitimate traditional ideology and to suppress its own. Lord Annan feared that 'the language of gentility may be imposed upon dramatists who are sincerely trying to evoke the manners and modes of different classes in society'.

The fight against censorship seemed at the time to be radical, but we should discern also the determination of the rising young intelligentsia to assert its own values and lifestyle by affronting traditional opinion; both this group and its ethos proved readily incorporable into English society. Moreover, the debate focused mainly upon sexuality, and in terms not of fundamental change but of individual freedom. Under this liberal banner the Lord Chamberlain was quite easily routed. He was reduced to absurd tinkering with dialogue; in Osborne's *Inadmissible Evidence* (1964) he ordered the deletion of 'off' from the line, 'Do you have it off with that girl of yours', and that 'arse' be changed to 'bum'. He acknowledged the quaintness of his standards in 1958 when he first permitted the *mention* of homosexuality: 'This subject is now so widely debated, written about and talked over that its complete exclusion from the stage can no longer be regarded as justifiable.' Nevertheless, whole scenes of *A Patriot for Me* (1965) were disallowed – although the story of an army officer reduced by role conflicts, emotional frustration and blackmail to sordid liaisons and then to suicide is hardly an inducement to homosexuality. The Royal Court constituted itself as a club and played to over 90 per cent houses, demonstrating that audiences did not wish to be 'protected'. The police successfully challenged the club device, and it seemed obvious to the reforming Parliament of 1966 that something must be done. Theatre censorship was abolished in 1968, marking the emergence of the liberal, intellectual middle class from the status of specialist minority to the mainstream of English culture.

Radicals and the absurd

The most insidious trap for radical theatre in the sixties was a tendency to attract likeminded audiences, who instead of being challenged were able to congratulate themselves on their commitment. This is probably the general case with attempts to promote change in Britain, and the new drama should perhaps be perceived as a means of reinforcement, not conversion. But this could sponsor a new complacency, as flattering as that in which conservative audiences had indulged before *Look Back*. Writers who intended a radical critique had to take account of this tendency.

In *Chips with Everything* (1962) Wesker used the Air Force as a microcosm of class relationships. His explanation of why the officers overtly despise the conscripts shows the problem: 'I deliberately said to myself, I am not going to make them rounded characters out of any sort of liberal impulse. However rounded I might make them, they still stood for what they did.' Wesker did not want to draw us into the officers' psychology so that we might understand and so sympathize and excuse. However, this allowed critics to dismiss them as 'caricatures', so Wesker's point was lost just the same. Thompson's identification with the lower-class conscripts and resistance to officer training is broken when his motive is uncovered: to be 'messiah to the masses'. Thus Wesker warns the labour movement of the dangers of betrayal by upper-class leaders whose main goal is self-aggrandizement. But the point was also applicable to many in the original audiences who had

182 Society and Literature 1945–1970

come to applaud a socialist play, for, even if they were not wealthy like Thompson, most were educationally privileged and destined for co-option into the middle class. Actually, it is unlikely that this point would be taken – that the audience would recognize itself in Pip. For while the play seems to present a cross-section of British society there is in fact a crucial gap: there is no one in it comparable to Wesker or his primary audience. The concluding stroke is effective none the less. The national anthem is played at the airmen's passing-out parade – so blurring into its customary performance at the ends of plays. Anyone experiencing an impulse to stand up shows respect to the class system which Wesker has exposed; and what about all other occasions when it is played at other plays? He or she may become sharply aware of the extent to which theatre-going is a middle-class activity.

After Haggerty (1970) by David Mercer is a series of traps for the liberated audience. We see that Bernard's left-wing lectures on theatre in Budapest, Moscow, Cuba and Prague are irrelevant to the problems of international socialism; the same applies to our own indulgence in theatre. But this is cut in with Bernard speaking to his working-class father (only Bernard is heard). The old man is not interested in Bernard's affairs, but we probably take this as indicating Bernard's separation from his working-class roots, and Bernard's impatience as a combination of guilt and metropolitan cynicism. This would be the typical structure for the politically conscious treatment of social mobility, allowing the audience a little gentle self-reproach as they identify with the successful younger person, together with satisfaction as they appreciate the proletarian solidity of the father.

The writer bent on pleasing would add an emotional reconciliation which acknowledges the problems and validity of both parties (compare Dennis Potter's celebrated television play, *Stand Up, Nigel Barton*, 1965). When Bernard's father arrives, this reading remains possible for a while, but gradually we realize that he is self-absorbed and bigoted, proud that his union broke the General Strike, insensitive and tyrannical in his respect for traditional family life. The idol is destroyed, but there is no satisfaction in his humiliation. The final comment on all of them is the news of the death of Haggerty, a black American who, we discover in the last line of the play, has been fighting for freedom in Africa. Commitment is possible, though none of the characters on the stage has made it; the proper focus of socialism is not anxiety about mythic proletarian origins but the struggle for freedom in the Third World.

The social challenge constituted by the new drama and its audiences was so uncertain that Beckett, Ionesco and Pinter were, in the minds of many, hardly separable from Osborne and Wesker. Ivor Brown linked *Waiting for Godot* (1955) and *Look Back* as parts of 'a deliberate cult of squalor';[17] *The Times* compared *Roots* to *Godot* as drama of non-communication and let slip the comment that *The Caretaker* (1960) is 'the least puzzling and the most pleasing play that Mr Harold Porter [*sic*] has yet written'.[18] Everything that was not Loamshire seemed part of a general threat to established decencies.

But the plays discussed so far locate their characters socially and are concerned with people in society. 'Absurdist' theatre purports to present the ultimate human condition. In the plays of Beckett and Ionesco (who was equally important between 1955 and 1965) our sense of time and place is systematically disturbed, and our notion of personality is undermined by characters who are invisible, turn into rhinoceroses, have whitened faces like clowns, live in dustbins or are buried up to the neck (in the debris of their own lives). The reliability of language, the prime means by which we constitute significance in our lives, is assaulted through parody, cliché, inconsequentiality, quotation, logic games and undefined menace. Existence is pointless, mysterious, irremediable and therefore anguished (see also the discussion in Chapter 4).

Such plays challenge conventional assumptions about the world, but politically – thinking of our initial question about the kinds of change the theatre of the period represented and helped to promote – they are conservative, for they tend to deny the relevance of political commitment and, indeed, the significance of the material factors in life with which it is usually concerned. This tendency was attacked by Tynan in his review of *The Chairs* and *The Lesson* at the Royal Court (1958). Ionesco replied: 'No society has been able to abolish human sadness, no political system can deliver us from the pain of living, from our fear of death, our thirst for the absolute.' He reversed Marx's dictum that social being determines consciousness: 'it is the human condition that directs the social condition, not vice versa.'[19]

Harold Pinter was the most successful dramatist of the period. His sense of idiosyncratic detail in the speech of different classes and of the dynamics of psychological tension suggest naturalistic rather than absurdist drama. One can envisage entire psychological explanations for strangenesses and inconsistencies in *The Caretaker* (1960) and *The Collection* (1961). But even in these relatively naturalistic plays we are held off from the action by a self-consciousness in the writing – the extraordinary outflow of language in *The Caretaker*, the symmetry of relationships in *The Collection*. Elsewhere Pinter is definitely absurdist: he introduces humanly inexplicable elements, like the blind Negro in *The Room* (1957) and Goldberg and McCann in *The Birthday Party*, which seem to point beyond the specific situation to a vague, general anxiety about ultimate reality. The mystery may originate in the depths of the psyche or in the supernatural, it is hard to say. Early plays like *The Hothouse* (written in 1958 but not performed until 1980) and *The Dumb Waiter* (1960) hint at the supernatural, the former in the sigh which passes through the building, the latter in the arbitrary demands from above. On the other hand, *The Lover* (1963) and *The Homecoming* (1965), where the characters slide between realistic and apparently symbolic roles, suggest individual sexual fantasy as the site of the mysterious forces that oppress and contort the world. But such attempts at interpretation quickly begin to look like a trap that Pinter has set for rationalist pride.

Absurdist drama was attacked as obscure by most traditional critics. But the new audiences, whose social validation depended upon academic attainment, welcomed intellectually demanding plays. As in the modernist classics of T. S. Eliot and James Joyce which came into vogue at universities, obscurity seemed the mark of a profound engagement with life. These plays challenged establishment complacency by declaring to a world under threat of extinction that life is more complicated and dangerous than is dreamt of in the philosophy of boulevard theatre. 'There is a kind of horror about,' Pinter remarked. However – and this perhaps appealed to the upwardly mobile audience – absurdist theatre does not require that disaffection be pushed through to action; indeed, it implies that any attempt would be futile. The overall drift was complicit with existing society.

Brecht and Artaud

Despite innovations in content and in absurdist drama, most plays were still written in the naturalistic mode, implying that stage action is a simulation of actual life, as if the audience is looking in at a real room through its fourth wall, seeing people doing the kinds of things people actually do (as opposed to speaking in verse or living in dustbins, for instance). While absurdists undermined naturalism because it inhibits access to what they regarded as the ultimate human condition, Brecht attacked it because it makes behaviour and relationships appear inevitable, rather than particular to a certain social system. His 'alienation' devices were designed to inhibit the audience's emotional identification with the characters and to stimulate an awareness that the action – and hence the real world – need not take one given form.

From 1956 Brecht was often invoked but mostly to doubtful effect. Cold War animus against his Marxism was reinforced when Brecht endorsed the suppression of a rising in East Berlin in 1953. Not much of his work was translated before 1962, and 'sympathetic' interpretations presented him as a liberal individualist trying to get out from under a weight of dogma. English productions of the plays were received uncomprehendingly: when the Royal Court did *The Good Woman of Szechuan* in 1956 Hobson reported that an audience prepared to adopt the mentality of a child of six would have a tolerable time. Any artistic form depends upon some readiness in the receiver to co-operate with its aims and conventions.

The Brechtian manner of John Arden's *Serjeant Musgrave's Dance* caused it to be generally misunderstood (takings still reached only 45 per cent of box office when it was revived in 1965). Arden's play has a cool, detached style; Hobson complained that it is not entertaining. It deters us from reducing political issues to personal problems by withholding in-depth motivation; *The Times* complained that it entrusts 'its message to characters who do nothing to win our sympathy'.[20] It denies us what Arden called the 'cosy point of reference' of an authoritative central character; Alan Pryce-Jones in the *Observer* thought it 'totally nihilist'.[21] Admittedly Arden leaves us for too long in ignorance of important facts but, like Brecht, he makes it reasonably clear what he wants us to think. Mrs Hitchcock and Attercliffe say plainly in the last scene, with the vitality of the village and the failure of Musgrave's project behind them, that Musgrave was wrong to replicate the punitive and arbitrary violence of imperialism: 'Aye, it's arsy-versey to what you said, but it's still an anarchy, isn't it?'; 'To end it by its own rules: no bloody good.' (The language is demotic without condescension, significant without pretentiousness, committed without shrillness or cliché.) Arden, here and until he took on a more Marxist analysis in about 1970, is a revolutionary anarchist. He asserts the goodness of human life, if only it can be released from false consciousness and the tyranny of current social systems. This is what Sparky sees just before he is killed. Because Arden leaves us to discern it for ourselves, it became a critical commonplace that he sits on the fence.

The impact of Brecht in the sixties was virtually smothered by the concurrent influence from America of 'happenings' and fringe groups like the Living Theatre ('performances, a great part of which were spontaneous when not actually random'),[22] and by the discovery of Artaud. This volatile French genius had also held that naturalistic plays are delusory, not because they hinder political awareness but because they obscure the spectator's supposedly violent primeval nature ('his taste for crime, his erotic obsessions, his savagery, his chimeras, his utopian sense of life and matter, even his cannibalism'). Artaud proposed to shock the spectator into awareness of such matters through incantation and ritual ('cries, groans, apparitions, surprises') and grotesque visual manifestations ('new and surprising objects, masks, effigies yards high'). He called it 'Theatre of Cruelty'.[23]

Peter Brook experimented with this approach with the Royal Shakespeare Company (RSC) and in 1964 directed Peter Weiss's play, usually called in Britain *The Marat/Sade*. In its original German production, this had seemed to be a Marxist indictment of revolutionary fascism. Brook made of it a play 'designed to crack the spectator on the jaw, then douse him with ice-cold water, then force him to assess intelligently what has happened to him, then give him a kick in the balls, then bring him back to his senses again' (preface). He said it was 'firmly on the side of revolutionary change' but, although the impact was terrific, quite what was to be changed to what was unclear.

The traditionally minded were duly shocked: the RSC had a series of battles with the Lord Chamberlain and in 1964 Emile Littler, a member of the RSC executive council and a powerful impresario, entered a public protest against 'dirty plays'. In May 1966 *Private Eye* gave theatre a double spread in its 'All-purpose Titillation Supplement' on 'Swinging London' ('an audacious, searing battle to keep up the flood of sensationalism. The old taboos have been toppled – but as brilliant, young, corrosive 59-year-old Peter Hall of the Royal Shakespeare Company states: "We shall soon find new ones"').

Radical disquiet with the ideological vagueness of Theatre of Cruelty emerged hesitantly in the left-wing journal, *Encore*:

> Any time now a naked man and a naked woman will appear on one of our stages (the Aldwych, of course) and say '****' or probably do it. We shall congratulate ourselves on living in a freer, more rational, more beautiful society. Is it enough?[24]

This reaction was suddenly powerful with *US* (1966): Brook and the RSC were condemned for making a self-indulgent Artaudian experiment out of the horror of the Vietnam war and for offering an inadequate political analysis. These accusations were not unfounded, but the virulent reaction suggests that the second-act questioning of the audience's integrity struck a vulnerable point. A young man who wants to burn himself as a gesture against the war is asked who will be changed:

> take me. I'm a suitable case. I vote left. I hold progressive opinions about homosexuality and capital punishment. I'm quite well-read, I have a University degree. I do my best not to buy South African oranges . . . and what the hell do you think I'll do tomorrow any different from what I did today – just because you burn yourself?

Here the characteristic RSC audience is represented to itself in its earnestness and its impotence (the play's title glosses as 'us' as well as 'USA'); and, if we are little changed by someone burning himself, what effect could any play have?

US was inadequate as a response to the Vietnam war, but it enraged audiences because it drew attention to the congenital frustrations of trying to change society through the theatre (or other arts). The more urgent the reference to real issues, the more theatre is likely to seem an inadequate substitute for the 'reality' of the newsreel; any commitment selects an already sympathetic audience; and the progressive audience (in our period) is generally split between its wish for a radical posture and its actual privileged position. Hence the uncertain political stance of many plays and the tendency – which is explicit in Theatre of Cruelty – to overrate the merely shocking. Charles Marowitz, initially Brook's collaborator, associated the Artaudian movement with impatience at 'the well-upholstered, self-esteeming cul-de-sac in which contemporary theatre found itself'.[25] Destruction of complacency seemed a valid substitute for positive thought. The RSC director, Peter Hall, admitted in 1966 to 'a particular feeling about the powerlessness of the intellectual in a political state';[26] themes of violence and metaphysical anguish ran through many RSC productions between 1960 and 1965. Audiences too felt frustrated at their exclusion from influence, first under an ageing Tory leadership, then under the managerial manipulation of Wilson. Theatre of Cruelty represented a desperate determination to make some – *any* – impact upon a society that seemed able to absorb all criticism.

In the longer term Artaud's influence made theatre generally less verbal (even Pinter's silences are verbal). Playwrights were freed to move between naturalistic and surreal effects, and to develop complex relationships with audiences. Already in *Saved* Edward Bond was using violence partly to intimidate the audience. Physical violence in *Lear* (1972) is of a piece with the violence done to Shakespeare's play (whose ethos Bond means to repudiate) and with a devastating concreteness of language, and it is all part of an analysis of the violence of political institutions. Some scenes of the play disgust; Bond wants to affront us because oppression is not just wars, prisons and walls (like the Berlin Wall); it is also an individual mental condition (Bond suggests in a flashback to the childhood of Bodice and Fontanelle that it derives from upbringing) of fear and selfishness. The reality of violence is made to intrude upon our consciousness because that is where it belongs, among our internalized assumptions. Cordelia – the apotheosis of 'love' in standard interpretations of Shakespeare's play, though she responds to her sisters' violence with an army – is in Bond's play a victim of such self-oppression, and in her determination to destroy Lear's system she only re-creates it. Lear tells her, 'Your Law always does more harm than crime, and your morality is a form of violence.' We may apply the thought to our own shrinking from the play: our sense of order and decency is in part a means by which we build walls against unpleasant reality. Shakespeare's Lear says, 'let them anatomize Regan, see what breeds about her heart. Is there any cause in nature that makes these hard hearts?' There is no answer; perhaps cruelty is inherent in humanity. Bond's Lear witnesses the autopsy of his daughter with astonishment and reaches opposite conclusions:

> I have never seen anything so beautiful. If I had known she was so beautiful. . . . Her body was made by the hand of a child, so sure and nothing unclean. . . . If I had known this beauty and patience and care, how I would have loved her.

So Bond wants the potential goodness of human life to emerge through his anatomy of violence. Walls can be removed if enough people see the need.

The politics of subsidy

There was, then, significant change in the English theatre. It reflected the changes in attitude and social grouping which accompanied the emergence of a new fraction in the middle class as it took up positions of influence in society. The movement only occasionally offered active opposition to the dominant ideology; on its favourite issue, freedom of sexual expression, it had rather an easy victory.

The economic and institutional vehicle of that theatrical change was subsidy. None of the plays of Arden or Bond was produced in the commercial theatre; they were all performed by subsidized companies and usually failed to cover even their immediate costs. Since Ibsen's time, all major developments in drama had taken place outside the main commercial system, but by the mid-fifties almost all the 'little theatres' had been closed as a result of rising costs. In the West End, 'shows' were vehicles for 'stars' and had to make an immediate 'hit', whereas Devine claimed 'the right to fail'. Tynan observed in 1954: 'Twenty-seven West-End theatres are at present offering light comedies and musical shows, of which perhaps a dozen are good of their kind. The number of new plays with a claim to serious discussion is three.'[27] Moreover, in the early fifties about half the West End theatres and even more provincial ones were controlled by three or four organizations, and these were interlinked by shared directors. This monopolistic tendency was developed in the sixties through a strong connection with commercial television. The directors of these companies did not appreciate the new plays; when ATV took over Stoll Theatres and Moss Empires in 1965, giving them twenty-two theatres in all, the chairman, Sir Robert Renwick, announced that he went to the theatre 'to be entertained and amused' and had no time for 'dirty plays'. Of seventy-four major productions (longer than four months) between June 1966 and June 1968, twenty-five were sponsored by interlocking companies associated with ATV.

Serious drama seemed impossible within this system. The principle of subsidy was established during the war, but until the formation of the English Stage Company at the Royal Court in 1955 it was used mainly by offshoots of major commercial producers with an eye to West End transfer. Arts Council support for the Royal Court started at £7000 in 1956, jumped to £20,000 in 1962, to £50,000 in 1965 and £100,000 in 1967. The RSC opened its London theatre in 1961 and its grant increased from £5000 in that year to £57,000 in 1963, £152,500 in 1966, £205,500 in 1967 and £280,670 in 1970. The National Theatre began work in 1963 with consistently larger grants. In 1968–9 the Royal Court received about £1 for every ticket sold when the average cost to the purchaser was 77p; the National's subsidy was 94p per seat when the average charge was 92p.

The period saw also an immense growth in subsidized provincial theatre. By 1968 the Arts Council was paying between £5000 and £50,000 to forty companies outside London; fifteen theatres were built between 1958 and 1970, all with public money. These companies varied a great deal, receiving as much impetus from civic pride as from the Royal Court. But they all manifested some pull towards the educated young audiences, sometimes accompanied by disputes between the artistic director and the board of local worthies.

Subsidy raises an obvious question of social justice: should the tastes of an affluent minority be financed from the taxation of people who have little opportunity, and probably little wish, to participate? A further question is why the state should finance theatre that intends to subvert its social and political structure. The suspicious will conclude at once that the state sponsors drama to keep people quiet; Osborne opposed a national theatre because 'the Establishment of the 1960s may try to promote a synthetic version of the really new theatre, with all its teeth drawn'.[28] And, indeed, Lord Goodman, Chairman of the Arts Council (1964–71), held that 'once young people are captured for the Arts they are redeemed from many of the dangers which confront them at the moment and which have been occupying the attention of the Government in a completely unprofitable and destructive fashion';[29] and Lord Eccles, Minister for the Arts in the Heath government, saw the arts as tranquillizers for 'minorities who are showing themselves bored, sulky, frustrated or angry'.[30] Perhaps radical thought was diverted into theatre when it might have been causing real changes in the social structure.

I perceive, rather, ideological inconsistency. The initial reason for subsidy, according to Lord Keynes in 1945, was that the artist 'leads the rest of us into fresh pastures and teaches us to love and to enjoy what we often begin by rejecting, enlarging our sensibility and purifying our instincts'. This hardly envisages The People Show. At certain points the Arts Council's alarm was apparent. In 1967 it refused to support the Royal Court over Bond's *Early Morning* because it might be party to a censorship offence; it discouraged the RSC's experimental work at the Arts Theatre in 1962 and the Court's studio, the Theatre Upstairs, in 1968; it failed to rescue the Arts Lab, a venue in 1968 for adventurous experiments by The People Show, Pip Simmons, David Hare and many others; it never gave Theatre Workshop funding commensurate with its reputation. But the main response of the traditional establishment was confusion, not quite comprehending that 'art' meant something new to the rising intelligentsia. When the managing director of Oxo presented £1000 to the Royal Court in 1958 he registered a 'slight criticism of policy and what is being done, and regretted the failure to discover a new Shakespeare whose work was devoid of sex, blasphemy, anti-monarchical opinions, and sensational things which don't make true theatre'.[31] But he still handed over the money.

Raymond Williams suggests three factors making for such complexity in the ideological formation. First, there may be an asymmetry between market conditions and the dominant social structure: a commodity may be immediately profitable within a market which, in its ultimate assumptions, is at odds with the ideology of that commodity. This occurred when commercial managements sponsored radical plays. Second, particular class interests may have a certain scope for oppositional production within the dominant order, especially when a class fraction is growing in size, confidence and influence. This is the principal mechanism, I have argued, in the case of *Look Back* and its successors. Observe, however, the paradoxical limitation of such a movement – namely, that its capacity to assert itself depends to an extent upon its potential contribution to the establishment (*Beyond the Fringe* was 'us' not 'them'), and it is precisely this which hinders the development of truly oppositional work. Third, certain institutions may have a privileged status that renders them relatively independent. This is the case with the RSC and National Theatre, but, while in the short term such institutions may promote oppositional work, in the long run their main symbolic effect is what Williams calls 'the slow building of *authority*'.[32] John McGrath (founder in 1971 of the 7:84 Company – 7 per cent of the population owns 84 per cent of the wealth) declared of the National Theatre, 'In its structure and its productions, it embodies a set of values and assumptions that are demonstrably those of the ruling class: even when it attempts ''left-wing'' plays – it gobbles them up into its high-cultural meritocratic maw.'[33] However they may dislike it, the major subsidized companies centralize power and resources and dominate creative outlets. They constitute a new theatrical establishment, spearheading the ideology of the class fraction which emerged with *Look Back* and moved towards its own positions of power.

The principals in this process were anxious about their role. Devine said in 1962 that to create challenging theatre the Royal Court 'had to become part of the Establishment against whom our hearts if not our faces were set'.[34] Peter Hall told the RSC in 1963 that even their name sounds establishment – 'antique, square, institutional, conservative, traditional'. But, he asserted, 'We are none of these things. We want to run a popular theatre. We don't want to be an institution supported by middle-class expense accounts. We want to be socially as well as artistically open.'[35] Yet Hall was so determined in his repudiation of the traditional middle class that he hardly noticed that he was helping to develop a new middle class. Repeated gestures were made towards other social groups, but crucial assumptions were not examined. To pick out one point, the Arts Council declared in 1970 that 'long periods of Bingo debase the theatre in the public mind [which public?] and reduce its value as a theatre'.[36] They did not consider the argument that, to involve the whole community, theatre ought to run alongside bingo. The RSC took drama in the form of half a dozen actors and a portable stage out to schools, youth clubs, evening institutes and town halls. But a gulf remained between the programme presented – a 'tour de force anthology recital, from *Lysistrata* to *The Birthday Party*, loosely schematized and played mainly for laughs'[37] – and the formality and intellectual demands of the main productions. By 1970 the new establishment threatened to dominate London. Although West End impresarios might dislike the plays, they were sponsoring them and taking them in from the subsidized companies in increasing numbers. That was the growth point of the business, including good proportions of American tourists.

The point is *not* that certain writers and directors were in bad faith but that English society has (or had until 1979) a great capacity to incorporate dissident movements. Each attempt to subvert the system is quickly granted, on certain conditions, a space, so becoming not just an aspect of the system but an evidence of its flexibility and beneficence. This power of incorporation has proved very difficult to evade.

By 1961 Wesker was established as a Royal Court dramatist whose work could transfer successfully to the West End, but he was determined to relate his writing to the labour movement. His Centre 42 sponsored six festivals with local trades councils in 1962, but *Their Very Own and Golden City* (1966) is his analysis of the overall failure of the project. Wesker's aim was radical, for he intended to finance the arts out of working-class (trade-union) funds. In the play the problem is failure of vision in the union leaders, who are described as the prefects of capitalism; Wesker does not face the further issues that 'art' is specific in form to class, and that even the concept is upper- and middle-class. In 1965 Centre 42 slipped into the role of umbrella organization for the operation of the Round House in Chalk Farm, London – mainly for the benefit of the youthful intellectual audience we have identified throughout. Wesker's play also points to the corrosive compromises that result from financial dependence upon government and business. This is the contradiction which beset radical theatre in the period: 'It's all patchwork . . . and then when it was done they'd heave a sigh of relief that they'd managed to stave off the real revolution for yet another century.'

John Arden went on from the Royal Court to the Chichester Festival Theatre in 1963 and the National in 1965, but already in 1963 he was involved in community drama in Yorkshire. At the end of *The Royal Pardon* (1966) two players refuse subsidy and the opportunity to act before the king: 'We two will attempt together a far more dangerous thing. / We will travel, hand in hand, / Across water and dry land – / We will entertain the people.' But Arden still believed that for a larger influence he must use 'the professional theatre with all its remoteness, its irrelevance, and its inability to attract a "popular" audience'. So in 1972 *The Island of the Mighty* was directed by David Jones for the RSC at the Aldwych, but Arden and the co-author, Margaretta D'Arcy, were so angry at changes which they felt weakened the political impact of the play that they picketed the theatre. Since then Arden has devoted himself to community projects, denying that professional theatre can promote significant change; he remarked in 1980 that *Serjeant Musgrave* has become a classic but the army is in Ireland.

Underground or fringe theatre, modelled partly on off-off-Broadway and sometimes stimulated by Americans, was the principal means by which artists tried to evade the established ethos. CAST started in 1966, but 1968 – with the student–worker insurrection in Paris, the invasion of Czechoslovakia, worldwide demonstrations about Vietnam, and sit-ins in many English colleges – saw a counter-cultural explosion. The People Show, Portable Theatre, Pip Simmons, Wherehouse/La Mama, Inter-Action and many others (thirty-two based in London by 1970) sought to develop oppositional plays, conditions of production and relationships with audiences. They performed in warehouses, pubs, universities and the streets, improvising performances, venues and organization. Some were determinedly political, some meant generally to shake up the audience with Artaudian violence of action and language. The obvious audience was the usual student–graduate sector, but some groups worked successfully in local communities, factories and building sites.

But even this attempt to break out has been partially absorbed by the major cultural institutions. Arts Council subsidy became available in 1968; by 1971 £91,000 was being divided between forty-five companies. Commerce was ready to welcome new trade, and the big breweries began converting pubs like the Bush. Established dramatists wrote for fringe groups, but few left the conventional theatre (John McGrath was an exception). The movement has been the opposite way. David Hare, Howard Brenton and Trevor Griffiths have all followed the same path from fringe companies in the sixties through the Royal Court Theatre Upstairs, Arts Council bursaries and progressive provincial companies like the Edinburgh Traverse and the Nottingham Playhouse (and, in Hare's case, progressive West End managements), arriving eventually at the National Theatre. They have tried to carry their commitment with them, but the transplant has not always taken well. Less dangerous than the temptation to be respectable may be the temptation to be outrageous in order to prove one has not sold out.

In 1973 Howard Brenton thought that the fringe might have to go underground, as the only surviving means of democratic communication. But by 1976 he was being performed at the National and saw fringe theatre as 'an artistic ghetto': 'I'd rather have my plays presented to 900 people who may hate what I'm saying than to fifty of the converted.'[38] The counter-proposition was put by Julian Beck of the Living Theatre, the American forerunner of the English fringe, when he celebrated the student occupation of the subsidized Théâtre de France in Paris in 1968. Beck wanted to deny 'the government the privilege of flattering both itself and the public into believing that the state maintains reputable avant-garde *contra sistemo* art. Any art that the government supports it exploits.'[39] Is Brenton gaining wider influence at the National, or is he helping the state to present a liberal front? Who is using whom?

In Trevor Griffiths's *The Party* (1973) English leftists bicker during the 1968 Paris upheaval. The accusation that intellectuals 'enjoy biting the hand that feeds you, but you'll never bite it off' seems to be endorsed by the play, as does the assertion, about the media, that 'the only thing you're allowed to put in to the system is that which can be assimilated and absorbed by it'. We wonder about the present play; is it subject to the same limitations? The published prologue moves beyond the naturalistic particularity of the rest of the play and promotes a general question about the relationship of politics, economics and entertainment by having Groucho quote from Karl Marx (alluding to the anarchistic slogan which appeared in Paris, 'Je suis marxiste, tendance Groucho'): 'Constant revolutionizing of production, uninterrupted disturbance of all social conditions, everlasting uncertainty and agitation distinguish the bourgeois epoch from all earlier ones.' Thus we are invited to perceive the superficiality of the play's political infighting, conducted, as it were, in the glare of the mass media (it is pointed out that the flat is lit like a television studio). We may think also that the analysis applies more broadly to the restless change, always oversold by the media, which characterized theatre generally in the period. Griffiths's prologue was cut from the National Theatre production.

Notes

1 See Raymond Williams, *Culture* (London and Glasgow: Fontana, 1981), pp. 71–81.
2 Kenneth Tynan, *A View of the English Stage* (St Albans: Paladin, 1976), p. 148.
3 *Observer*, 21 February 1954, p. 11.
4 *The Times*, 19 February 1954, p. 5.
5 Harold Hobson, *The Theatre Now* (London: Longman, 1953), p. 168.
6 Quoted in John Russell Taylor (ed.), *John Osborne, Look Back in Anger: A Casebook* (London: Macmillan, 1968), pp. 37, 39, 38, 45, 46.
7 In Tom Maschler (ed.), *Declaration* (London: MacGibbon & Kee, 1957), p. 164.
8 Quoted in T. R. Fyvel, *Intellectuals Today* (London: Chatto & Windus, 1968), p. 92.
9 *The Times*, 29 June 1960, p. 4.
10 *The Times*, 1 October 1958, p. 6.
11 *Sunday Times*, 25 October 1959, p. 25.
12 *Sunday Times*, 14 June 1959, p. 23.
13 *The Times*, 25 May 1956, p. 3.
14 *The Times*, 15 October 1958, p. 8.
15 *Prompt*, 1 (1962), p. 8.
16 *Encore*, 38 (1962).
17 Ivor Brown, *Theatre 1955–6* (London: Reinhardt, 1956), p. 8.
18 *The Times*, 31 May 1960, p. 4.
19 Eugène Ionesco, *Notes and Counter-Notes* (London: Calder & Boyars, 1964), p. 95.
20 *The Times*, 23 October 1959, p. 18.
21 *Observer*, 25 October 1959, p. 25.
22 Bernard Levin, *The Pendulum Years* (London: Cape, 1970), p. 188.
23 Antonin Artaud, *The Theatre and its Double* (New York: Grove Press, 1958).

24 *Encore*, 56 (1965).
25 Charles Marowitz and Simon Trussler (eds), *Theatre at Work* (London: Methuen, 1967), p. 184.
26 Ibid., p. 155.
27 *Observer*, 19 September 1954, p. 15.
28 Quoted in Taylor, op. cit., p. 64.
29 Quoted in Ronald Hayman, *The Set-Up* (London: Eyre Methuen, 1973), p. 248.
30 Quoted in ibid., p. 245.
31 Quoted in Terry Browne, *Playwrights' Theatre* (London: Pitman, 1975), p. 52.
32 See Williams, op. cit., pp. 101–3, 74, 223–5.
33 Quoted in Catherine Itzin, *Stages in the Revolution* (London: Eyre Methuen, 1980), pp. 125–6.
34 *Prompt*, 1 (1962), p. 12.
35 Quoted in David Addenbrooke, *The Royal Shakespeare Company* (London: Kimber, 1974), p. 63.
36 *The Theatre Today* (London: Arts Council, 1970), p. 14.
37 Addenbrooke, op. cit., p. 68.
38 Quoted in Oleg Kerensky, *The New British Drama* (London: Hamilton, 1977), p. 225.
39 Julian Beck, *The Life of the Theatre* (San Francisco, Calif.: City Lights, 1972), p. 91.

Further reading

Addenbrooke, David. *The Royal Shakespeare Company*. London: Kimber, 1974.
Armstrong, William A. (ed.). *Experimental Theatre*. London: Bell, 1963.
Bentley, Eric (ed.). *The Theory of the Modern Stage*. Harmondsworth: Penguin, 1968.
Brown, John Russell (ed.). *Modern British Dramatists*. Englewood Cliffs, NJ: Prentice-Hall, 1968.
Browne, Terry. *Playwrights' Theatre*. London: Pitman, 1975.
Caute, David. *The Illusion*. London: Deutsch, 1971.
Elsom, John. *Post-War British Theatre*. London: Routledge, 1976.
Elsom, John. *Post-War British Theatre Criticism*. London: Routledge, 1981.
Elsom, John. *Theatre Outside London*. London: Macmillan, 1971.
Hayman, Ronald. *The Set-Up*. London: Eyre Methuen, 1973.
Hinchcliffe, Arnold P. *British Theatre 1950–70*. Oxford: Blackwell, 1974.
Itzin, Catherine. *Stages in the Revolution*. London: Eyre Methuen, 1980.
Marowitz, Charles, Milne, Tom, and Hale, Owen (eds). *The Encore Reader*. London: Methuen, 1965.
Marowitz, Charles, and Trussler, Simon (eds). *Theatre at Work*. London: Methuen, 1967.

McGrath, John. *A Good Night Out*. London: Eyre Methuen, 1981.
Taylor, John Russell. *Anger and After*. London: Methuen, 1962; rev. edn, 1969. Harmondsworth: Penguin, 1963.
Taylor, John Russell. *Look Back in Anger: A Casebook*. London: Macmillan, 1968.
Tynan, Kenneth. *A View of the English Stage*. London: Davis-Poynter, 1975. St Albans: Paladin, 1976.
Wandor, Michelene. *Understudies*. London: Eyre Methuen, 1981.
Williams, Raymond. *Culture*. London and Glasgow: Fontana, 1981.
Williams, Raymond. *Drama from Ibsen to Brecht*. London: Chatto & Windus, 1968. Harmondsworth: Penguin, 1973.
Worth, Katherine J. *Revolutions in Modern English Drama*. London: Bell, 1972.

7 Thrills and frills: poetry as figures of empirical lyricism

ANDREW CROZIER

Contexts in canons

If we want to ask questions about the context of poetry, with the idea, perhaps, that the broader our frame of reference the better our knowledge, we should find ourselves at the same time having to ask the question: What poetry? Some modes of contextual criticism commonly encountered avoid this in practice. One, for example, will point to self-evident social factors which can be exhibited in their due place beside a standard choice of texts. Another infers a total historical and social reality determining all literary productions uniformly, able without difficulty to incorporate within itself even those productions that resist such determination: from this point of view the literary productions of a given period are typical and more or less equivalent. Both these positions, even when adversary, treat poetry as an unproblematic unity, knowable as such in a way largely independent of any comprehensive survey. Neither position asks of itself why it attends to this poetry rather than that, for as a result of an inclusive embrace of text and context the only poetry in evidence is whatever is at hand. That other poetry might never have been written. Neither position interrogates its own context (is poetry not part of the context of criticism?) and thus must operate with implicit commitment to unexamined and even disowned judgements of literary status.

Yet there is a quantitative phenomenon (which, incidentally, suggests that notions of status and quality often have more to do with prescription and taste than judgement) that can put into proportion the question of what our critics refer to. It is not often enough remembered that in recent years, and maybe for much longer, poetry has been the art with probably the greatest number of practitioners in this country: entrants to poetry competitions and participants in writers' circles and creative-writing classes are a fraction of the total. The mass of these poets are, of course, without ambition, and the private nature of their activity means that they are not concerned with making a quality product; but this is not the point. Not only do these poets hardly know what the quality product is; when it is pointed out to them they tend not to recognize what makes it so very different from what they write themselves. Unless they are ambitious to win prizes, they certainly do not rush to buy it. If we dismiss these poets as amateur, as self-preoccupied, or as having old-fashioned standards of taste, we do not remove their significance. We have not justified the direction of our attention.

This is not just the question of a distinction between high art and popular culture. Nor are the questions raised here to be resolved by contrasting the critical privileging of literature as high art and the disparagement of popular culture. The pressures behind such an observation are obvious enough, but to proceed from a general point about the social production of literature to a complaint about the élitism of its criticism is to go on too fast. What literature? and What poetry? remain questions unasked within a blanket notion of high art; nor are questions about the relation of criticism, as a mediator of contexts, to the production of its subject allowed to be put. Yet everyone engaged in the academic study of English knows how criticism has redesigned the tradition of English literature throughout this century. Where recent literature is concerned, and criticism shares the immediate context of its production, such relations are intensified. The poetry commonly talked about – the standard, canonical work – cannot be simply located in a non-literary context if it owes not only existence but status to the way in which that context operates in intimacy, through secondary discourse, with its production. Not to proceed too fast, therefore, we should bear in mind that criticism itself is contextually produced, before being an agency through which literature is determined.

The criticism of contemporary literature typically represents cultural values as artistic values, and so governs the perception and status of what is regarded as artistically valid. There is a notional admission that art directs its own discourse, but most criticism, in the guise of artistic judgement, is doing no more than affording its sanction to culturally and socially approved modes of discourse. Present-day criticism of the poetry of the period 1945–70 has its origins, still, within the period itself; indeed, when we examine its origins we see how closely they were involved with a section of its subject. It would appear, specifically, that currently approved modes of discourse established themselves in poetry in the early and middle fifties. In order, therefore, to understand why the canon for our period exists in the form in which it does, we need to consider it in relation to its formative critical context. Two points of focus – the canon as it is received today and as it emerged and was codified – provide the starting-point of this essay: superimposed, they provide an image of the self-consciousness, so to speak, of the canonical poetry of the period. But when we trace the terms by which the canon was defined it becomes apparent that they are also those by which it was validated; controversy never infringed certain agreements, and these largely unexamined positions cover major exclusions of poetic discourse. In terms of the poetic history of the period the present-day reader is ill served indeed, but this problem cannot begin to be overcome until we see it in its critical context.

But what is the canon? Do I make exaggerated claims for its existence? These are questions readers may already have answered from their own knowledge. In his monograph on Seamus Heaney (1982) Blake Morrison provides a current version, registering the status of his subject, placing him in the company of his peers, and marshalling an array of established authorities to underwrite the orthodoxy he describes.

> Seamus Heaney is widely believed to be one of the finest poets now writing. To call him 'the most important Irish poet since Yeats' has indeed become something of a cliché. In Britain he is as essential a part of the school and university syllabus as are his post-1945 predecessors Philip Larkin and Ted Hughes; in America scholarly articles reflect a growing interest in his work; on both sides of the Atlantic influential critics . . . have pressed large claims on his behalf.[1]

It is worth noting, in passing, the slight shiftiness of tone in this passage ('is . . . believed', 'part of the . . . syllabus'); Morrison is never wholly behind what is being claimed. But this is only local colouring to an argument which, it is clearly felt, need not be made: the constellation of Larkin, Hughes and Heaney is assumed, and it is as 'one of the finest poets now writing' that Heaney belongs there.

What we should attend to in particular are the implicit strategies of this argument, which strip from the notion of a canon of excellence any suggestion that the criteria involved might not be universal. First of all, the argument is contained within an unspecified concept of quality, 'the finest poets'. It accomplishes itself by means of ostensibly neutral chronological markers ('since Yeats', 'post-1945'); yet, while 1945 is an important date in social history (the election of a Labour government, the end of the Second World War – although neither was directly an event in Irish history, surely), 'Yeats' is a function of literary history. The notion of an autonomous literary history is implied by the concept of succession, Yeats–Heaney, Larkin–Hughes–Heaney, yet such succession is not simply chronological but is concerned with authority and status and, it would seem, relations of descent; a version of tradition, in other words, though not that of Pound or Eliot. Something British perhaps? Whatever the case, the argument derives its force more from its air of unassuming conviction than from anything it says about the poets in question, and it functions rather like those systems of radio interference used to jam other signals. The message that is allowed to come through is the persuasive notion of major quality, quite unbiased, simply the best. It is a salesman's message (seeking in fact to develop the market for a series of primers on 'Contemporary Writers'), appealing to a variety of tastes, a variety of English-language cultures, but appealing above all to the taste for quality. (It should be remembered that the appeal of quality is always pitched towards the individual consumer.)

The most compelling strategy of the argument as a whole is the way it associates the authority of period and tradition with the generosity of contrast and internal diversity. The canon, within limits, is able to evolve. Some years ago, before the decisive advent of Heaney, it was usual to encounter the name of Ted Hughes twinned with that of Thom Gunn. Larkin and Hughes are frequently perceived as antithetical, the one tame and insular, the other barbaric and invoking elemental powers. Heaney is Irish. There is a host of subsidiary poets available to be conscripted by exponents of the canon if they are keen to diversify. Morrison himself mentions Geoffrey Hill, and is bravely revisionist in his account of Heaney, arguing that in the more recent verse his sympathies are Republican.

Morrison has the merit of providing us with the canon in pure, concentrated form: Larkin, Hughes, Heaney. But he appears somewhat halfhearted in his commitment to it, and it might appear that the critical position it embodies has become decadent, the terminology a

codified, rhetorical strategy. If we look at the canon nearer the moment
of its inception the difference in tone is striking. In the next section of
this essay I show that, while proponents of the canon initially exploited
the notion of period much as Morrison does today, they used the notion
of contrast in order to dissociate, to signal protest rather than cathol-
icity. In a similarly protestant manner, far from any suggestion of an
apostolic succession, it was implied that they were renewing connections with an older tradition disrupted by recent literary events.
Donald Davie, for example, who has seen himself as the theorist of that
moment of protest (the 'Movement', as it was commonly known) wrote
about Larkin with committed rhetoric.

> I think that everyone knows, really, that Philip Larkin is the
> effective laureate of our England. Other poets may criticize
> what Larkin does with the truths he discovers, what attitudes
> he takes up to the landscapes and the weather of his own
> poems; but those landscapes and that weather – none of us,
> surely, fails to recognize them? And this is just as true if we
> think of landscapes and weather metaphorically; we recognize
> in Larkin's poems the seasons of present-day England, but we
> recognize also the seasons of an English soul – the moods he
> expresses are our moods too, though we may deal with them
> differently.[2]

'Everyone', 'our England', 'our moods': the collective pronouns are
powerfully attached; even the question of Larkin's special distinction is
placed in terms of a native institution. Davie published these remarks
in 1963, when Larkin's reputation still effectively rested on a single
book, published in the provinces.

The appeal to Englishness may reinforce values placed on the
concrete and specific (and, indeed, Davie goes on to say of a poem by
Ted Hughes that its landscape lacks such local definition: it could be
England but it might equally be Ireland), but at the same time the
argument annexes poetic quality to an exclusive sense of cultural possession. Clearly, the present-day canon, although its values are no less
exclusive, is not possessive in quite this way. But to what extent might
Davie's praise of Larkin address the qualities of the Movement as a
whole? Does Movement poetry in fact elaborate and celebrate the recognition and enjoyment (however wistful) of common cultural property?
In the next section of this essay I consider the arguments put into play
following the theoretical and polemic initiatives of Robert Conquest's

anthology of Movement verse *New Lines* (1956),[3] but it will be as well
to preface that discussion with some consideration of the qualities there
disclosed by the Movement in its most vigorously codified form.

A recurrent impulse of the poets associated in *New Lines* is to appre-
hend or, at least, allude to the discrete: this impulse centres both the
topics and the mode of discourse of their poetry. The art object or the
cultural site (both generally foreign) or the moment of experience
(again, often in a remote setting) furnish occasions for the majority of
their poems. 'Afternoon in Florence', 'Baie des Anges, Nice' (titles of
poems by Elizabeth Jennings and D. J. Enright respectively) exemplify
one aspect of this preoccupation with the discrete. The type of occasion
for moral-aesthetic reflection found by Davie in 'A Head Painted by
Daniel O'Neill' is modified and brought closer to contemporary life (as
we might expect) in Philip Larkin's 'Lines on a Young Lady's Photo-
graph Album'. In 'The Minute', by John Holloway, 'He scarcely saw
the moment when . . . make one bright / Minute: and then the thing
was done.' Such discrete occasions are partially seen as potential with
expressive discourse; what they might say to the poet is taken up and
considered in a poem. But – and this seems inevitable in view of the
poets' lack of intimacy with, even estrangement from, whatever it is
that provokes them – their own discourse does not readdress the
worlds of discourse to which they allude. It does quite the opposite, in
fact. Occasions, however necessary they may be to poets, are not felt to
be trustworthy. They are not full with a world of realized experience.
The components of the moment of realization in Holloway's poem can,
without misrepresentation, remain obscured by my ellipsis, for the
point is that experience of them was wryly deficient. In Enright's 'The
Interpreters', 'those critics for whom the outside is a dreadful bore' are
condemned, while a reality of surfaces is esteemed, both the grass
which covers a 'senseless' mess, and the 'really' meant.

> Good lord, if a poet really meant what he said,
> we should all be out of a job – why on earth
> would he sing of the merely real? – the papers have taken
>   up that chorus –
> 'the agonies, the strife of human hearts'? – why,
>   Hollywood will do that for us.

But the irony of Enright's 'merely real', a reality that is exclusively
human, rebounds, surely, from the allusion to Keats, for Enright's

reality ('the peasants look at their rotting cabbages, / a gang of clods are building a block of flats') is conscientiously remote and diminished.

In these poems we detect in the poet's authority a relentless determination of poetic discourse and foreclosure of its intended audience. The discourse is emphatically singular in many cases: the first-person pronoun 'I' is characteristic, we notice, in Thom Gunn as well as in Larkin; while 'we', as uttered by Davie, for example, implies a restricted group, and is far from being generously inclusive. If we include ourselves we do so by self-election. 'How dare we now be anything but numb?' concludes his 'Rejoinder to a Critic', a poem of casuistic argument in which Davie figures the effects of 'Love' as the radioactive fallout from an atomic bomb burst, and suggests – since love and hate are both 'versions of / The "feeling"' that the critic enjoins – that a modern answer to Donne's question 'Who's injured by my love?' would be 'Half Japan!' It is hardly possible to feel that 'we' here implies a communal injunction, so beset is it by the thickets of feeling conjured up by the critic. Furthermore, numbness is a state of such nullified response that communication might seem out of the question. No, the discourse here is set, typically, towards a few others who can be imagined as sharing the moments of privileged contemplation such poems envisage. 'We' is not 'us', the English, but rather 'you and I', English poets. Donald Davie and John Donne.

It might be supposed that a poetics of objects, sites and moments placed its exponents in the tradition of enfeebled Romanticism, the decadence of conventional poetic emotions; and to a certain extent the poets of the Movement are to be understood in this light. But at the same time they place themselves outside that tradition by earnestly demystifying its conventional occasions, by finding nothing there, nothing below the surface. The profound or sublime are closed options. In 'Near Jakobselv' Robert Conquest is able to contemplate the unfamiliar, alien landscape of an Arctic summer not with horror but in a mood bordering on complacency. Here, as elsewhere, the expressive discourse potential in the occasion is found to reside less in the occasion itself than in its conventional status. This bifurcation – in which ostensible occasions are virtual fictions – is recognized and exploited by Kingsley Amis in 'Here is Where'.

> Here, *where the ragged water*
> *Is twilled and spun over*
> *Pebbles backed liked beetles,*

Bright as beer-bottles,
Bits of it like snow beaten
Or milk boiling in saucepan . . .

Going well so far, eh?
But soon, I'm sorry to say,
The here-where recipe
Will have to intrude its *I* . . .

But this irony, which becomes increasingly emphatic ('Scream the place down *here*, / There's nothing *there*') cannot elude its dependence on the very conventions it rejects. We might attribute this ambivalence to the social origins of the Movement poets (reference to which is made, in passing, in the next section of this essay), suggesting that the cultural institutions around which they sustained their careers were not theirs by birth. Be that as it may, it will be apparent that ambivalence of this sort is likely to be attended by an incongruity between poetic occasion and motive that is fraught with disruptive pressure in need of containment.

It is in these terms, I believe, that the formal characteristics of Movement verse, which Conquest makes prescriptive, are best understood, rather than in a straightforward congruity of form and content. The high regard for regular rhyme and stanza displayed throughout *New Lines* does not engage notions of finish, of the polished object; the poems are not discrete events in the sense that they correspond as such to their discrete occasions. They are discrete, rather, in the way they wrap around their author-subject. Their occasions are for the most part treated with scepticism, and the texts distort and buckle as a consequence of inner tension. Traditional forms are invoked not so much for the freedom they can confer as for support. They define the space in which the self can act with poetic authority, while at the same time, in the absence of assurances provided by conventionally felt poetic experience, they secure the status of the text.

From our retrospective point of view our questions concern not only how best to read Movement verse but also how to explain its success in determining and underwriting the emerging canon. Within the constraints operating in Movement verse we would expect to find that individual poets wrote with different degrees of flexibility and inclusiveness. I would suggest that Larkin exploited Movement ambivalence most fully, and was thus best able to retain the terms and formal procedures of its discourse without exhibiting them as limits. Davie's remarks, I think, implicitly recognized this, although I might put the point another way, and say that Larkin's objects, sites and moments are English and thus intimately his.

To summarize the argument so far, I might say that the present-day canon has its roots in the Movement. But if Blake Morrison were to owe anything to Donald Davie, say, his position nevertheless exhibits a falling away from the rectitude and seriousness of Davie. Yet, were I to mount a dispute, across almost two decades, between two such opponents – in the knowledge, for example, that Davie's praise of Larkin involves some rather damaging remarks about Hughes – it would amount, I fear, to no more than an internal, sectional difference. Both are positioned, in relation to what they admire, towards the same mode of poetic discourse: a necessary response to actual pressures at one time, no doubt, but now very much a preferred manner.

The Movement as controversial nexus

We no longer see the Movement as a pressure group or a publicity stunt; it has acquired historical status. Blake Morrison has published a useful survey (*The Movement: English Poetry and Fiction of the 1950s*, 1980) which offers a representative account of the literature of the decade. His treatment of the Movement falls in line with frequent claims that the term itself is a misnomer – that there was no membership, no push or direction, no common programme or general agreement on principles. All this is quite helpful, even if it stands in the way of any reconstruction of Movement networks and tactics we might wish to make, for if no Movement as such can be said to have existed, and we can only approximate the typical features of its poetry and not judge individual departures from a standard, the way is open to seeing the work of a particular poet as typifying the poetry we think of, however vaguely, as being Movement. Many signs point to Philip Larkin as an appropriate choice: not only does he figure largely in much Movement documentation; his writing confirms and clarifies much of its polemic. In other circumstances I might not treat the Movement and Larkin as in some sense commutative, but here my concern is with the extent to which the Movement's self-definition was set strategically against the poetry of the previous decade, and the concurrence of this Movement disposition with polemics otherwise directed against the Movement. Larkin's career, with its early, rejected affiliations with the rhetoric of forties poetry, is exemplary in the way it incorporates and stabilizes such antagonisms.

It is not necessary to go into circumstantial detail here – the series of pamphlets published out of Oxford by the Fantasy Press, the role of the *Spectator*: Morrison documents it all fully. But it will be useful to remind ourselves of his account of the Movement's ideological characteristics: the Low Church and middle-class origins; the concern with classlessness and upward social mobility; the hostility to the 'posh' and the 'phoney', and the nostalgia for traditional order; the connection with provincial universities. All these bespeak a high degree of social rootlessness, and a complementary degree of personal isolation and self-dependence. They also imply a social matrix largely made up of males. Certainly, the Movement provoked a number of squeamish reactions to what was felt as its posture of tough and aggressive philistinism. More forcefully, it was also argued against the Movement that the refusal of ideas, the empirical derivation of poetry from exclusively personal experience, made for a socially conservative poetry, uncommitted and without dedication.

But if Larkin provides a standard for Movement poetry, and inaugurates the canon of post-war English poetry, it is in Robert Conquest's propaganda that Movement positions are generalized and made exclusive. The Movement effectively demonstrated its existence to the general reader in 1956 with Conquest's anthology *New Lines*. It was reprinted within months, and again the following year. It was sharply attacked by Charles Tomlinson in a 1957 review article in *Essays in Criticism*,[4] and provoked a counter-anthology of 'poets unafraid of sensitivity and sentiment', *Mavericks*, edited by Howard Sergeant and Dannie Abse (1957),[5] intended to demonstrate that the Movement did not have a monopoly in poets born after 1920. (Typical 'mavericks' were Jon Silkin and W. Price Turner.) A. Alvarez's anthology *The New Poetry* (1962; revised in 1966 and still in print)[6] engaged the Movement from a rather more up-to-date position but included five of Conquest's nine poets. Conquest brought out a revised and updated *New Lines – II* (1963),[7] with many more poets, to produce an even greater overlap between *New Lines* and *The New Poetry*. Both include Ted Hughes, Alvarez's strongest anti-Movement contender. It has been argued that *New Lines* appeared after the Movement had shot its bolt, and that it should not be taken as definitive – both nice points which I would not try to dispute. Conquest claimed considerable achievement already for the poets in his first anthology, while noting that several of them had yet to publish substantial collections of their work. By any accounts

New Lines was able to reach a considerable and new audience, and most of the poets went on to establish careers for themselves, if they had not done so already.

What we see in the sequence of response and reaction following the publication of *New Lines* is not, needless to say, the internecine feuding of small, conspiratorial groups of poets, let alone the successful dominance of a single group (the event feared by the editors of *Mavericks*). It is something much more like the establishment of a new kind of literary professionalism, utilizing the cultural prestige of poetry to diversify into new markets – universities, the media, the secondary education syllabus – in a manner already established in the USA, with the poet playing the role of cultural entrepreneur. As in any boom (the professionalism I describe was more a feature of the sixties than of the fifties, of course) such an economy rolled forward under its own momentum, and Movement poets, unless they were especially recalcitrant, found themselves merged with their successors. Davie's 1963 remarks about Larkin, or his 1962 polemic dialogue with Alvarez in *The Review*,[8] in which he advocates the moral and aesthetic resistance of objects (very much with Tomlinson's poetry in mind) against Alvarez's insistent personalizing of experience, can be seen as attempts to resist such dispersals of poetic energy.

Because he served as the major publicist of the Movement, although declining to invoke the authority of its unofficial name, Conquest's Introductions to his two anthologies are of special interest. He may vulgarize ideas put forward by Davie in his occult role of theorist in *Purity of Diction in English Verse* and *Articulate Energy*,[9] he may not have a very generous appreciation of the poets he brought together (distinguishing Amis and Wain by name, say, rather than Davie and Larkin), but he provides the Movement with an immediate and polemic frame of reference by asserting its newness, and in doing so initiates the present-day canon attributed to finely made judgement. In 1956 Conquest starts from the journalistic proposition (somewhat disingenuous in hindsight) that each decade has its characteristic poetry, and stakes a claim to the fifties, asserting of *New Lines* that it represents 'a general tendency . . . a genuine and healthy poetry of the period'. But he claims more than this: not only is *New Lines* contemporary; fifties poetry, as represented by *New Lines*, is better than the poetry of the previous decade. In addition, as 'healthy' might have warned us, even more is at stake. Uncovering the pathology of the forties in terms of its 'images of sex and violence', Conquest remarks

9 Jazz and Jive

10 The Twist

that to 'combat this trend was not a purely artistic task'. How the task was conceived, whether in moral or political terms, will emerge later. What Conquest goes on immediately to say, however, suggests that his quarrel is not just with the poetry of the forties but with most of twentieth-century writing: 'When a condition of this sort takes hold it sometimes lasts for decades. The writers remembered later are odd eccentrics – the Kiplings and Hardys.' Announcing 'a general tendency, perhaps of lesser talents', rather than a collection of individual eccentrics, Conquest is implicitly claiming that the Movement, the poetry of the fifties, represents a return to literary standards inscribed in social normality.

Conquest sets the poetry of the fifties in reaction to that of the forties through a series of binary contrasts: empiricism versus theory, intellect versus feeling. The forties poets gave the id too much of a say in things; they attempted to delete everything from their writing except emotion and submitted to the 'debilitating theory that poetry *must* be metaphorical'. Even more than 'technical and emotional gifts', poets must have 'integrity and judgement enough to prevent surrender to subjective moods or social pressures'. What distinguishes fifties poetry is that it 'submits to no great systems of theoretical constructs nor agglomerations of unconscious commands. It is free from both mystical and logical compulsions and – like modern philosophy – is empirical in its attitude to all that comes.' Reference is also made to 'reverence for the real person or event' and 'refusal to abandon a rational structure and comprehensible language'. None of this is argued through; positions are affirmed as though their truth were self-evident. We might consider that any view of 'social pressures' that presents them in an invariably negative light is likely itself to have developed in response to social compulsions, and that corollary notions of integrity and the person will equally have unconscious social derivation. The proclaimed affinity with 'modern philosophy' (a rare instance of Conquest's claims to representative status involving reference to contemporary nonliterary concerns) does little more than seek prestige for uncommitted attitudes. The reference to rational structure, on the other hand, seems to echo the ideas of the American critic Yvor Winters (whose Thomist logic we might expect Conquest to disdain) to which Davie had responded with enthusiasm in the late forties.

It need not concern us much that Conquest's arguments in 1956 were incoherent and question-begging; what matters is that he codified a successfully assertive group position based on exclusion and prejudice. His arguments in the Introduction to *New Lines – II* show how the needs of the situation had changed. 'The influences making for distortion in poetry are now different from what they were seven years ago.' It was no longer necessary to take up a position against the previous decade, nor to claim attention as representative of the moment. (It was, after all, no longer the fifties, and part of Conquest's intention now was to forestall new claimants.) In retrospect, Conquest argues, the importance of *New Lines* was not topicality but rather its demonstration that 'as against the work of the past few decades, a good deal of contemporary poetry had returned to the cardinal traditions of English verse'. Conquest's rejection of the modern tradition is now explicit. The authentic English tradition is still vulnerable, however, for 'a great deal is still being written which affects to be founded on new, or at least different, attitudes'.

This disclosure of position, while it confirms what was implicit in the Movement's beginnings, also serves to underline divergences within it at a point where poetry and criticism peel away from one another. The point might be put thus: when the Movement lost whatever poetic integrity it initially possessed, its polemic apparatus was detached and naturalized as critical commonplace – that the modern movement was over, the need for experiment no longer existed. (In his conversation with Alvarez, on the other hand, Davie could remark, referring to Pound, Eliot and Yeats, 'Let's go back, then, to them, and go forward from there.') Conquest does not pause to define his tradition but says that it has fallen into decline from time to time through the imposition of critical fashions. What he objects to are pretensions to extend the range of that constant tradition, and the concomitant esteem of novelty, as he sees it; the poet's relationship with tradition is normally unselfconscious. Such arguments allow Conquest to generalize the authority of *New Lines*; it is more appropriate, now, not to appear embattled, but to lay claim to as much as possible.

His polemic in 1963 is directed primarily at arguments put forward by Alvarez in his Introduction to *The New Poetry*, and the dispute is no longer between generations (within the perspective of history) but internal (within 'the traditions of English verse'). Conquest reinforces this internalization both by taking pains not to identify his adversary and by presenting his adversary's position as that of a critic (i.e. wilfully modish) rather than an anthologist. Alvarez's arguments thus appear as those of a depraved taste and its prescriptive criticism – as another example of that systematic criticism which pretends to make its judgements 'derive rigorously from the nature of the poem discussed'. (Judgement, in other words, derives from the critics, and we judge of critics by their taste.) What Conquest objects to is the demand for powerful feeling at the expense of 'balance and proportion', suggestions that 'the circumstances of modern life . . . open up hitherto unsuspected psychological depths', and the recommendation of European and American poets as models for English poetry. Against these, Conquest argues that

> the human condition from which the poetry of one country springs cannot be readily tapped by that of another. The British culture is receptive to immigration, if not to invasion: but it remains highly idiosyncratic. It is part of our experience, and for that no one else's experience, however desirable, can be a substitute.

The adaptability of Conquest's polemic was its great strength; the care not to identify too precisely what was argued against, and to make it instead a projection of the case in hand, pre-empted many possibilities of disagreement. The assertion of an unspecified, native tradition underpinned claims to be authoritative and inclusive, so that the most disabling argument against Alvarez was not that he sanctioned bad poets but that he might corrupt or mislead good ones. To disagree successfully with Conquest – to forestall, that is to say, the possibility of any disagreement being reconciled and generalized by the inclusiveness of the terms in which he argued – would have entailed taking issue with his version of history. Any disagreement about 'modernism', for example, would remain a matter of recuperable detail if it failed to challenge his view of tradition. Yet this polemic strategy, so absorptively coercive, was so little substantiated in detail that its pretensions seem hardly to have commanded notice. On the other hand, both Tomlinson and Alvarez were ready, with Conquest, to write off the poetry of the forties as 'vicious' (Tomlinson), 'English poetry . . . at its nadir' (Alvarez).

The differences between Tomlinson's and Alvarez's opposition to *New Lines* are worth attention; neither of them, however, denies its coherence (as, in a sense, the editors of *Mavericks* did by challenging its claim to be representative). Furthermore, the particular qualities they object to – for Tomlinson its 'suburban mental ratio', for Alvarez its 'gentility' – are roughly identical. But although this pinpoints something about Movement poetry in general there is no broader agreement between them. They do not share a point of view. Tomlinson considers the 'myth' surrounding the Movement poets, that they represent the average man and write for a middlebrow public, but concludes instead that they are making for themselves 'another cosy corner . . . in our watered down, democratic culture', and that they thus hardly differ from the forties poets (he instances Tambimuttu's editorial line in

Poetry London) who propounded an artistic democracy of the unconscious. He objects to the Movement's parochialism, failure of nerve,
and merely negative virtues, and deplores the lack of 'high and objective criteria' that allows *New Lines* to be taken for 'a significant literary
fact'. This lack of objectivity, in self-awareness as much as in critical
standards, is Tomlinson's main concern, the key to all the Movement's
deficiencies. The poets in *New Lines* 'show a singular want of vital
awareness of the continuum outside themselves, of the mystery bodied
over against them in the created universe'.

Regard for the presence of the object, in Tomlinson's own poetry,
was the issue which prevented Davie and Alvarez reaching agreement
in their 1962 conversation. What Tomlinson objects to as the imposition
of a poet's 'mental conceit of himself' (their 'suburban mental ratio' in
the case of the *New Lines* poets) on 'that which is beyond himself'
might be seen, moreover, as the very thing argued for by Alvarez in *The
New Poetry*, with the difference only that risk and extremity are the
'mental conceits' preferred to gentility. Alvarez's hope for poetry, a
combination of the 'psychological integrity and insight' of D. H.
Lawrence and the 'technical skill and formal intelligence' of T. S.
Eliot, need not detain us; nor need the inconsistency of his explanation
of the failure of the experimentalism of 'Eliot and the rest' to 'take on'
in England – both because it had been 'an essentially American
concern' and because of the operation of a series of 'negative feed-
backs'. (By this he means, I think, that English poets reacted against
experimentalism, although to say this doesn't tell us why they did so.)
Alvarez, with some circumspection, can justify experimentalism when
it is able to 'open poetry up to new areas of experience', but the
distinction implied between this and unjustified experiment is not
explored. (As usual, we wonder why such distinctions need not apply to
writing in conventional forms.) His argument is that 'negative feed-
backs' (which presumably have kept English poetry closed to those
'new areas of experience') can be short-circuited without having to go
back to Eliot: American poetry in the forties, unlike English poetry,
had assimilated the experiments of the twenties, and this new poetic
generation, represented at its best by John Berryman and Robert
Lowell, exemplifies a 'new seriousness' English poetry sorely needs.
The revised edition of *The New Poetry* (1966) added Anne Sexton and
Sylvia Plath to Alvarez's model of the American vanguard. (It is worth
noting, while American influences on English poetry are in question,
that Alvarez had no truck with many American poets who emerged in

the fifties. Charles Olson, Robert Duncan, Robert Creeley and Edward Dorn, for example, heirs to the practices of Ezra Pound and William Carlos Williams, were noticed with interest by Tomlinson and Davie, among others, although generally disdained by English critical opinion.)

Alvarez's argument may depend on the notion of new experience, but he is not setting up as an advocate of experiment; nor need he, since although English poetry has not assimilated the experiments of 'Eliot and the rest' American poetry has. In an important sense, therefore, his disagreement with the Movement is less radical than Tomlinson's. Tomlinson does not employ any such crude notion as 'the experimental', but he goes beyond rejection of the personal and social values implicit in Movement poetry and argues that a willed or manipulated self-image (a failure of objectivity) impedes the realization of a work of art. Alvarez, on the other hand, objects to the inadequacy of the self-image of the English poet ('the post-war Welfare State Englishman') rather than its aesthetic consequences. Gentility, he argues, the 'belief that life is always more or less orderly', is 'a stance which is becoming increasingly precarious to maintain' in the face of 'the more uncompromising forces of our time', 'forces of disintegration which destroy the old standards of civilization'. Alvarez, pointing to the scale of twentieth-century evils, concentration camps, genocide, the threat of nuclear war, looks back as far as the mass slaughter in trench warfare of the First World War. This might strike us as powerfully persuasive evidence were it in fact the 'new experience' he had in mind. What Alvarez is in fact impressed by are parallels between modern experience of these evils and perceptions derived from psychoanalysis, and 'our recognition of the ways in which the same forces are at work within us'. The forces of disintegration, that is to say, are not social, political or economic, but psychological (see also Chapter 4); but what this psychological insight is made to require of poetry is that it treat all events as projections of the poet's psyche. 'Dominant public savagery', 'the full range of his experience' – the import of such phrases reduces to the statement that 'the writer can no longer deny with any assurance the fears and desires he does not wish to face'.

Alvarez's espousal of what is commonly termed 'confessional' poetry, his advocacy of personal risk and extremity, even suicide, are notorious but consistent with his argument that psychoanalysis constitutes an unavoidable new area of experience for poetry. His praise of Robert Lowell, particularly the Lowell of *Life Studies*, is understandable, for Lowell is pre-eminently a poet in whom the confusions and violence of the age (these are question-begging notions, of course) are figured out in terms of his own disturbance. But, leaving aside any mis-givings this may provoke – for example, that in such poetry the poet takes rather too much (of our experience, say) upon himself or herself – Alvarez's special pleading should not obscure the fact that he shares a broad agreement with Conquest about the proper mode of discourse of poetry. The agreement is so fundamental, in fact, as to be in danger of passing beneath notice. Both Movement and 'confessional' poetry share a discourse which operates through the personal lyric, often dramatic in its presentation, and employs an elaborate figurative language to draw together the self and its objects. The site of Con-quest's disagreement with Alvarez, therefore, suggests that his 'English tradition' is concerned less with any maintenance of tra-ditional poetic decorum than with an ideological preference among self-images.

When Alvarez contrasts Larkin's 'At Grass' and Hughes's 'A Dream of Horses', in order to consider the 'kind of success' different styles allow, the distinctions he discovers are less convincing if we pause to consider the similarities between the two poems. Both are surfeited with extended figurative devices which tie the things referred to – horses, in each case – to the speakers of the poems: in Larkin's poem the speaker is an implied observer whose presence is reinforced by inter-jected qualifications and reservations, 'perhaps', 'what must be'; in Hughes's poem the speakers are a chorus of stable lads. In both poems the horses are allegorized by the speakers' double view of them: in Larkin's poem racehorses retired to grass are seen against after-images of their fame and glory on the course; in Hughes's poem the speakers dream of powerful, overwhelming horses unlike the pitiful hacks they mind. Both poems are allegories of an absent fullness of being, although Larkin, as we might expect, is the more ambivalent in his treatment of this conventional theme. His devices undercut the glories associated with the race meeting, and imply that the horses, although approach-ing the end of life, have more authenticity in their anonymous retire-ment than in any role they played in racing and its annals. Hughes, by contrast, uses his devices for emphasis and amplification, in a way that deflects the suggestion (rather commonplace, nevertheless) the poem might be making that the grooms' relations to their charges are inverted in dream. Alvarez's conclusion that Hughes's horses, unlike Larkin's, 'have a violent, impending presence' may indicate a prefer-ence but is not very much to the point. What presence there is in

Hughes's poem is a presence of dream images. But this is a minor issue. Both poems, as allegories, ask to be read not for their presentational immediacy but for what they say about life. What differentiates the poems is their approach to the nostalgia of diminished being (and here, possibly, remarks about suburban mental ratios and Welfare State Englishmen have some bearing). Larkin suggests that although we may experience such feelings we should not allow ourselves to be too affected by them, whereas Hughes, I take it, suggests that we can imagine or dream ourselves out of them. Neither poet questions the sources or conditions of such feelings, but takes them for granted. Arguably, however, the personal lyric is not a mode conducive to asking such questions; nostalgia is, so to speak, fully naturalized within the mode, and irony the only restraint able to be applied against it.

Twenty years after Davie's recognition of Larkin's effective custody of 'our England' as poetic subject-matter, Larkin is being seriously canvassed as the next poet laureate. The only cynicism such views admit is the suggestion that the laureate's official duties are now excused. Davie's bestowal of laurels was, by comparison, tongue-in-cheek and mildly subversive. He was not looking for official recognition of England's most distinguished poet. It cannot be disputed, surely, that this is how Larkin is perceived today – not only distinguished but quintessentially English, insular almost, and not easily appreciated by American readers. His common sense has moved from being that of the common man, as Alvarez recognized it, to that of the political Right. He puts pretentiousness and the second-rate in their place. But these are no more than the terms in which his general esteem has been negotiated. (What strikes *me* most in Larkin's poetry is a torpid apprehensiveness about death in the living moment, and a refusal of any compensations for this; it's a moving but idiosyncratic affective conformation.) His recognition of 'our England', polluted rivers, cheap consumer goods, and relics of spiritual and national grandeur, is uniformly marked by regret. He is far from being a documentarist, however. Instead, his poems seek to reinsert the values of which they collect the residual signs within the unconscious lives of ordinary people. It is as though, if the landscape and institutions of post-war England are the dumb reminders of a better past, that past at least lives on in its people, latent but unexpressed.

The lyric self cannot stand for either term of this transaction, though it can to an extent collude with both. In 'Church Going', for example, Larkin's speaker aligns himself ('Bored, uninformed') with those for whom a sacred edifice can have little meaning, and a secular wit plays ironically over his account of a sightseeing visit: 'Hatless, I take off / My cycle-clips in awkward reverence'. But, for all the ignorance he claims, this visitor displays in passing some knowledge of church fitments – font, lectern, plate and pyx. Such ambivalence disturbs much of the language of the poem, which runs a gamut of plainness, sarcasm and portentousness, so that we are uneasily aware of the incomplete adjustment of the poet's intentions and the serviceability of his persona; at best we might feel 'his' wit is a form of discomfort. The poem appears to intend an optimistic assertion of spiritual persistence, 'someone will forever be surprising / A hunger in himself to be more serious', but what that seriousness might mean, what it is that is never 'obsolete', is expressed in a frigid mixture of abstractions: 'all our compulsions meet, / Are recognized, and robed as destinies.' Compulsion may turn into destiny, the profane become sacred, but the process seems to be automatic, dispensation perhaps rather than discipline. The poem does well to end, on an altogether less transcendent note, affirming the secular, graveyard wisdom that everyone must die.

'Church Going' uses comparatively little figurative language and instead adjusts its tone to expository shifts of feeling. Although it is an established anthology piece, and did much to get Larkin noticed, it is not really typical of his work in its discursive procedures. What is typical (and, as I argue, is typical in one way or another of what is perceived as the canonical poetry of the period) is what we saw in 'At Grass', the use of verbal figures as devices to readjust the observer's position towards the objective relations perceived. (This is the same type of substitutive device, but more extendable and controllable, as the grammatical figure 'Hatless, I take off my cycle-clips', and like that, too, as often as not produces an effect of aloof wittiness.) In 'The Whitsun Weddings', another anthology piece, the mode is fully developed. The poem details events on a train journey from the provinces to London, and this synoptic trajectory might be considered as an emblem of the poem's theme; we see the commonplace view from the carriage window but also, exceptionally, a series of departing honeymoon couples seen off at successive stations by their wedding guests. It is all unremittingly 'our England', with a sense of hallucination in the heat and sun, and the people are generalized through grotesque detail which is always on the verge of registering distaste. But the poem's figures, starting with those which present the passage of the train through the landscape, emphasize meeting and incorporation; the people observed may be coarse and vulgar but they are included within a figure greater than themselves, marriage is still ritual and sacrament despite its secular trappings.

But only the poet sees this (in this poem we hardly feel it necessary to observe a formal distinction between poet and speaker), and he sees it not only as observed event but also as complex simile ('I thought of London spread out in the sun, / Its postal districts packed like squares of wheat') replete with connotations of sexual surrender and fecundity, dispersal and unity ('spread', 'packed'), the whole and the part. (Yet what exactly are 'squares of wheat'? Fields? Not English fields, surely. Grains? Breakfast cereal?) Like 'Church Going', 'The Whitsun Weddings' is expository, yet in this case the different stages of the poem are drawn together by the consistency of the figures. Furthermore, the figures accomplish the poet's participation in what is observed. But at the same time we might feel that his participation is also imposition, a projection in the face of alternatives too appalling to contemplate ('An uncle shouting smut; and then the perms, / The nylon gloves and jewellery-substitutes'). Moreover, we might also feel that just as the description of the ordinary, secular life of these people is selective (and admonitory), so the redemptive figures are somewhat worked up, fanciful rather than felt. In the television programme 'Philip Larkin at 60' (*The South Bank Show*, ITV, 30 May 1982) Larkin, appearing only as cuffs and hands, took the viewer through his notebooks to show how, searching for an expression of 'fruitfulness', he arrived at 'packed like squares' from 'spread like fields' via 'packed like fields'. Not that there is anything necessarily wrong with such a derivation; it merely goes to show how Larkin's plainness conceals a studied indirectness. But this example also confirms the way the creative energy of the personal lyric is focused in its invention of figures; and the energy of the figures, the rewriting of the world as it is, is made to guarantee the authenticity of the person, the subject. But such guarantees hold good only for the subject, not for his experience; we are asked to trust the poet, not the poem.

Beyond controversy

Since 1945 the major poetic controversies, through which current poetic concerns have received their most effective public exposure, occurred within the decade bracketed by the publication of the first *New Lines* anthology and the revised edition of *The New Poetry*. By and large our sense of the situation of poetry today is conditioned by the arguments of 1956–66. The extent to which those arguments still determine our sense of poetic achievement since the war underscores the suggestion that, for all the differences and disagreements implied by those arguments, certain basic, undeclared – even unrecognized – agreements bound the controversialists together. Positions taken up on behalf of the Movement had the power and flexibility to absorb and merge with those of its successors; the non-partisan, individualist strategies of Movement poets enabled them, when the time came, to transcend their collective moment in the mid-fifties. (Donald Davie, apparently, suggested 'Divergent Lines' as an apt title for the representatives of the old guard in *New Lines – II*.) *The New Poetry*, once it is conceded that the qualities of the American models it advocated were not reflected in the work of its English poets, is *New Lines* thinned and agitated.

It is surely worthy of consideration – to set against the notions of variety and pluralism and vital difference which controversy might seem to substantiate, of different poetic discourses pursuing different goals – that our three canonical poets, Larkin, Hughes and Heaney, share the same publisher, are apparently thought to possess similar market potential, and imply the same sort of readership. If we accept unreservedly the proposition that they are our best poets, if perhaps we feel it appropriate that Faber and Faber, with their prestigious backlist including Eliot and Auden, should dominate the poetry market, then what notions of continuity and pure quality are we dealing with? Might we not find, in view of the resolution and incorporation of the controversialists' differences within our current view of the period, that their unreflected agreement that the poetry of the forties was an unmitigated disaster is also not to be taken at face value? Should we not question the notion of a homogeneous 'poetry of the forties', and might we not also suppose that such a myth possessed advantages for its promulgators? Yet from what position, in relation to any view of what is canonical, can we begin to ask such questions? What is the evidence to consider? At this point I do no more than propose a few materials as a start to answering such questions.

The two most important events of the forties were the war and the Labour government which administered the return to peacetime conditions. As far as publishing was concerned, both books and periodicals, it seems correct to see both these events as largely similar in their effects: the war encouraged an audience for the arts, and publishers, despite economy measures, were able to carry on their business. On the

11 The 2nd National Jazz Festival, at Richmond (1962)

face of it there was a boom in literary publishing, of poetry especially, which benefited not only established firms such as Faber and Faber but also smaller, speculative enterprises such as the Fortune Press and the Grey Walls Press. There was a rash of magazines, anthologies and annuals. Post-war austerity seems to have perpetuated the conditions in

12 Hyde Park 'Happening' (1967)

which this sort of publishing flourished, whereas the relaxation of austerity (the availability of consumer goods and the new patterns of spending that ensued) seems to have reduced the market for poetry, even while publishing in general expanded (see Chapter 5). Within a comparatively short period of time a number of small literary publishers and magazines either went out of business or found themselves forced to operate on a considerably reduced scale: Grey Walls Press, Falcon Press, *Poetry London*, *Poetry Quarterly*. The mass-market *Penguin New Writing* folded. It was reported that Routledge could not continue Geoffrey Grigson's book-format periodical *The Mint* because they overestimated sales by thousands. Depression in the poetry market seems to have lasted into the mid-fifties: Conquest makes the point, in *New Lines*, that less poetry was published than formerly, and that contributors to the anthology had, for the most part, published only in pamphlet format with small presses. But if this reminds us, parenthetically, that the Movement was an attempt to win recognition for new writers, it was an attempt upon virtually abandoned territory. Many poets who began their careers in the forties had found themselves without publishers in the fifties.

For other reasons, too, the Movement's ambitions met with little resistance. Many poets of the previous generation had stopped writing, or had put their literary careers on ice (while establishing themselves in new post-war jobs, for example), or were in the process of remaking their style. In the latter category we might mention Roy Fuller (although the changes are less drastic than is sometimes suggested), Norman MacCaig or, rather later, W. S. Graham. In the former categories, not always possible to distinguish exactly, we might think of Charles Madge, Kenneth Allott, F. T. Prince, Nicholas Moore, David Gascoyne and J. F. Hendry. (An even earlier generation, that of Spender and MacNeice, was able to maintain its impetus. Arguably, it was sufficiently well established to receive little effect from the war or its aftermath.) The most prestigious career to terminate, however, in a way that seemed to mark the end of an era, was that of Dylan Thomas. The Movement, of course, held Thomas in particular disrepute, and gave the impression that it thought his premature death a deserved consequence of lifestyle and poetic style combined. He and his 'followers' (a somewhat mythical company of scapegoats), and the mindless romanticism for which it was held they stood, were made to bear the burden of responsibility for the low standards of poetry in the forties. Leaving such judgements to one side for the moment, it is worth noting that whereas Movement poets often reflect their times in more or less direct ways – in their individualist concept of the 'ordinary' man, for example, or their tentative recognition of consumers' pleasures – and repudiated any connections they may have had with the poetry of the forties, the poets of the forties were, for the most part, poets of the late thirties in the first instance, and responded to the war not in an empirical fashion, as though it were some unprecedented novelty, but as the fulfilment of their worst fears and predictions. Many of these poets, albeit in rather an obscure way, saw the transition to peace as requiring a search for solutions to the same set of problems for which the war had failed to provide a solution.

According to such a logic, while 1945 may be a date of the first order in our social and political life, it may not serve us as well when we try to reconstruct a context for poetry. But, equally, we may find no other date which serves us better. If we think in terms of generations, however, it is possible to argue that poets born after 1920 (the threshold adopted for *New Lines*) were able to repudiate their war experience, that having had their careers delayed by wartime conditions they set out to make up for lost time. Donald Davie says as much of himself in his recollections *These the Companions* (1982).[10] Poets born after 1908, on the other hand, but before 1920, would tend to stand in a very different relation to the war. (And in many cases their regular careers were postponed not only by wartime but by pre-war conditions.) The post-1920 generation would all, in one important respect, begin as survivors. The poets of the earlier generation, on the other hand, would have experienced war in part as a threat to survival, in part also as a prolongation and culmination of their pre-war experience. If, briefly, we can imagine Roy Fuller and Donald Davie as mess-mates (naval service took Fuller to East Africa and Davie to Russia), then we might see how, although empirically their wartime experience would be similar, their respective stances towards it must have been different in ways having little to do with personality.

But this in itself would not explain why the generation of 1908 had such a poor hold on the post-war poetic world. Indeed, to all appearances that generation flourished in the late forties. It was extensively documented, for example, in the USA by Kenneth Rexroth in his 1949 anthology *The New British Poets*,[11] but yet significantly this remarkable anthology was not brought out in an English edition. If we wished to make a representation of the diminishing presence of this generation of poets, its rapid acceleration towards vanishing-point in the fifties (ignoring, that is to say, the re-emergence of some of its members in the late sixties, at a time when other poets of an even earlier generation were breaking silence), we might note the rapid eclipse of Dylan Thomas's reputation after his death, and the publication of probably the last collection of forties poetry, in the 'bad' sense, W. S. Graham's

The Nightfishing (1955). In the same year Philip Larkin's *The Less
Deceived* was published by the Marvell Press in Hull, and further
impressions were very quickly called for. Graham, by then, must have
seemed to Larkin's readers very much a back number. It would appear
that in 1955 vested interests in the publishing of poetry no longer
addressed the most promising market. We should bear in mind, also,
the charges made by Tomlinson, that *New Lines* was the culmination of
a sustained publicity campaign, and consisted only of OK names. If the
Movement took issue with what it conceived of as the 'London literary
racket', then perhaps we should see the Movement as, in turn, not only
an academic literary racket but also the creator of a new audience for
poetry, in schools and colleges and among teachers of English.

When we look at the poetry of the forties we find that the collective
and interlocutory manner of address which we associate with Auden,
and the phrase-making habit, are strongly persistent. We might feel
that these are modes of candour and generosity, but equally we might
note that neither the mode nor the associated quality of feeling is
characteristic of Movement poetry. If we consider Roy Fuller as an
example of such persistence, we might also note that his attempts to
detach himself from his pre-war politics (Marxist) and aesthetics
(mildly surreal), and to establish his themes as those of the poet as
private citizen, although they direct much of his subsequent career,
remain liable to the pull of contrary experience and of an imagination
that cannot wilfully forgo its past. His best poems are those in which
such conflicts are played out. In '1948', for example, (*Epitaphs and
Occasions*, 1949) panic overtakes the poet while he reads in his garden.

> I hear behind the words
> And noise of birds
> The drumming aircraft; and am blind till they have gone.

But although his panic subsides ('blind till they are gone') the poet
goes beyond the personal occasion of the poem to consider our tenure
on peace ('behind' is exact and anticipatory in its perceptual and moral
ambiguity).

> It is as though the lease
> Of crumbling peace
> Had run already and that life was as before.[12]

But this is not the kind of forties poetry so powerfully objected to in the
fifties and sixties. It may be irresolute, and it may end with a trope

('The gnawed incredible existence of a dream') which seems persuas-
ively to refer to normality as a dream from which we will be woken, but
it is civil and decorous none the less.

When Robert Conquest deplored 'the theory that poetry *must* be
metaphorical' he was being caustic, but not using his terms with any
exactitude. (Larkin and Hughes, as we have seen, rely on figurative
devices, on metaphor and simile.) What Conquest was gesturing
towards, I think, was the extensive use in forties poetry of images and
symbols, and we can best understand his objections to such procedures
in the light of his claimed empiricism. Dylan Thomas's images, and the
connections he establishes between them, cannot be empirically veri-
fied by appeal to a world independent of the poem – independent in
theory, though sanctioned in practice by the poet's warrant that it is
that real world, shared (but at a distance) with the reader, to which the
poem refers. Such verification requirements, which lie behind objections to Thomas's poems, do more than assume the incompatibility of
language and reality; they require that poetry observe the prevailing
contractual usages in language and hence that it be bound by the
commonsense meanings of the times. (Alvarez's arguments, for all
their radical posture, failed to address themselves to the preconditions
of poetic meaning, which involve the position of discourse within
language. Any language use, even the most unconsidered or apparently nonsensical, entails some immediate seizure of reality.) Hughes's
'A Dream of Horses' observes a clear-cut distinction between real world
and dream world; we may move between one and the other, as we wake
or sleep, but we know which is which. (Such knowledge, of course, is
not operative in both worlds and implies a confident demarcation of
reality.) In Fuller's '1948' the distinction, for him and for us, is more in
doubt. Thomas, on the other hand, insisted that his poems should be
read literally; to take him at his word would be to commit a serious
assault upon the empirical sanctions of meaning.

The collective and interlocutory manner, as I have called it, does not
assume the need for empirical verification; it looks no further than the
experience and expectations of the group implied or addressed. Hence
the power of phrase-making, the group acting as the poet's resonating
board; hence, also, the tendency to semantic drift, commonly noticed
in Auden's pre-war poetry, for example. But if we see this manner as a
compromised attempt to restore to poetry a social reference without, at
the same time, reintroducing the authority of the poet's subjectivity, as
I believe we must, we can see other attempts to redefine the subject

matter of poetry which go further in their displacement of the discursive centrality of the self. It is in this light that we should approach the work of the poets associated with the 'New Apocalypse', the poets most typically associated with the vices of the forties. The term 'Apocalyptic', broadly used to refer to the poets influenced by Thomas, now has exclusively pejorative overtones. I will not begin to describe the Apocalypse as a movement, but it is important to note in passing that it emerged in anticipation of the outbreak of war, and that the poets most closely involved with its publications and responsible for its programme (in so far as their critical writings can be said to constitute a programme) – J. F. Hendry, for example – tend to deny Thomas's influence. Instead it makes more sense, for the time being, to think of the Apocalypse in terms of a style and its practitioners, bearing in mind Conquest's objections to what he thought of as metaphor. The mode is lyric, but treats the person as a site in which experience is to be acted out as conflict. It presents a dense, often violent rhetoric, from which the guiding and controlling presence of a speaking subject – constructing the poem's framework of interpretation around its personal authority, and furnishing its empirical experience as the horizon of the poem's range of reference – is excluded. The self (the subject, the poet) does not stand at the centre of and mediate the reader's experience of the poem. That which, in grammatical relationships, is consigned to the role of the predicated, defined and subordinate, is afforded scope for its own resistance and counter-action. We might think of this as occurring in the space vacated by the figures of conventional rhetoric. (Hence, I believe, some of our experience of difficulty and obscurity when we read such poetry.) This theory does not, needless to say, suggest that such poems have written themselves, that they have no human author, but rather that the poet does not constitute at one and the same time the poem's protagonist and boundary. No surrogate enactment of the poet's intelligence is provided as part of the poem's interior, and instead the poem claims to represent the whole person. Through such a mode the things referred to in the poem participate actively in what is imagined, they are not merely figurative devices, and the poet is acted upon as well as acting – an experiencing creature rather than a mastering intelligence.

In this passage from *The Nightfishing*, for example (chosen both because it is a late example and because Graham stood somewhat on the fringe of the Apocalyptic movement, and thus illustrates the diffusion of the manner), sea, fishing boat and fishermen exist in a relation one to another of active resistance.

> See how, like an early self, it's loath to leave
> And stares from the scuppers as it swirls away
> To be clenched up. What a great width stretches
> Farsighted away fighting in its white straits
> On either bow, but bears up our boat on all
> Its plaiting strands. This wedge driven in
> To the twisting water, we rode. The bow shores
> The long rollers.[13]

These relations are not simply observed, they impinge upon and constitute themselves through the writing. So there are moral as well as formal issues in question here: the personification of the natural world; the vigorous, energized language; the release of individual words ('shores' in the passage above) into equivocal syntactic and semantic relations, which are consequences of the way the poem's discourse marginalizes the self. We may think, with Conquest *et al.*, that these are examples of poetic vices, but that does not allow us to think that they are devices employed for their own sake, rather than means employed to accomplish a distinct mode of discourse. In the poetry of Nicholas Moore or David Gascoyne the commonsense data base of the empirical self is eluded by less overtly disruptive means, in particular by presentation of a non-authoritative self, socially marginal or suffering. If we wish to recuperate their poetry (and I do not see how we can afford to neglect it), it will entail severe criticism of the terms in which the accepted canon of post-war poetry has been constructed.

Different examples

In the poetic tradition now dominant the authoritative self, discoursing in a world of banal, empirically derived objects and relations, depends on its employment of metaphor and simile for poetic vitality. These figures are conceptually subordinate to the empirical reality of self and objects, yet they constitute the nature of the poem. Poets are now praised above all else as inventors of figures – as rhetoricians, in fact – with a consequent narrowing of our range of appropriate response. Poetry has been turned into a reserve for small verbal thrills, a daring little frill round the hem of normal discourse; objects and relations in the natural and social worlds have an unresistant, token presence; at its most extreme, they serve as pretexts for bravura display. It does not wish to influence the reader's perceptions and feelings in the lived world: its intersection with that world is attenuated and discourages reading back; transformation is confined within the surprises and routines of rhetoric. The poems written by Craig Raine (in whom the Larkin–Hughes–Heaney canon extended itself in the late seventies) are the appropriate illustrations of this argument.

It may be felt that the case I am advancing depends on more substantiation than has been provided so far. By way of further example, therefore, here are some lines from Heaney's poem 'The Barn' (*Death of a Naturalist*, 1966), a poem which deals with the transference of enclosure and menace from a building to the intimacy of one's own feelings.

> Threshed corn lay piled like grit of ivory
> Or solid as cement in two-lugged sacks.
> The musty dark hoarded an armoury
> Of farmyard implements, harness, plough-socks.

The figures are applied in this opening stanza as an enrichment of description, but the same figurative technique is used to produce the space in which to effect the transfer from the elaborate figure of the barn itself to the speaker's affective life.

> Then you felt cobwebs clogging up your lungs
>
> And scuttled fast into the sunlit yard.
> And into nights when bats were on the wing
> Over the rafters of sleep, where bright eyes stared
> From piles of grain in corners, fierce, unblinking.

Here the figure is functional ('the rafters of sleep, where'); elsewhere figures project the speaker's terror.

> I lay face-down to shun the fear above.
> The two-lugged sacks moved in like great blind rats.[14]

The tropes proliferate and are uniformly highlighted, like consumer goods in a shop window, but they are uncoordinated (unlike Larkin's, say); the effect is gratuitous and draws attention finally to the poet's rhetorical ingenuity. Everything is of a piece, irrespective of what is being said. Our sense that the details bind together into a more complex meaning derives not from the figures but from the attenuated presence of autobiographical anecdote.

By way of contrast, here is an example of poetry from the middle of our period in which figures play a minor role. The following lines are from Charles Tomlinson's 'Geneva Restored' (*Seeing is Believing*, 1960), and we might note the careful, sustained description of the city's environs, with its suggestion that language might be compatible with what it refers to rather than necessarily appropriated to the special register of the poet's sensibility.

> Limestone, faulted with marble; the lengthening swell
> Under the terraces, the farms in miniature, until
> With its sheer, last leap, the Salève becomes
> The Salève, juts naked, the cliff which nobody sees
> Because it pretends to be nothing, and has shaken off
> Its seashore litter of house-dots. Beneath that,
> This – compact, as the other is sudden, and with an
>   inaccessible
> Family dignity: close roofs on a gravel height,
> Building knit into rock; the bird's nest of a place
> Rich in protestant pieties, in heroic half-truths
> That was Ruskin's.[15]

We might feel that the poet has his imagination reined in here; alternatively we might feel that his attention has been directed to good purpose. We might also feel that he is satisfied to let his language become so identified with his material as to court the risk of tautology, until we notice that the repetition of 'the Salève', coming as it does at the beginning of a new line, transforms the thing into its proper name by the formal capitalization of the first letter of the definite article: 'The Salève'. Not only is the poem's point of intersection with the world realized in detail, and in terms of particular, local qualities, the place is also remembered to possess a history, to be charged with it indeed as associations, with Protestantism, with Ruskin, which feed into the present. Yet none of these, it can be argued, owes its presence to the poet's intervention; they occur because the poet finds them interesting and they sustain the poem accordingly.

Tomlinson's poem, highly literal, informed by respect for the presence and character of things, is one example of a discourse unlike that of the dominant canon. But his is not the only one. In *Thomas Hardy and English Poetry* Donald Davie, although from a somewhat exclusive concern with landscape, writes about other poets, from the sixties, who conduct their writing in ways quite independent of the norms of the canon. It is a comment on the narrowness of our critical culture that such challenges have not been more fully recognized and taken up.

Notes

1 Blake Morrison, *Seamus Heaney* (London: 1982), p. 11.
2 Donald Davie, *Granta*, 68, 1229 (1963); repr. in *Thomas Hardy and English Poetry* (London: Routledge & Kegan Paul, 1973).
3 Robert Conquest (ed.), *New Lines* (London: Macmillan, 1956).
4 Charles Tomlinson, in *Essays in Criticism*, 7, 2 (April 1957).
5 Howard Sergeant and Dannie Abse (eds), *Mavericks* (London: Editions Poetry and Poverty, 1957).
6 A. Alvarez (ed.), *The New Poetry* (Harmondsworth: Penguin, 1962; rev. 1966).
7 Robert Conquest, *New Lines – II* (London: Macmillan, 1963).
8 *The Review*, 1 (1962).
9 Donald Davie, *Purity of Diction in English Verse* (London: Chatto & Windus, 1952) and *Articulate Energy* (London: Routledge & Kegan Paul, 1955).
10 Donald Davie, *These the Companions* (Cambridge: Cambridge University Press, 1982).
11 Kenneth Rexroth (ed.), *The New British Poets* (New York: New Directions, [1949]).
12 Roy Fuller, *Epitaphs and Occasions* (London: John Lehmann, 1949).
13 W. S. Graham, *The Nightfishing* (London: Faber, 1955).
14 Seamus Heaney, *Death of a Naturalist* (London: Faber, 1966).
15 Charles Tomlinson, *Seeing is Believing* (London: Oxford University Press, 1960).

Further reading

Bedient, Calvin. *Eight Contemporary Poets*. London: Oxford University Press, 1974.
Brown, Merle E. *Double Lyric: Divisiveness and Communal Creativity in Recent English Poetry*. London: Routledge, 1980.
Davie, Donald. *Thomas Hardy and English Poetry*. London: Routledge, 1973.
Dodsworth, Martin (ed.). *The Survival of Poetry*. London: Faber, 1970.
Hamilton, Ian. *A Poetry Chronicle*. London: Faber, 1973.
Homberger, Eric. *The Art of the Real: Poetry in England and America since 1939*. London: Dent, 1977.
Morrison, Blake. *The Movement: English Poetry and Fiction in the 1950s*. London: Oxford University Press, 1980.
Press, John. *Rule and Energy*. London: Oxford University Press, 1963.
Raban, Jonathan. *The Society of the Poem*. London: Harrap, 1971.

Schmidt, Michael, and Lindop, Grevel (eds). *British Poetry since 1960: A Critical Study*. Manchester: Carcanet Press, 1972.
Stanford, Derek. *The Freedom of Poetry*. London: Falcon Press, 1947.
Thwaite, Anthony. *Contemporary English Poetry*. London: Heinemann, 1959.
Treece, Henry. *How I See Apocalypse*. London: Lindsay Drummond, 1946.

8 Novels and the novel

STUART LAING

Most literary-historical accounts of novels become accounts of 'the novel' – a search for lines of development, a tradition, a stream, a progression, its 'rise', its 'turn', its 'death'. This is as true of post-war fiction as it is of the English novel as a whole. Initially 'the post-war novel' was a 'reaction against experiment'; the novels and pronouncements of Snow, Amis, Wain, Angus Wilson, Braine and Sillitoe were variously presented in evidence. This is now discredited, partly because it became clear that there was not much to react against (such inter-war novelists as Waugh, Greene, Orwell and Isherwood clearly prefigured the styles and concerns of the post-war 'reactionaries') and partly because the sixties produced much writing that did not fit the model (by John Fowles, B. S. Johnson, Doris Lessing and others). Indeed, the reaction against the 'reaction' model has been so strong that more recent accounts such as Bergonzi's *The Situation of the Novel* (1970) and Bradbury and Palmer's *The Contemporary English Novel* (1979) have tended to sweep some novelists (Wain, Storey, Sillitoe) entirely off the map. Attention has tended to refocus either around 'post-modernism' or simply on the general fact of fictional self-consciousness – 'the novel now, with its shifted range of possibilities . . . is in a general ferment'.[1]

It is hard to disagree with this comment except by querying the usefulness of 'the novel' itself as an organizing term. For, if a history of post-war novels is to be possible, novelists' formal choices need to be understood in relation both to the varying degrees of conscious and unconscious pressure on them to contribute to the development of 'the novel' in general, and to the demands of the particular forms of experience (and therefore of language) which they are seeking to represent. The lack of consensus on these issues within the period produced a wide range of forms of writing, not easily reducible to a single unilinear development. 'The post-war novel' is, then, not a single organism with a variety of manifestations; it is, rather, the site of conflicts, differences and a range of diverse literary projects.

The forties: austerity and insecurity

Work published in the late forties has particularly suffered neglect as a result of the subsequent critical search for the direction of 'the post-war novel'. The lack of a dominant fictional mode in the period is, however, better understood as part of a general cultural instability than as an automatic indication of a literary backwater. Certainly the cultural position of novels in 1945 was insecure. Publishing conditions (as well as the time constraints, on writers, of wartime activities, military and civilian) had discouraged the production of extended works of fiction during the war; poems, short stories and documentary reportage were preferred forms. At another level, many of the most prominent inter-war novelists were no longer active. The deaths of James Joyce and Virginia Woolf in 1941 symbolized the end of one particular possibility. Already Joyce seemed to have progressed, in *Finnegans Wake* (1939), where few could follow, while Virginia Woolf's *The Years* (1937) seemed to suggest some retreat from her earlier critiques of traditional realism. Forster's decision to write no more novels remained. Isherwood and Huxley had emigrated. Upward's promise never materialized, while both Orwell and Waugh (like many others) found the war a major disruption of their previous patterns of writing. Waugh never completed the novel he was writing in 1939; the unfinished manuscript was later published as *Work Suspended* (1942) with the prefatory comment that it had been abandoned because in wartime 'the kind of people he wrote about would cease to be of interest'.[2] Orwell was more sweeping – stating in January 1941 that 'only the mentally dead are capable of sitting down and writing novels while this nightmare is going on'.[3] Both returned to writing fiction during the war, but with the traces of this sense of a major cultural hiatus clearly in evidence.

During the late forties there was, then, little evidence of any consensus about a novelistic aesthetics upon which practice might be founded. The modernist experiment had passed by and the left-wing literary climate of the thirties had failed to develop an adequate social-ist novel – the competing demands of political tendency, social realism and aesthetic structure never being reconciled. As the war made committed political writing irrelevant (by defining all literature as political in the sense of being intrinsically opposed to fascist barbar-ism), so the reportage element was absorbed easily into war docu-mentary. The novels of the late forties offer, in the face of this, a variety of approaches to the problem of re-establishing directions – both for individual writers and for the purposes of novels in general.

Philip Toynbee's *Tea with Mrs Goodman* (1947) appears particularly self-conscious about this task. This short novel (published by *Horizon* and recalling Cyril Connolly's famous first editorial in 1940 – 'our standards are aesthetic and our politics are in abeyance') deliberately avoids explicit representation of the war experience or contemporary social reality. A combination of Bloomsbury setting (a Woolfian tea party presented through seven separate consciousnesses), thirties rhetoric (as in references to the 'Truly Strong Man' of Auden's early poetry and echoes of Day Lewis's secularization of Hopkins's diction) and early forties romanticism (in the development of sustained mythic and religious imagery) produces a remarkable, almost self-parodic, mandarin style, characterized by frequent rhetorical questions and exclamation marks. In retrospect, however, this attempt to gather together and re-energize divergent strands of recent literary movements seems to summarize the end of certain inter-war developments rather than to mark a transition to new beginnings.

It was two more established writers, transforming their existing prac-tices in response to wartime conditions, who produced the most distinc-tive and symptomatic novels of the forties. Both Evelyn Waugh's *Brideshead Revisited* (1945) and George Orwell's *Nineteen Eighty-Four* (1949) are uncompromising negative statements about imagined post-war worlds which threaten the central elements of their respective value systems. Waugh's novel maintains a balance between using the narrator Charles Ryder as a device to present the decline of the March-main family and being concerned with the effect of the family (and the house) on Ryder. Ryder's eventual career as an 'architectural painter' who, in the thirties, is 'called to all parts of the country to make portraits of houses that were soon to be deserted or debased'[4] throws some light on Waugh's attitude to his material. A nostalgia for twenties Oxford and aristocratic settings is accompanied by a presentation of decay through internal weakness, changing economic patterns (as embodied in Rex) and, finally, the social levelling of the organized war effort.

In his Preface to the 1959 edition, Waugh recognized the degree to which the novel's 'gluttony' for 'the splendours of the recent past, and for rhetorical and ornamental language' was a product of 'the period of Soya beans and Basic English' in which it was written. *Nineteen Eighty-Four* is equally a product of that period, although it seeks to extend its implications, not to react against them. After the schematic and (for Orwell) experimental *Animal Farm* (1945) Orwell had confidence in an approach that could combine his previously essentially separate political and literary motivations. *Nineteen Eighty-Four* builds on the central thesis of Burnham's *The Managerial Revolution* (1941) (see Chapter 2) to construct an opposition between the political and the human – the latter a post-Lawrentian concept with 'the sex instinct' at its centre. The anti-hero of Orwell's pre-war novels is now totally sympathetic within a rationed and bombed wartime London organized through totalitarian propaganda whose central mechanism is the control of language itself. Its corruption and ability to make (and unmake) history suggest writing (Winston's diary, Goldstein's book) as the central test of freedom and site of struggle.

This perception of the degree to which language constructs reality leads, however, not (as in early modernism or some sixties novels) to the questioning of the status of a primary 'real' but to an implicit valuing of a natural, direct language founded on truth to experience (as embodied in the 'plain style' of Orwell himself). O'Brien defines the key principle of totalitarian philosophy as 'collective solipsism' by which 'reality is inside the skull';[5] against this, Orwell, through Winston, defends 'the validity of experience', 'the very existence of external reality' and, above all, 'common sense', which is for the Party 'the heresy of heresies'.[6] *Nineteen Eighty-Four* sets out the terms for much fifties writing both by closing the door on active relations between literature and politics and by its deep suspicion of anything other than 'common sense' language and 'the empirical mode of thought'.[7]

Between Waugh's pre-war Arcadia and Orwell's post-war nightmare there were, of course, novels concerned directly with the war experience itself, although P. H. Newby writing in 1951 (in a British Council pamphlet, *The Novel 1945–51*) found little to impress him. In fact he found few novels of any kind about 'the horrors of war'. He suggested that this absence was due to 'the nature of total war itself, the fact that it spared no one and that many civilians suffered more than soldiers'.[8] Unlike the First World War, there was no gap of experience to be bridged, no tremendous hidden knowledge to be communicated. Novels about the Second World War tended rather to see it as a context which destabilized and intensified interpersonal relationships, as in Elizabeth Bowen's *The Heat of the Day* (1949) – an elaborate network of character studies in the manner of Henry James or E. M. Forster. Interest centres on the competing claims of personal relations (Stella's love for Robert) and the public good (Robert's political treason). The main action is set in London in 1942 after the dramatic experience of the Blitz has passed. Instead –

> This was the lightless middle of the tunnel. Faith came down to a slogan, desperately reworded to catch the eye, requiring to be pasted each time more strikingly on to hoardings and bases of monuments. . . . No, no virtue was to be found in the outward order of things: happy those who could draw from some inner source.[9]

The opposition here (slogans and hoardings against 'some inner source') echoes Orwell's more explicit delineations. However, Stella's moral problem is left rather unresolved both by Robert's difficulty in explaining his motives – 'You talk vaguely', Stella complains,[10] with good reason – and by his suicide. Some resolution is attempted by carrying the action forward to 1944 and D-Day and paralleling this with references to future new lives (an inheritance, a baby) for the supporting characters.

Graham Greene's *The End of the Affair* (1951) depends on a somewhat similar representation of a wartime London in which personal relations seem distorted, magnified and, often, suspended in time. However, the issues at stake are ultimately very different. The Catholic solution offered by Greene since *Brighton Rock* (1938) is now pressed very hard. The seedy urban locations and pessimistic readings of human nature of Greene's thirties fiction easily adapted to wartime and post-war conditions in *The Ministry of Fear* (1943) and, especially, *The Heart of the Matter* (1948). Here a specific stage of colonialism is offered as a paradigm for the exposure of general truths – 'here human nature hasn't had time to disguise itself'.[11] Scobie's moral dilemmas, failures and ultimate integrity constitute a late instance of a tradition of self-doubting liberal imperialist fiction running through Conrad, Forster and Orwell. This tradition was about to be overtaken by the history of decolonization and British withdrawal and, in literary terms, by the view from below, from Achebe, Soyinka and Ngugi, whose work begins from the point of contradiction between British cultural norms of language and literature and the need to represent the experience of the colonized as opposed to the colonizer.

Greene himself is one of the few novelists mentioned in Newby's survey who continued to develop new areas of work in the fifties and sixties. This is one reason why from a post-1954 position it has proved very difficult to see the forties novel as anything other than the culmination of pre-war directions or a series of false starts for the post-war novel. Newby's 1951 perspective is, then, of considerable value. Although not very enthusiastic about the general quality, he did assess the 'two most interesting novelists now writing in English' as Ivy Compton-Burnett and Henry Green. Both were established pre-war writers, although this was much more the case with Ivy Compton-Burnett, whose prolific production over a fifty-year period has only confirmed the narrowness of her range.

For Henry Green, on the other hand, the forties were the major period – seven of his nine novels were published between 1939 and 1952. Green's novels follow his own dictum that 'the novelist's approach must be oblique'; they demand attention more for their linguistic constructions and patterns of minor incidents than for their addressing of substantial issues of moral choice or social analysis. A characteristic procedure is the foregrounding of forms of disability and of perceptual distortion, both in central characters and in the environments presented. Blindness, deafness, old age, the effects of patterns of light, all suggest difficulties of recognition. In *Back* (1946) the predicament of Charley Summers, returning from the war (after four years as a prisoner), seeking personal and social reintegration, generates a pattern for the whole novel of the recognition of similarities and identities and the achievement of adequate replacements for loss. Charles finds echoes of Rose (his lover who died during his imprisonment) in roses (the object), in the word 'rose' (= has risen), in Rose's son (who may be his own) and in Rose's half-sister and double, Nancy. Towards the close of the novel Charles is unsure whether Nancy really is Rose (the ending almost suggests it does not matter either way). Nancy herself gradually takes Rose's place with Rose's parents and takes Charles on as a replacement for her own husband killed in the war. More generally through the whole text is the issue of Charles's adaptation to a new physical identity – his artificial leg replacing that blown off before his capture.

Green has been identified by Nathalie Sarraute as an early practitioner of the *nouveau roman*, and recent critical accounts have identified his major achievement as the 'defamiliarization' (of normative
reality) so much praised by the Russian formalists. In accepting these
assessments, however, it is important to note that, while Green is no
social realist, his forties novels depend on the construction of marginal
or temporary and unstable social environments for their settings.
Caught (1943) is centred around the London Fire Service in the Blitz,
Back on the problems of post-war readjustment, and *Concluding*
(1949) is set in a future in which the state has created new and arbitrary
forms of social institutions. There is a sense in which Green's already
established pre-war aesthetic procedures found the forties full of
appropriate situations and settings. If there is ever a serious attempt to
map the forties as a distinctive period of forms of writing, Henry Green
is the novelist most likely to profit from it.

First novels in the fifties: keeping control

In retrospect, forties fiction is characterized by the absence of new
novelists who later developed into established literary figures. By
contrast, in the early fifties a number of writers emerged who were to
form the core of a new, distinctively post-war generation and who, in
most cases, have continued to publish novels for nearly three decades.
Between 1950 and 1954 alone, first novels were produced by Angus
Wilson, Doris Lessing, John Wain, Kingsley Amis, Iris Murdoch and
William Golding. This wave of new writers tended to obscure work of
the forties and, at the same time, stimulated the quest for a unilinear
account of 'the novel'. In fact, if there is a common feature here, it is an
uncertainty about the role and voice of the novelist and a tendency to
incorporate such issues into novels. But they are unevenly perceived
and diversely expressed.

Of these new writers, Golding has proved by far the most difficult to
fit into any overall map of the novel. His books have resisted the labels
of both realist/traditional and modernist/experimental. His early
works combine a secure narrative position (the famous shifts of point of
view at the end – to the naval officer in *Lord of the Flies*, the new
people in *The Inheritors* or the discoverers of Martin's body in *Pincher
Martin* – depend for their effect on this initial security) with settings
deliberately removed from contemporary social life by situation, distance or time. His first three novels all imply their truth by a deliberate

reversal of texts of high-bourgeois optimism (*Coral Island*, Wells's *Outline of History* and *Robinson Crusoe*), with an underlying project of constructing fables to 'scrape the labels off things . . . to show the irrational where it exists'.[12] *Lord of the Flies* (1954), written in the wake of Golding's experiences of and reflections on the Second World War, takes up the negative implications of *Nineteen Eighty-Four* – history as nightmare, as recurrent examples of man's innate propensity for evil and destruction. His two subsequent novels explore component parts of the boys' collective experience and in doing so raise questions about the role of language. In *The Inheritors* (1955), the two prehistoric tribes (and species) embody different aspects of innate human nature; the central distinction between Neanderthal and Cro-Magnon (modern) man is in their modes of thought and speech. Modern man is more imaginative, adaptable and resourceful but, as a consequence, more susceptible to evil.

The analysis of the essentially human is narrowed in *Pincher Martin* (1956) to one man on a barren rock. As the narrative emphasis shifts to Martin's desperate and minute attempts at survival, so language is seen as the central mechanism: naming the parts of the rock is a necessary precondition of controlling it. The final reversal to a 'normal' perspective indicates the central role of consciousness and language in Martin's construction and sustaining of his world. In *The Spire* (1964) the issue is returned to a social setting and to the construction of the material world – the spire itself. Issues which in *Pincher Martin* threatened to dissolve the security of narrative position and of linguistic forms are now made more controllable by placing Jocelin's motives within the context of social and material constraints. Golding's later work suggests both a wish to return his general statements to particular social worlds and a need to avoid the more extreme (solipsistic) implications of Martin's isolation and breakdown.

Pincher Martin in fact shows Golding at his closest to that aspect of the modernist project which seemed most relevant in the fifties: the idea of man as isolated individual in a world without meaning. Samuel Beckett's novels are the exemplary instances of this. In the trilogy, originally written in French in the late forties and published in English as *Molloy* (1955), *Malone Dies* (1956) and *The Unnamable* (1958), Beckett presents individual voices speaking (and writing) of situations of physical and mental extremity. The increasing pressure towards silence in Beckett's work is the logical consequence of what Alvarez summarizes as the search for 'a language without reverberations', 'a transparent medium, drained of all local and associative colour'.[13] The aim appears to be the creation of an objectless discourse, which does not, however, celebrate the liberation of language from a referenced reality but rather despairs at the lack of such a consequential solidity.

The reverse (and complementary) image of such a universalized despair is a self-consciously non-transcendent view of contemporary society as the domain of a commonsense everyday reality which must be negotiated. The Movement novels of the fifties invoke such a world through the figure of the young hero (probably provincial and lower-middle-class in origin) on his way to success at the (humorous) expense of a variety of established figures and values. Philip Larkin's *Jill* (1946) has been hailed as a precursor of these, although it is set in the war and deals with Oxford, and the hero ultimately proves ineffectual. William Cooper's *Scenes from Provincial Life* (1950) has also been claimed as a key document, but its pre-war setting and tremendous smugness deprive it of the critical edge of John Wain's *Hurry on Down* (1953) and Kingsley Amis's *Lucky Jim* (1954). Despite some disclaimers to the contrary, the linking of these two authors and texts was not simply the fantasy of literary journalism. Both had been at Oxford in the forties, both were (in the early fifties) provincial university lecturers, and it was on a radio programme edited by Wain that Amis's novel (or a section of it) was first made public. There are a number of formal similarities between the novels. Both take as hero a graduate in his early twenties and present the action exclusively from his point of view. Both are comic critiques of the institutional frameworks the heroes inhabit and, in the conclusions, London is the arena of possible fulfilment and resolution.

In *Hurry on Down* Charles, in 'the jungle of the nineteen fifties', rejects his respectable middle-class upbringing and education, while avoiding the mistakes of 'all the expensive young men of the thirties' who had looked

> through two telescopes at the same time – one fashioned of German psychology and pointed at themselves, the other of Russian economics and directed at the English working-class. A fundamental sense of what life really consisted of had saved him at any rate from such fatuities.[14]

The 'real' is then offered as the refutation of the conceptual. Charles's critique is, by definition, non-political. Compare a similar dismissive comment in Cooper's *Scenes from Provincial Life*: 'For some reason or other political sentiment does not seem to be a suitable subject for literary art. If you doubt it you have only to read a few pages of any novel by a high-minded Marxist.'[15]

In both *Hurry on Down* and *Lucky Jim* the detailed social commentary (discussed in Chapter 2) is accompanied by some unease about the status of the overall project of being a serious writer. In *Lucky Jim* this is general and related to the evaluation of 'culture'. Poetry, art and music possess no claims for respect; their practitioners are arrogant (Bertrand), stupid (Welch), ridiculous (Michel) and spiteful (Johns). In *Hurry on Down* that unease is limited but more specific. The only scene in which Charles is not the protagonist is a literary society meeting at which Froulish, a would-be novelist, describes his 'Work in Progress' (the name by which *Finnegans Wake* had been known in the thirties – Froulish's novel also is not intended to be finished for fifteen years). It is at least 'twelve times' the length of the average novel, and questions about its 'plot and characters' induce contemptuous laughter in the novelist. It has no title, is concerned with 'psychic currents', not physical lives, and is 'expressed chiefly through patterns of imagery'.[16] The meeting is used to indicate an equal criticism of Froulish's absurd posturings and of the simple realist objections of the local curate and schoolteacher (who recommends a course of Thackeray). Froulish himself finally becomes Charles's colleague in a team of radio comedy scriptwriters. Both *Hurry on Down* and *Lucky Jim* in fact make it clear that the choice of 'traditional' conceptions of narrative, character and language is not a display of middlebrow ignorance but a registering of a specific position in the field of aesthetic politics.

The issue recurs in Amis's second and third novels. In *That Uncertain Feeling* (1955) the figure of Probert and his verse drama *The Martyr* occupy a similar role to that of Froulish and his novel. Amis's hero notes that 'the whole business was rather on the symbolical side. Words like "death" and "life" and "love" and "man" cropped up every few lines, but were never attached to anything concrete or specific.'[17] As with Jim Dixon in *Lucky Jim*, John Lewis's job as a librarian implicates him in the task of cultural dissemination; the issues of cultural evaluation (his favourite reading is *Astounding Science Fiction*), personal integrity and general social commentary are then fused together in the rejection of Elizabeth's patronage. This fusion is most explicit in Amis's *I Like it Here* (1958) through Garnet Bowen's attempt to discover the identity of a modernist (Jamesian) novelist, Wulfstan Strether, living in Portugal. Here a general rejection both of 'abroad' and of self-conscious aesthetic positions is presented. Bowen is cynical about his own work as a literary (mainly critical) hack, and Amis's preference for the comic (embodied in Fielding) as against the tragic modernist ethic is expressed directly and in the novel's form. A passage of Strether's prose (presented for the reader's appreciation of parody) is condemned by Bowen as lacking 'clarity, common sense, emotional decency and general morality'.[18] By the mid-fifties the Orwellian values had shifted into the terrain of a comfortable insularity.

Both Iris Murdoch and Angus Wilson were linked in the fifties with the Movement novelists – the former because of the persona of Jake and the comic, picaresque form in *Under the Net* (1954), and the latter for statements in praise of eighteenth- and nineteenth-century novels at the expense of twentieth-century modernists. While these reasons may now seem insufficient, a rather different similarity suggests the existence of some common ground in the desire to define the proper concerns of the novelist through debate within the novel itself (even the hero of *Scenes from Provincial Life* is a published novelist).

Murdoch's *Under the Net* charts Jake's transition from being a 'literary hack', mainly concerned with translating, to a belief (in the manner of Sartre's *Nausea*) in the possibility of an authentic personal literary creativity. The precondition of this transition is the experiential recognition of the truth of Hugo's proposition that 'each thing' should be seen as 'absolutely unique', that while 'everything had a theory . . . yet there was no master theory'.[19] Jake's discovery that Anna (whom he loves) is pursuing Hugo, and not vice versa, shocks him into truth: 'Anna really existed now as a separate being and not as part of myself.'[20] The corollary of this in Iris Murdoch's explicit aesthetic position has been to emphasize the need to recognize 'the real impenetrable human person' ('Against Dryness') and to define love as 'the extremely difficult realization that something other than oneself is real' ('The Sublime and the Good').[21]

In the light of this, however, many of her novels seem to suggest a paradox or at least a problem of execution in that the extravagances of her characters, plots and settings are often far from the solid social networks of a writer such as George Eliot – whom Iris Murdoch has cited as possessing the 'godlike capacity for so respecting and loving her characters as to make them exist as free and separate beings' ('The Sublime and the Beautiful Revisited').[22] Part of the answer lies in the extreme nature of her concept of the 'otherness' of individuals and

characters. This leads, often, to the systematic production of a cata-
logue of eccentric isolates who are then held together, as in *The Flight
from the Enchanter* (1955), not so much by the notion of an underlying
social reality as by a set of almost diametric patterns of emotional
attraction and repulsion. Her novels tend to conduct arguments about
the need for a severe empiricism rather than being themselves embodi-
ments of such a principle through the fictional worlds presented. Even
in *The Sandcastle* (1957), a novel in some respects conventional enough
in form to be compared by one critic to *Brief Encounter*, the figure of
Rain Carter acts simultaneously to disturb Mor's routinized existence
and to suggest certain aesthetic and philosophical issues which relate to
the novelist's practice. The debates about the ethics and purposes of
portrait painting – of the difficulties of trying to show what the
subject's face and self is 'like itself and not treat it as a symbol of our
own moods and wishes'[23] – parallel Mor's problems in relating to
Rain. Here the central issue of the novelist's aesthetics is transferred to
become a problem for the characters; it can then be offered for the
reader's contemplation without causing any disturbance of the security
of the controlling narrative position.

Angus Wilson's first novel *Hemlock and After* (1952) is also constructed around the problems of the stance of the contemporary writer.
The opening ceremony at Varden Hall (a new state-supported centre for
young writers) is the scene for Bernard Sands's self-doubt about the authenticity of his own motives, for varying degrees of social disintegration
and the invasion of the interior of the hall itself by a troop of homosexual
poseurs. The problem here is Wilson's own – how to accommodate
perceptions of irreducible evil and unconscious energies and pressures
within a rational 'liberal humanist' programme (at another level Wilson
has himself spoken of the need to reconcile a George Eliot approach with
'a kind of Dickensianism' within his texts). The issue is focused around
homosexuality, which is shown both as the source and justification of a
broad liberal tolerance and as having allegiances with disruption, sadism
and cruelty, paedophilia and the completely 'evil' Mrs Curry. It is
homosexuality too, with its lack of a 'natural' style of behaviour, which
generates awareness of role playing, acting and mimicry – all elements
central to the direction of Wilson's later work. Again, in *Hemlock and
After* these problems are controlled by articulating them as problems of
the characters rather than of the text itself.

Of all the first novels of the fifties, Muriel Spark's *The Comforters*
(1957) is perhaps most explicit in its introspection about the novelist's

own position. Caroline's conversion to Catholicism coincides with her realization that she is a character in a novel (in her own book on 'form in the modern novel' she is having trouble with the chapter on realism). The novel closes with her decision to write a novel (which is, of course, *The Comforters* itself); the substance of the plot (centring on the discovery by Caroline's fiancé, Lawrence, of his 78-year-old grandmother's diamond-smuggling gang), however, suggests not a chaos of raw experience needing novelistic form but a pattern of intricate and hidden order awaiting detection. Ruth Whittaker[24] has noted how Muriel Spark's work suggests an underlying assumption similar to that of the somewhat uncharacteristic later sections of Greene's *The End of the Affair*, where the narrator notes: 'we are inextricably bound to the plot, and wearily God forces us, here and there, according to his intention, characters without poetry, without free will.'[25]

In the light of this, the 'problematic' nature of *The Comforters* denotes not so much a commitment to exploring the difficulties of reconciling the novel's fictional and mimetic functions as a need to get certain issues out of the way. Muriel Spark has remarked:

> I didn't think much of novels – I thought it was an inferior way of writing. So I wrote a novel to work out the technique first, to sort of make it all right with myself to write a novel at all – a novel about writing a novel . . .[26]

The technique established allowed her to avoid both the need to present a contingent social reality (the need for a certain density of material detail and psychological characterization) and the infinite openness of presenting the novelist as world-creator. The phone calls from Death in *Memento Mori* (1959) and the Catholic emphases of the historical retrospection in *The Prime of Miss Jean Brodie* (1961) and *Girls of Slender Means* (1963) create the patterns of meaning which allow economy of scale and the ultimate subordination of character to plot.

Unknown worlds: conflicting voices

In the light of the number of writer protagonists in the pages of fifties novels, it is not surprising to find John Braine subsequently advising would-be novelists to avoid the 'ultimate sin of writing a novel about a novelist'.[27] This may be partly a rather simpleminded attitude to formal complexity, but it is also a recognition that there are other social worlds to be explored. In other writers, this awareness helped to push concern with questions of voice into new formal directions. Again we see a range of responses to pressures more immediate and diverse than the development of the genre 'novel'.

Angus Wilson suggests the nature of these further social worlds (and the problems of including them in his own novels) when, in *The Middle Age of Mrs Eliot* (1958), Meg is faced with all that is excluded by her own highly selective view of England.

> Americanization, rock 'n' roll, Teddy boys, angry young men, new towns, housing estates, television, these formed the substance of all their talk and questions of home. Meg tried to answer as well as she could, but really she wanted to tell them that her life was not lived in the pages of popular newspapers. . . . She felt suddenly as though the world at home was as remote and dangerous as this unknown Asian world that had struck out at her so cruelly.[28]

In *Late Call* (1964) Wilson attempts to map the more accessible aspects of this other world – the new-town ethos, the impact of television, middle-class youthful revolt (*Look Back in Anger* and CND). However, the issue was not simply that of a more contemporary social content but also that of the difference between life as lived in 'the pages of popular newspapers' and life as lived in serious novels and by novel writers and readers. The quantitative domination of television in the area of leisure and the new, apparently irrational, youth subcultures both provided difficult challenges to novelists' claims to be able to chart cultural directions. In *Late Call* Harold (the secondary school headmaster) perceives a situation of 'more vulgarized popular taste, increasingly remote minority culture'[29] and attempts to create appropriate educational strategies as outlined in his book of teaching theory, 'The Blokes at the Back of the Class'. These 'blokes' (whether the traditional working class or the adherents of new youth subcultures) remained, however, resolutely on the fringes of the fiction of Wilson and most fifties novelists. It was rather in the provincial realist novels of the late fifties and early sixties that they were, briefly, pulled into the centre.

Initially these novels apparently involved simply a further downward extension of the social milieu of the Amis/Wain/Osborne hero. In *Room at the Top* (1957) John Braine's hero, Joe Lampton, is in transition between his working-class origins and a new middle-class identity, combining worldly success with private guilt. The novel provided a point of connection between the middle-class world of the Movement and the working-class heroes of Alan Sillitoe, David Storey and Stan Barstow. However, the shift in subject-matter raised considerable problems concerning the gap between the cultural pretensions of a serious novel and the nature of the social world presented – particularly that of designating an appropriate language. The difficulty was, as Sillitoe remarked, 'how to write a book about a man who hasn't read a book'.[30] The first novels of Sillitoe and Storey suggest different ways of resolving this. In Sillitoe's *Saturday Night and Sunday Morning* (1958) a third-person narrative position allows a range of metaphorical language which is constructed to convey Arthur Seaton's experience (and others' experience of him) without attributing to him an implausible range of articulacy. The novel's language in fact merges an idea of the energy and directness of Nottingham working-class speech with a more general verbal extravagance. The novel's linguistic range (within the first three pages Arthur is compared to 'a tall thin Druid', 'an earthquake machine' and 'a fully dressed and giant foetus') points forward to the move, in Sillitoe's later work, beyond work and leisure in working-class Nottingham. Criminal subculture (*The Loneliness of the Long-Distance Runner*, 1959), national service in Malaya (*The Key to the Door*, 1961) and latter-day Lawrentian wandering in London and Algeria (*The Death of William Posters*, 1965) provide both areas of individual freedom and a perspective to totalize and evaluate the contemporary working-class situation.

David Storey's *This Sporting Life* (1960) is, by contrast, constructed directly on the basis of Arthur Machin's problems of self-expression. Within the first-person narrative, his voice suggests restriction, difficulty and absence; at one point he comments, 'I give over trying to think', as the novel lapses into frustrated silence. He turns to stereotyped pulp fiction to provide ways of naming and living his own situation as local sporting hero; the dissonance between these idealized worlds and his own unfulfilled reality implies the unsatisfactory nature of both. The narrative voice of *Flight into Camden* (1960) is more articulate, but the central experience is again one of restriction. Margaret, a miner's daughter, caught between the examples of her brother (now a university lecturer) and her mother's traditional role-fulfilment, attempts to escape through an affair (and a room in London) with a married teacher. The failure of the relationship and Margaret's breakdown point forward to the recurrent theme in Storey's fiction of making sense of the gap between working-class roots and the upward mobility implied by a successful education.

Storey's pessimism contrasted sharply with Sillitoe's celebratory rhetoric. Contemporary reviewers were particularly concerned about how far Sillitoe endorsed the anarchistic antisocial tendencies of his heroes. The problems of assessing Arthur Seaton's character are taken up explicitly in John Fowles's *The Collector* (1963), where the imprisoned Miranda asserts that 'the most disgusting thing of all is that Alan Sillitoe doesn't show that he's disgusted by his young man'.[31] The collector, Clegg, is an amalgam of elements from the late fifties / early sixties lower-class hero. His lack of parental roots recalls Braine's Joe Lampton; his lack of language recalls Storey's Arthur Machin; and even his view of Miranda as an idealized object ('seeing her always made me feel like I was catching a rarity')[32] is recognizably similar to that of Stan Barstow's Mr Average, Vic Brown, in *A Kind of Loving* (1960): 'the way I think about her is sort of clean and pure and soft.'[33]

The originality of *The Collector* lay, however, in its opposition of two voices (both recognizably of 'our' society) which speak different languages and talk past each other. They talk across an absent centre of solid middle-class discourse (Miranda's art-student life, support for CND and hints of sexual liberation mark her out as in fact more socially marginal than Clegg). This opposition, alongside the clearly foregrounded echoes of *The Tempest*, both in the text's construction (the characters' names, Clegg's coincidental adoption of Ferdinand as a pseudonym) and in Miranda's thoughts, indicates a novel demanding attention at the level of its formal construction.

The Collector was one of a number of novels which, in the early sixties, offered new directions by putting into play conflicting voices or areas of experience within a single novel. The most ambitious was Doris Lessing's *The Golden Notebook* (1962). That the heroine, Anna Wulf, is a novelist with a problem is the novel's least innovatory aspect. It is rather the way that the problem becomes the determining principle of the novel's form that sets it apart. It is a novel intended 'to talk through the way it was shaped' (1971 Introduction). The four notebooks develop areas of Anna's experience which are either absent from or marginalized in the typical 'conventional short novel' (of which the 'Free Women' skeleton is an example). Reality is understood to present itself through conflicting textual forms – newspaper, film, dream, diary, memory, stories – and Anna is shown as living by means of a variety of different languages: the colonial memory, the Communist Party, herself as subject of woman's sexuality, psychoanalysis, contemporary world affairs (Korea, Quemoy, Africa), her search for a fundamental level of reality from which to write.

The novel is clearly a product of the political and cultural displacements after 1956 (*Anger*, Suez, Hungary). Anna speaks, in 1957, of 'a phenomenon in the arts I'm damned if I'd foreseen', recognizing that 'little novels or plays about the emotions don't reflect reality'.[34] For Lessing this helped to create the space to rework the options for 'free women' – worked through in *The Grass is Singing* (1951) to closure and in the *Children of Violence* novel sequence (1952–69) towards openness – into a novel which would 'give the ideological "feel" of our mid-century' (1971 Introduction). This, however, is undertaken with many hints of an underlying desperation. The novel seems an unwilling enterprise – the only alternative to formlessness or silence. Anna's separation of herself into four notebooks is the only way to avoid chaos. While the 'Golden Notebook' and 'Free Women' sections offer a resolution for Anna, the novel contains a persistent worry that it may become one of 'the novels about the breakdown of language like Finnegan's Wake'.[35]

The memory of Joyce's achievement indeed haunts English post-war novelists. Apart from the parody in Wain's *Hurry on Down*, there is Garnet Bowen in Amis's *I Like it Here* comparing two months abroad to 'making a determined start on *Finnegan's Wake* – an experience bound in itself to be arduous and irritating, but one which could conceivably render available a rich variety of further experiences'.[36] Even Jim Dixon is a reader of Joyce, remembering, when faced with Bertrand, a 'sentence in a book he'd once read'[37] which proves (if Amis's reader is knowledgeable enough) to be from the 'Citizen' section of *Ulysses*. If Joyce was not to be copied, then he apparently could not be simply ignored. An even more curious aside occurs in Barstow's *A Kind of Loving*, where Vic, browsing through the bookshelves of his brother-in-law, an English teacher, opens *Ulysses* (which 'didn't mean a thing to me') at Molly Bloom's soliloquy and is impressed simultaneously by its sexual explicitness (just like 'these things what sometimes get passed on hand to hand on mucky bits of typing paper') and its form ('there's no commas or full stops or anything and all the sentences run into one another just the way they do when you're thinking yourself, I suppose').[38] Vic is, however, dissuaded from reading it on the grounds of its difficulty; instead he is given a Hemingway.

In the sixties Joyce was allowed to come down from the bookshelves. The competition of visual media (film being taken seriously, the expansion of television), a new openness to European and, particularly, American influences, the sociological and literary rediscovery of the working class, the post-*Chatterley* trial atmosphere and a reawakened interest in novels' formal properties (both from novelists and within academic criticism) – all created space for active appropriation of Joycean techniques. Anthony Burgess, in particular, found Joyce's linguistic inventiveness an important and liberating example. In Burgess's *Nothing Like the Sun* (1964) Stephen Dedalus's autobiographical reading of Shakespeare expands into a whole novel using the same mock-popular Elizabethan language. *A Clockwork Orange* (1962) invents a subcultural slang for a Sillitoe hero pushed to the limits. The novel embodies a fear of a future in which liberalism and literature will have no place. While fifties novels tend to have heroes who are about to begin intellectual creation, Burgess's hero is engaged in destroying it. Preoccupation with extreme cultural philistinism is a repeated concern of sixties novelists – see Fowles's story 'Poor Koko' in *The Ebony Tower* (1974), as well as *The Collector* and B. S. Johnson's *Albert Angelo* (1964).

B. S. Johnson too takes Joyce as a necessary starting-point. *Travelling People* (1963) at times suggests an uneasy amalgam of a fifties picaresque hero and plot with a mixture of styles derived from Joyce and Sterne. Henry Henry is an avid reader of *Ulysses*, but the range of techniques Johnson employs (including interior monologue, a film script, letters, Johnson's comments on his own narrative performance) do not seem to be articulated with Henry's major preoccupations. More marginal areas of the clash of values and cultural levels (as both Henry's educated radicalism and the local Welsh community provide critiques of the Stromboli Club upper-crust ethos) point forward to *Albert Angelo*. The most quoted aspect of this novel is the shift towards the end into an explicit recognition of the fictionality of the hero and his problems, as against the actual experiences of Johnson himself which form the 'raw material'. Equally important, however, are the ways in which the earlier sections seek to present a clear opposition between Albert's educated discourse as would-be architect and teacher, and the illiterate essays, letters and jokes of his secondary school pupils. It is their undermining of Albert's control and identity which confirm the need for Johnson to retreat from fictional illusion to the validity of unquestionable personal experience. In this respect, Beckett offered Johnson a way forward which avoided either complete silence or a return to a more traditional realist form. Both *Trawl* (1966) and *The Unfortunates* (1969) depend on a single voice uniting present events, past memories and the process of their transcription in terms of a primary reality – Johnson's own mind.

Fowles's *The Magus* (1966), by contrast, develops the implications of this increasing concern about the relations between the fictional and the real in the opposite direction – emphasizing the fictional nature of reality rather than the reality which fiction tries to hide. Knowledge of the truth about Conchis's games and theatre is persistently deferred as a range of extreme experiences (public and private) are told or shown to Nicholas Urfe. The novel can be read as a kind of answer to Amis's *I Like it Here*. In place of Strether and his pretentious novel 'This Rough Magic' is Conchis, another relic of the great age of modernism, with the role of a Prospero to be taken seriously. While Bowen returns to a comfortable, limited marriage (and the feeling that he was 'exactly the same man as he was before'),[39] Urfe is granted, or achieves, the heroic existential moment of freedom and choice.

The Magus confirmed the range of possibilities for English fiction in the sixties – international reference, the inclusion of history, the areas of fabulation and fantasy, the deferral of a reference to the primary real. It also suggested political and social limitations which Fowles was willing to recognize when Mrs de Seitas defends the god-game – 'We are rich and we are intelligent and we mean to live rich, intelligent lives'.[40] It is not merely coincidence that Johnson's retreat to reality takes place in a London secondary school while Fowles's celebration of the fictive occurs in a well-appointed villa on a Greek island.

At the crossroads: forms and ideologies

Established fifties novelists reacted to the new opportunities of the sixties in a variety of ways. Both Iris Murdoch and Muriel Spark found themselves with already established procedures for reducing the wider range of experiences and aesthetic possibilities to manageable proportions. For Anthony Powell too the existing formal structures of the *Dance to the Music of Time* novel sequence, rather than any responsiveness to social change or aesthetic fashion, determined the pattern of his work (the sequence had begun in 1951 and was at its halfway point with the sixth volume, *The Kindly Ones*, in 1962). In the third trilogy (published during the sixties and concerned with the period of the war) Powell's evocation of inter-war, upper-middle-class society through a relatively uninvolved narrator (Nicholas Jenkins) did, however, begin to give way to a sense of Jenkins himself as the central figure, the arch-survivor whose very adaptability and lack of definition allow him to sustain a tone of amused neutrality even while the old world collapses around him. The final three volumes (published in the early seventies) deal more episodically with post-war society. In the last of the whole sequence, *Hearing Secret Harmonies* (1975), Powell's original structural metaphor, whereby the pattern of human life is regarded as a dance which simultaneously expresses and transcends the fact of mortality, proves a remarkably appropriate image for sixties religiosity – the world of drugs, cults, new universities and middle-class youth culture.

Kingsley Amis's response to the new climate of the sixties was more immediate, reflecting perhaps a less secure (or more flexible) sense of the significance of novelistic form. He seemed torn between a mapping of the developing 'permissive' society from a Lucky-Jim-type perspective, in *Take a Girl Like You* (1960) and *I Want it Now* (1968), and a rather tentative exploration of the new freedom to work in a wider range of genres, particularly those popular forms his fifties heroes always preferred – serious exploration in *The Anti-Death League* (1966), apparently less serious in the Bond pastiche, *Colonel Sun* (1968). Angus Wilson's response was more wholehearted. In *No Laughing Matter* (1967) he finally abandoned the single central sympathetic character which, even in the futuristic *The Old Men at the Zoo* (1961), had provided security of perspective for the reader. *No Laughing Matter*, with its range of voices, literary styles and parodies and attempt at a developmental account of the 'ideological feel' of twentieth-century history (with specific dates which, as in *The Golden Notebook*, throw the reader back to an assumed general historical knowledge for comparison), is a novel in which the novelist's still often contradictory range of aesthetic concerns becomes the determining principle of the formal organization, rather than remaining as issues to be debated by the characters.

By the end of the sixties it was clear that this kind of 'problematic' novel had to be recognized as more than an occasional oddity. In 1969 David Lodge, writing in *Critical Quarterly*, attempted to map the wider range of formal choices now being made by English novelists. Lodge's essay 'Novelist at the Crossroads'[41] moves beyond the conventional binary (realist/experimental) opposition to suggest that, as pressure came to bear on the central 'compromise' of realism, so possible alternative routes branched off in different directions – both towards the 'non-fiction' novel and towards 'fabulation'. In addition, a fourth choice available was for novelists to 'hesitate at the crossroads' and 'build their hesitation into the novel itself'. Lodge's central metaphor is helpful in suggesting a certain plurality of options, but it also clearly leads on to the evaluation he proposes. Realism is 'the road on which [the English novelist] stands.' It is the main road, and Lodge concludes with 'a modest affirmation of faith in the future of realistic fiction', continuing: 'if the case for realism has any ideological content it is that of liberalism.'

A distinctive feature of Lodge's essay is an uneasy movement between discussion of the novel in general and 'the English novel' in particular. The view that the English novel was provincial in relation to the European (especially Russian and French) tradition had long been current, if not universally agreed. Now in addition there was concern that American post-war novelists (including Mailer, Bellow, Barth, Pynchon and Vonnegut) were not merely much more energetic and ambitious than their English counterparts but also technically superior and aesthetically more self-aware. This anxiety is even more explicit in Bernard Bergonzi's *The Situation of the Novel* (1970). Lodge's defence of realism and liberalism can thus be understood too as an assertion of English cultural identity now under threat not only (as had been the case since the thirties) from the allegedly low quality of American popular culture but equally from the high quality of contemporary American literature. Lodge, by implication, called for an English novel which would match American ambition and technical achievement without losing a humanist commitment.

1969 saw the publication of one novel that might almost have been written to illustrate Lodge's argument and answer his call – Fowles's *The French Lieutenant's Woman*. From a centre of realism (plot, character, density of social detail), Fowles secures the novel in a bedrock of historical truth (poetry, footnotes, statistics) and suggests its essential fictional character (the three endings, the appearance of the novelist himself). This last area leads on to the 'hestitations', particularly in the much-quoted 'Who is Sarah?' chapter 13. The integration of these elements occurs through the idea of a historical shift from a (quite traditionally conceived) mid-Victorian ethic to mid-twentieth-century notions of freedom, hazard and Fowles's own brand of existentialism. This progression is simultaneously an epochal shift, character development (in Charles) and the basis of Fowles's self-confessed problems of narrative authority – how the writer as world-creator can also create characters that can embody the principles of freedom (a problem which, in different terminology, had much preoccupied Iris Murdoch).

It would be tempting to see Lodge's essay and Fowles's novel as summaries of the issues at stake for English novelists by the end of the sixties. One reason for resisting the temptation lies in Lodge's equation of 'realism' with 'liberalism', particularly as he further remarks that 'the aesthetics of compromise go naturally with the ideology of compromise' (Bergonzi makes a similar point in analysing the 'English ideology' in *The Situation of the Novel*). Two basic assumptions made here are open to challenge: the positing of fixed relations between literary forms and political/philosophical positions (are they 'naturally' linked?) and the view that compromise and liberalism are adequate and desirable positions. The latter is for Lodge not so much facile mid-sixties optimism as a deliberate response to a perceived crisis; as a *Critical Quarterly* editorial put it, also in 1969, it was now time that 'moderation must become militant in its own defence'.

There were, however, other ways of defining the crisis and its attendant political and literary forms. Socialist novelists during the period subscribed neither to Lodge's assumptions about the meanings of available formal choices nor to ideas of liberal compromise. Particularly after 1956, issues largely closed since the late thirties were reopened in the context of a new political and cultural climate. *The Golden Notebook* suggests some of the problems which then arose. Differences between Anna's self-doubts and the proletcult socialist realism of the 'Comrade Ted' stories reflect the difficulties of integrating a literature of working-class realism with writing designed to demonstrate the need for, and the route towards, socialism. In the late fifties, while Sillitoe, Storey and Barstow revitalized the former (in a way much depoliticized as compared to Tressell or many thirties novels), John Berger's *A Painter of Our Time* (1958) shows a Hungarian painter (through the textual form of the diary) approaching political issues obliquely through the problem of aesthetic form. Berger's later novels address this question increasingly through their own form, culminating in *G* (1972), where the juxtaposition of modes of writing (fiction, autobiography, history, essay) is paralleled by the attempt to make Giovanni stand as an exemplification of a particularly significant set of historical moments. Arguably, without the narrative commentary such an exemplification could not succeed, but this is only to point out why, for Berger, a Lodgean realism would not be enough. David Caute's novels also attempt to link the particular individual to notions of historical process. *Comrade Jacob* (1961) and *The Decline of the West* (1966) are realist presentations of situations of sharp political conflict. *The Occupation* (1971), however, shifts the focus to considering the production of political-intellectual work itself and to a form that undercuts the kind of realism Caute had previously employed.

Both Berger and Caute had moved a considerable distance from more traditional ideas of the socialist novel as presentation of working-class situations and consciousness. Raymond Williams, on the other hand, clearly sought to maintain contact with this tradition in both *Border Country* (1960) and *Second Generation* (1964), which present the psychological and political consequences of the move from working-class community to middle-class intellectual. *Border Country* is more accessible precisely because there the move is also of physical location (country/city) and from childhood to adult independence. *Second Generation* has to work much harder to contain all the issues (often through weighty dialogue) within the realist form – issues that are more pressing because the two worlds (of industry and university) now coexist within the same city.

For all three writers, however, their novels are part of more general intellectual projects which go beyond the desire simply to contribute to the English novel's development or even to appropriate it for socialism. Berger's novels can be better understood by seeing them in relation both to his art criticism and, more particularly, to his book-length essays on a country doctor, *A Fortunate Man* (1967), and on European immigrant workers, *A Seventh Man* (1975), where the unusual combination of photographic, descriptive, reflective and autobiographical material poses problems of categorization similar to those encountered in *G* – particularly in relation to Berger's self-presentation as observer and narrator. Caute's *The Occupation* was designed as part of a trilogy (published simultaneously) – the other two texts being a play and a dramatized critical essay. This again has to be put alongside Caute's work as a historian; and Williams's novels are a significant but partial aspect of his work in 'politics and letters' and cultural studies.

The issues underlying novelists' formal choices can, in fact, never be reduced to a concern with the health or future direction of the novel genre in itself, even though the very fact of writing a genre study (like this one) tends to reinforce the likelihood of such a reduction. Equally, formal choices can never be simply read off in terms of their inherent ideological content (whether realism as liberalism, realism as socialist humanism or post-modernism as revolutionary practice). While Lodge's essay and Fowles's novel suggested the possibility of a specific set of protocols for the contemporary English novelist, in the early seventies writers such as Alan Burns, B. S. Johnson and David Storey simply did not see their practice in such terms. Burns's 'cut-up' method in *Babel* (1969) and *Dreamerika!* (1972), Johnson's return to multiple viewpoints in *House Mother Normal* (1971) and Storey's use of unselfconscious and stark realism to present breakdown in *Pasmore* (1972) indicated a considerable diversity of formal possibilities for appropriation rather than a dominant direction for that imaginary organism 'the English novel'.

Notes

1 Malcolm Bradbury (ed.), *The Novel Today* (London: Fontana, 1977), p. 20.
2 Christopher Sykes, *Evelyn Waugh* (Harmondsworth: Penguin, 1977), p. 309.
3 *The Collected Essays, Journalism and Letters of George Orwell*, vol. 2 (Harmondsworth: Penguin, 1970), p. 72.
4 Evelyn Waugh, *Brideshead Revisited* (Harmondsworth: Penguin, 1951), p. 216.
5 George Orwell, *Nineteen Eighty-Four* (Harmondsworth: Penguin, 1954), pp. 214, 212.
6 Ibid., p. 68.
7 Ibid., p. 156.
8 P. H. Newby, *The Novel 1945–51* (London: British Council, 1951), p. 13.
9 Elizabeth Bowen, *The Heat of the Day* (London: Cape, 1949), pp. 87–8.
10 Ibid., p. 272.
11 Graham Greene, *The Heart of the Matter*, Collected Edition (London: Heinemann/Bodley Head, 1971), p. 31.
12 Quoted in V. Tiger, *William Golding* (London: Calder & Boyars, 1974), p. 30.
13 A. Alvarez, *Beckett* (London: Woburn Press, 1974), p. 75.
14 John Wain, *Hurry on Down* (Harmondsworth: Penguin, 1960), p. 38.
15 William Cooper, *Scenes from Provincial Life* (Harmondsworth: Penguin, 1961), p. 17.
16 Wain, op. cit., p. 66.
17 Kingsley Amis, *That Uncertain Feeling* (London: Gollancz, 1955), p. 109.
18 Kingsley Amis, *I Like it Here* (London: Gollancz, 1958), p. 112.
19 Iris Murdoch, *Under the Net* (Harmondsworth: Penguin, 1960), pp. 61, 58.
20 Ibid., p. 238.
21 Iris Murdoch, 'Against Dryness', *Encounter* (January 1961), and 'The Sublime and the Good', *Chicago Review* (Autumn 1959).
22 Iris Murdoch, 'The Sublime and the Beautiful Revisited', *Yale Review* (December 1959).
23 Iris Murdoch, *The Sandcastle* (Harmondsworth: Penguin, 1960), p. 77.
24 In Malcolm Bradbury and D. Palmer (eds), *The Contemporary English Novel* (London: Edward Arnold, 1979).

25 Graham Greene, *The End of the Affair*, Collected Edition (London: Heinemann/Bodley Head, 1974), p. 203.
26 In Bradbury (ed.), op. cit., p. 132.
27 John Braine, *Writing a Novel* (London: Eyre Methuen, 1974), p. 44.
28 Angus Wilson, *The Middle Age of Mrs Eliot* (St Albans: Granada, 1979), p. 97.
29 Angus Wilson, *Late Call* (London: Secker & Warburg, 1964), p. 65.
30 In K. Allsop, *Scan* (London: Hodder & Stoughton, 1965), p. 60.
31 John Fowles, *The Collector* (London: Pan, 1965), p. 241.
32 Ibid., p. 5.
33 Stan Barstow, *A Kind of Loving* (London: Corgi, 1982), p. 29.
34 Doris Lessing, *The Golden Notebook* (St Albans: Panther, 1973), p. 61.
35 Ibid., p. 299.
36 Amis, *I Like it Here*, p. 23.
37 Kingsley Amis, *Lucky Jim* (London: Gollancz, 1954), p. 50.
38 Barstow, op. cit., p. 99.
39 Amis, *I Like it Here*, p. 207.
40 John Fowles, *The Magus* (London: Cape, 1966), p. 563.
41 David Lodge, 'Novelist at the Crossroads', *Critical Quarterly*, 11, 2 (1969).

Further reading

Bergonzi, Bernard. *The Situation of the Novel*. London: Macmillan, 1970; rev. edn, 1979.
Bradbury, Malcolm. *Possibilities*. London: Oxford University Press, 1973.
Bradbury, Malcolm (ed.). *The Novel Today*. London: Fontana, 1977.
Bradbury, Malcolm, and Palmer, D. (eds). *The Contemporary English Novel*. London: Edward Arnold, 1979.
Burns, A., and Sugnet, C. (eds). *The Imagination on Trial*. London: Allison & Busby, 1981.
Firchow, Peter (ed.). *The Writer's Place*. Minneapolis, Minn.: University of Minnesota Press, 1974.
Gindin, James. *Post-War British Fiction*. Cambridge: Cambridge University Press, 1962.
Gordon, Giles (ed.). *Beyond the Words*. London: Hutchinson, 1975.
Hayman, Ronald. *The Novel Today 1967–75*. London: Longman, 1976.
Karl, Frederick. *The Reader's Guide to the Contemporary English Novel*. London: Thames & Hudson, 1963.
Lodge, David. *The Novelist at the Crossroads*. London: Routledge & Kegan Paul, 1971.
Newby, P. H. *The Novel 1945–51*. London: British Council, 1951.
Rabinovitz, Rubin. *The Reaction Against Experiment in the English Novel 1950–60*. New York: Columbia University Press, 1967.
Vinson, James (ed.). *Contemporary Novelists*. London: St James Press, 1972; rev. edn, 1976.

Index